"Feeling make you,
out there in the open space.
He coming through your body,
Look while he blow and
feel with your body . . ."

Big Bill Neidjie.
Surviving elder of the Bunitj clan.

PHOTOGRAPHING AUSTRALIA WITH STEVE PARISH

National Photographic Marketing
Queensland Australia

SILVERTON
ICE
DUBLE HEDER
15
PARLOR
ICECREAM
enjoy
FA

AND MILK
BAR
DRINKS
PARLOR
Peters
OPEN

P*HOTOGRAPHING AUSTRALIA* is, I believe, unlike any book yet published in this country.

This is more than just a book of Australian photographs, a book to teach you how to go about taking photographs, or a book which tells you something of how the photographer, Steve Parish, feels about his photography.

It is all of these things, but most of all, this is a book which will stir a desire that we all have: a desire to create.

From these pages flows the inspiration to 'go, wander, explore and discover.' Steve Parish will awaken you to the magic around us; the land, its flora and fauna, and its people.

It is all there, waiting for you.

I hope that this book will motivate you, as it has me, to start planning now to 'make tracks' and photograph Australia.

Rob Tolmie

Robert Tolmie
MANAGING DIRECTOR
NATIONAL PHOTOGRAPHIC MARKETING

CONTENTS

Kego lives in a tiny settlement called Oodnadatta. It used to be a reasonably busy little place, but that was back when the Ghan Railway passed through town. Now, like so many other towns out there, it's a lonely, desolate, nowhere kind of place.

Each year Kego heads 250km south from Oodnadatta to another outpost called William Creek. He goes to "av'a go" at winning the annual gymkhana.

Even when I am very low, this picture gives me a real lift. When I look at this single image I am reminded that, as a photographer, it is my attitude that governs my success or failure. You see, Kego lost the race by more than ten lengths. But his face is the face of a winner!

PHOTOGRAPHING AUSTRALIA

I *HAVE SPENT* twenty five years making pictures and seventeen years sharing them with people. During this time I have had a great many people tell me that they would love to become actively involved in making pictures. What puzzled me for a long time was why so few went on to fulfil that ambition.

I now believe that there are two main reasons. Firstly, many people consider that they do not have the technical expertise necessary to operate sophisticated-looking equipment. Secondly, many believe that they do not have the necessary creative ability. To an extent, both kinds of skills are needed. What is often not appreciated is that a change in attitude may well be all that is really required.

I was twenty nine before I discovered that I could, with the right kind of attitude, attain levels of achievement well beyond my wildest dreams. I found that if I dropped the word *can't* out of my vocabulary and my thinking, if I simply let go, all the old tensions associated with learning vanished.

This book is about learning; learning to see, touch, hear and feel a living landscape. It also deals with how you can transfer your feelings onto films in a way that will enable you to relive the magic forever.

I hope that the words and images in this book will motivate you to make tracks. While you are out there wandering, exploring and discovering, do yourself a favour. Take a break and pat yourself on the back. Reward yourself, because you are one of the very few who ever get motivated to fulfil a personal desire.

Steve Parish

Steve Parish
BRISBANE, 1986

WANDERING OUTBACK

W*HEN MY MIND* drifts down dusty highways to the outback, I feel the urge to pack up and wander. Out there I can stop for an hour, a day, or a week. I can sit by a billabong, marvel at a tabletop hill, traverse a rugged mountain range, climb a sand dune, cross a stony desert or a grassy open plain.

I can sleep beneath the stars, sure of being woken by a chorus of crows or galahs. I can follow tracks in the sand all day long, or I can lie on my back in the grass, marvelling at the complexities of a flower. In the cool of the evening, I can watch a red hot day beneath cobalt blue skies change slowly to vermilion.

I can do all of these things, but most of all I can roam with a sense of total freedom. Out there I can scream out loud and no one can hear me.

NAMBUNG NATIONAL PARK, THE DESERT BY THE SEA, WESTERN AUSTRALIA.
60th sec., f5.6, 15mm, 64asa.

LAKE CALLABONNA, SOUTH AUSTRALIA.
60th sec., f1.2, 50mm, 64asa.

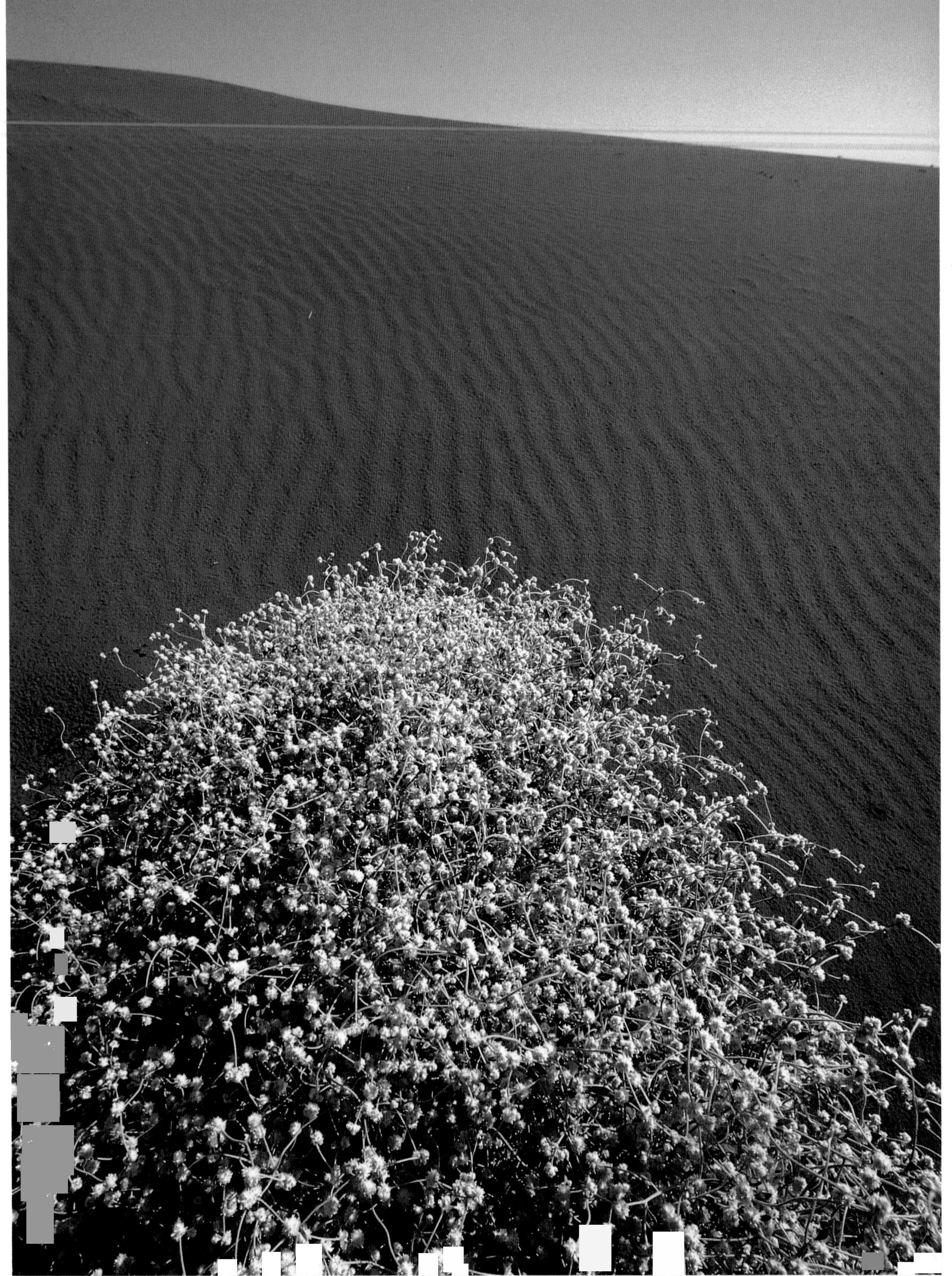

'LIVING' HEART, SIMPSON DESERT, NORTHERN TERRITORY.
125th sec., f5.6, 15mm, 64asa.

THE 'DEAD' HEART

I*T ALWAYS SEEMS TO ME* that the much-used term 'dead heart' is applied to Australia's centre by people whose experience of this arid part of the world has been acquired from the windows of air-conditioned buses in transit from Alice Springs to Ayers Rock. Those who use the phrase probably travel in mid-summer and probably never get out of their buses.

Wildlife in arid regions does not generally present itself in parade form beside a busy road; nor does it wander, fly or crawl about in the middle of a hot day. So if you want to see animals, try moving about in the early mornings and late afternoons, preferably in winter, autumn or spring.

As with all of Australia's wild places, finding elusive animals does require some skills—certainly not a university degree, but using commonsense and having the desire to look is essential. My approach to finding wildlife is to relax and let the environment I am in happen around me. I simply do not try. Quick movements, noise, too many people and so on, are perceived as aggressive vibrations, and animals which have evolved hundreds of different ways of staying alive, will most certainly vanish, probably before you even knew they were there.

So, if you want to turn a bit of 'dead desert' or 'boring bush' into an encounter experience, try sitting alone on a rock or log for an hour or two. Sit quietly and relax, camera at the ready. Look at the ground around you, the sky above, and keep an eye on surrounding foliage and grasses. I'll bet you get a visitor. If you do not, try sitting a while longer. This is called being patient. Its reward will be the cheapest 'high' you have ever experienced.

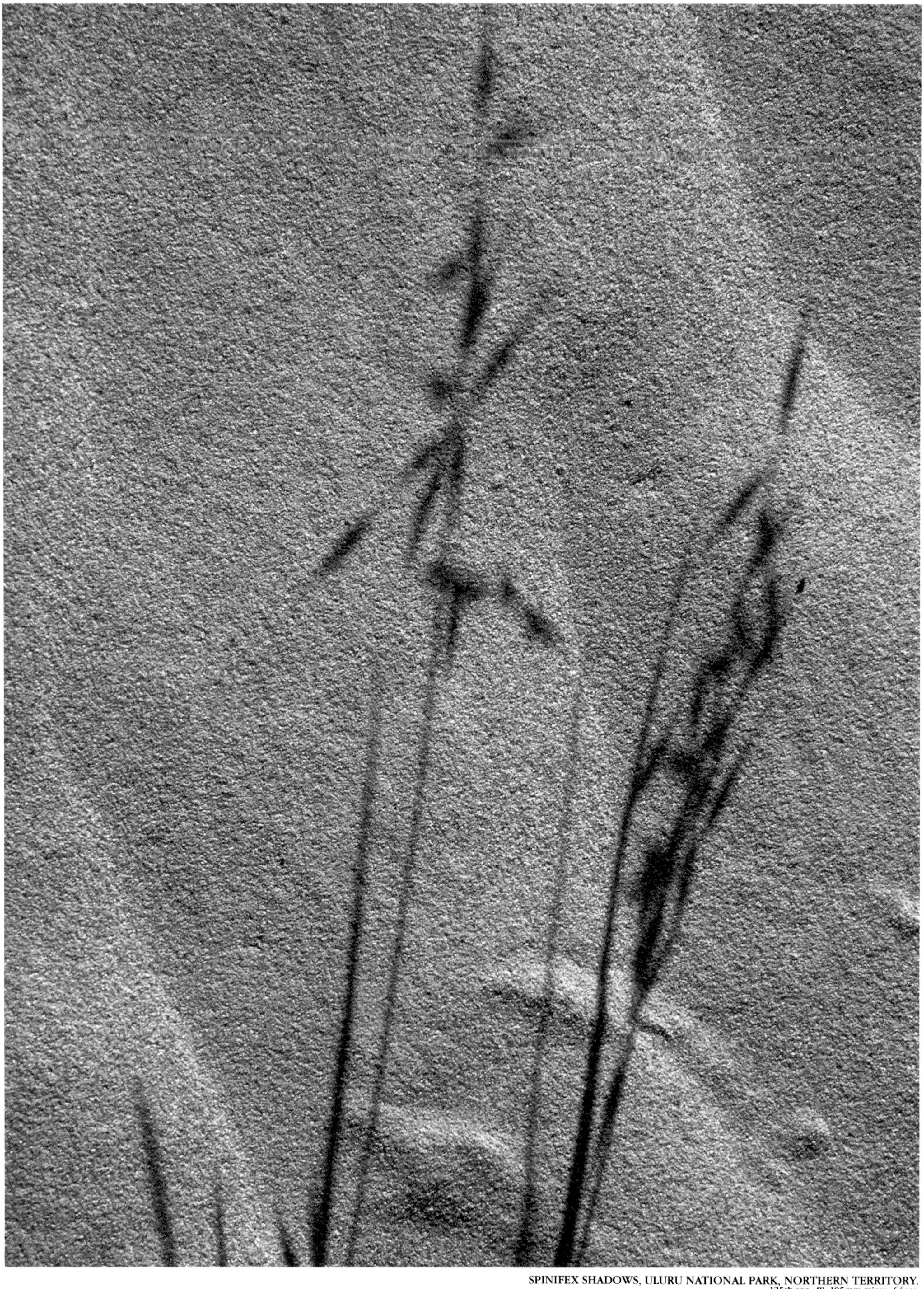

SPINIFEX SHADOWS, ULURU NATIONAL PARK, NORTHERN TERRITORY.
125th sec., f8, 105mm micro, 64asa.

Wind ripples, sand shadows, animal tracks, landscape shots, wildflowers and wild animals. Tight, graphic photos relating earth and sky. The possibilities for making pictures in the sandy desert environment are as limitless as one's imagination.

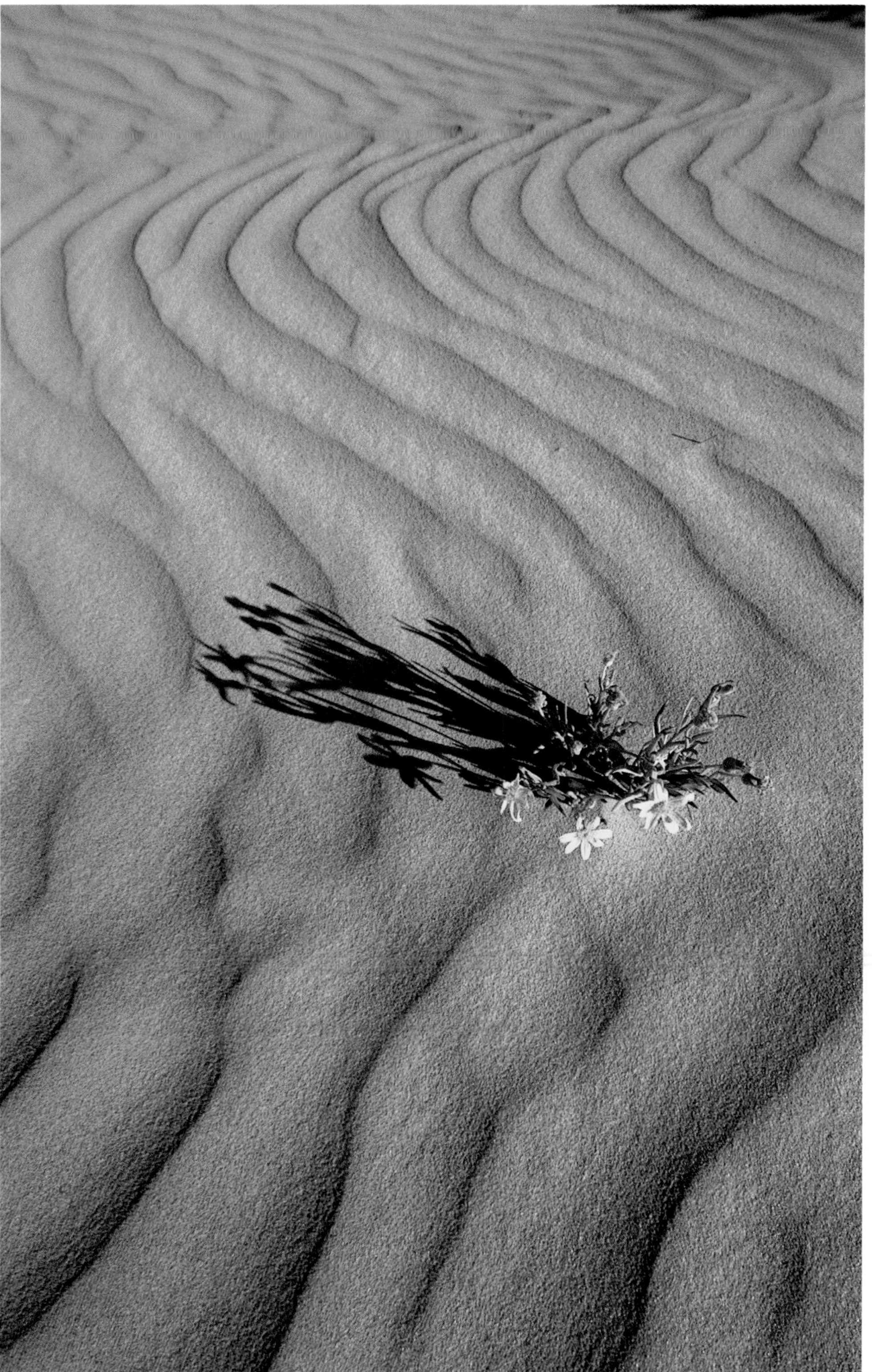

DESERT WILDFLOWER, SIMPSON DESERT, QUEENSLAND.
60th sec., f5.6, 24mm, 64asa.

SPINIFEX AND TERMITE MOUND, THE PILBARA, WESTERN AUSTRALIA.
60th sec., f8, 135mm, 64asa.

SAND GOANNA, THE PILBARA, WESTERN AUSTRALIA.
125th sec., f8, 80 - 200mm zoom, 64asa.

Spinifex is a plant that is as symbolic of Australia as the gum tree. It may not be recognised as such, but it should be. Spinifex covers some two thirds of the Australian landscape, primarily in areas of low rainfall. Under low light conditions, I find it impossible to resist as a subject for my camera.

An array of birds, mammals and reptiles finds sanctuary among its mats of needle sharp vegetation. Here a large predatory sand goanna found some difficulty searching out prey.

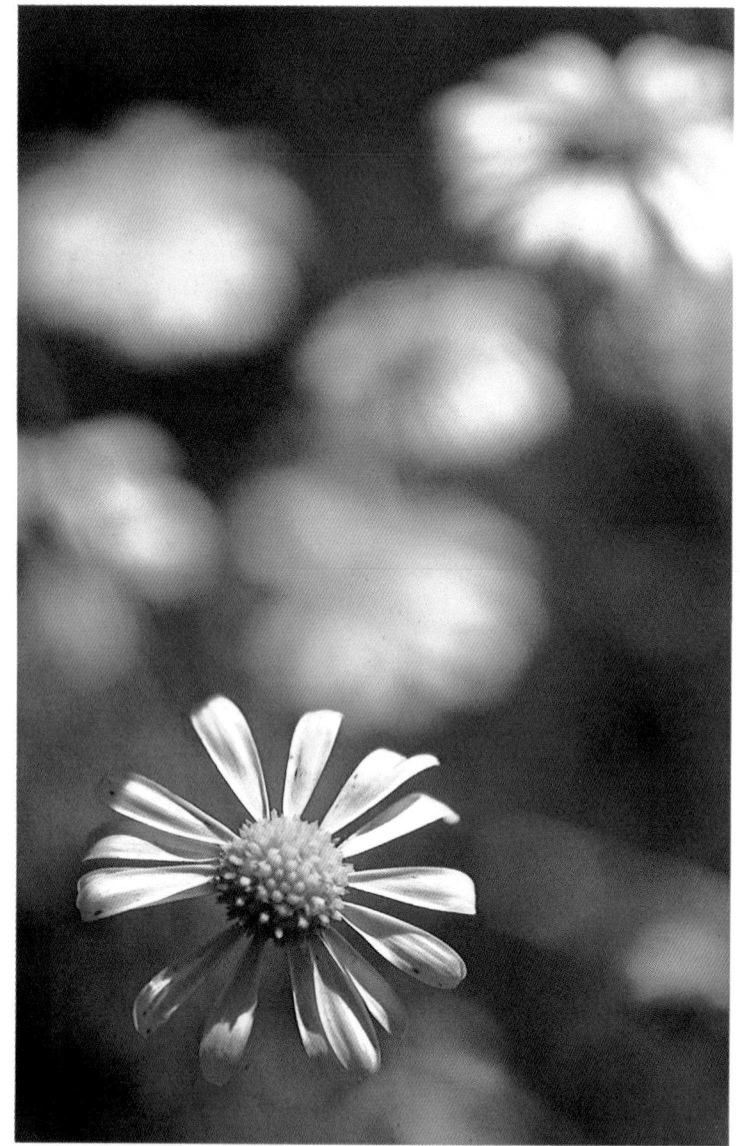

DESERT FLOWERS, BULLOO, QUEENSLAND.
125th sec., f2.8, 55mm, micro, 64asa.

DESERT FLOWERS, ULURU NATIONAL PARK, NORTHERN TERRITORY.
125th sec., f4, 105mm, 64asa.

The desert is such a big, awe-inspiring landscape that I sometimes find focusing in micro very difficult. Each time I do make the effort, I find I have entered into another world—a world of delicate intricacy, an intimate world where I cannot help feeling great humility.

DESERT FLOWERS, TANAMI DESERT, NORTHERN TERRITORY.
250th sec., f4, 105mm micro, 64asa.

KATAJUTA (THE OLGAS) FROM ULURU (AYERS ROCK), NORTHERN TERRITORY.
60th sec., f5.6, 400mm IFED, tripod, 64asa.

I find Katajuta spiritual and sensuous. It is one of Australia's most photographed landscapes, but it is impossible to capture on film the real life experience of a dawn walk among those monstrous domes. That is the challenge of landscape photography: to capture in a single photograph the feeling of such a magnificent wild place.

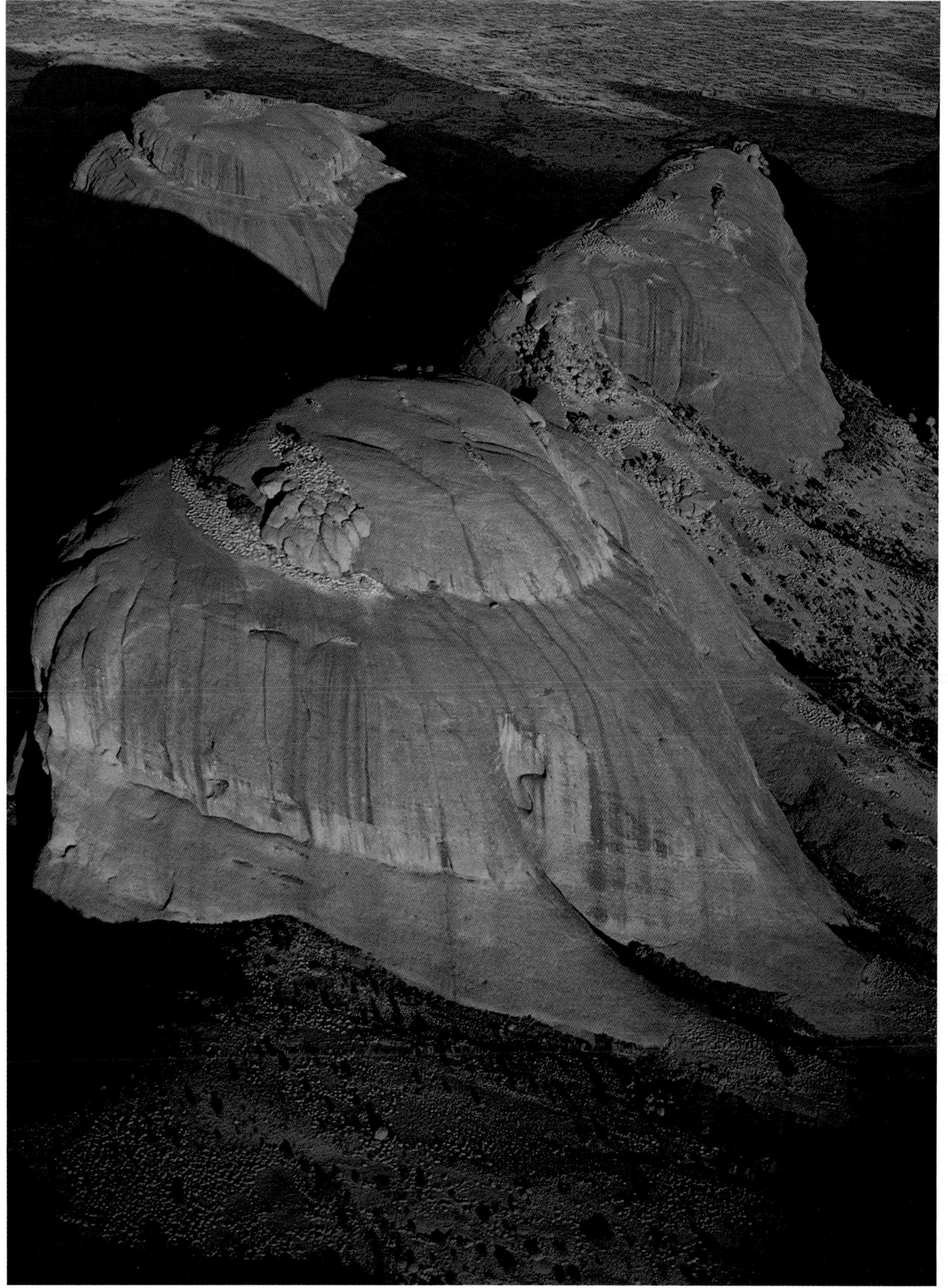

KATAJUTA FROM THE AIR, NORTHERN TERRITORY.
250th sec., f2.8, 24mm air, 64asa.

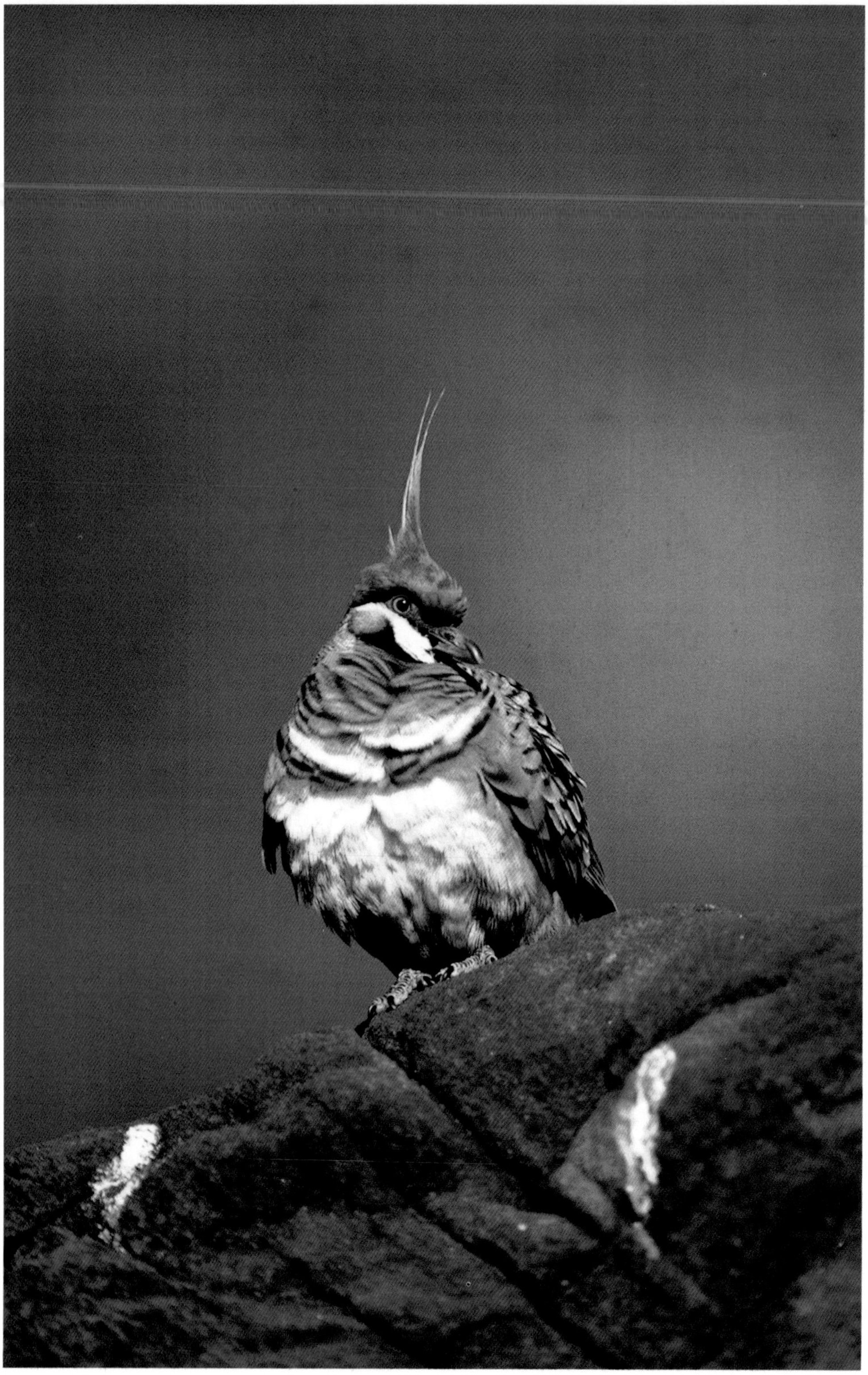

SPINIFEX PIGEON, KATAJUTA (THE OLGAS), NORTHERN TERRITORY.
125th sec., f5.6, 600mm IFED, tripod, 64asa.

It had been an extremely cold night and this Spinifex Pigeon was more occupied with warming up than with my approach. This picture captures the colours, and textures of the red centre.

The thing that impressed me most about this encounter was the relationship of size between Ayers Rock and the Nankeen Kestrel. I wanted to say 'bird of the rock,' not 'bird on a rock,' so I composed the image in a way that I felt placed equal emphasis on each.

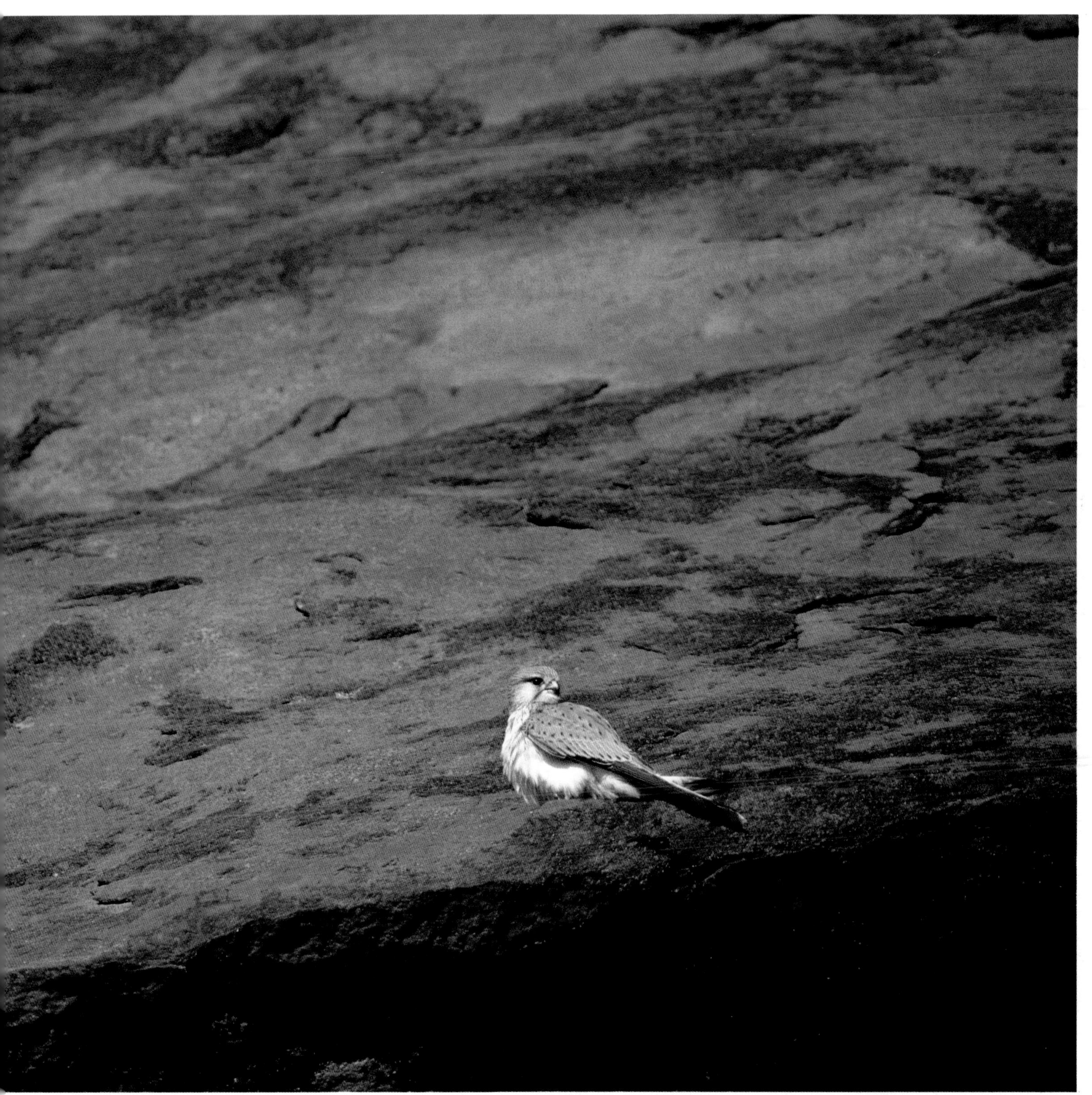

NANKEEN KESTREL, ULURU (AYERS ROCK), NORTHERN TERRITORY.
125th sec., f5.6, 600mm IFED, tripod, 64asa.

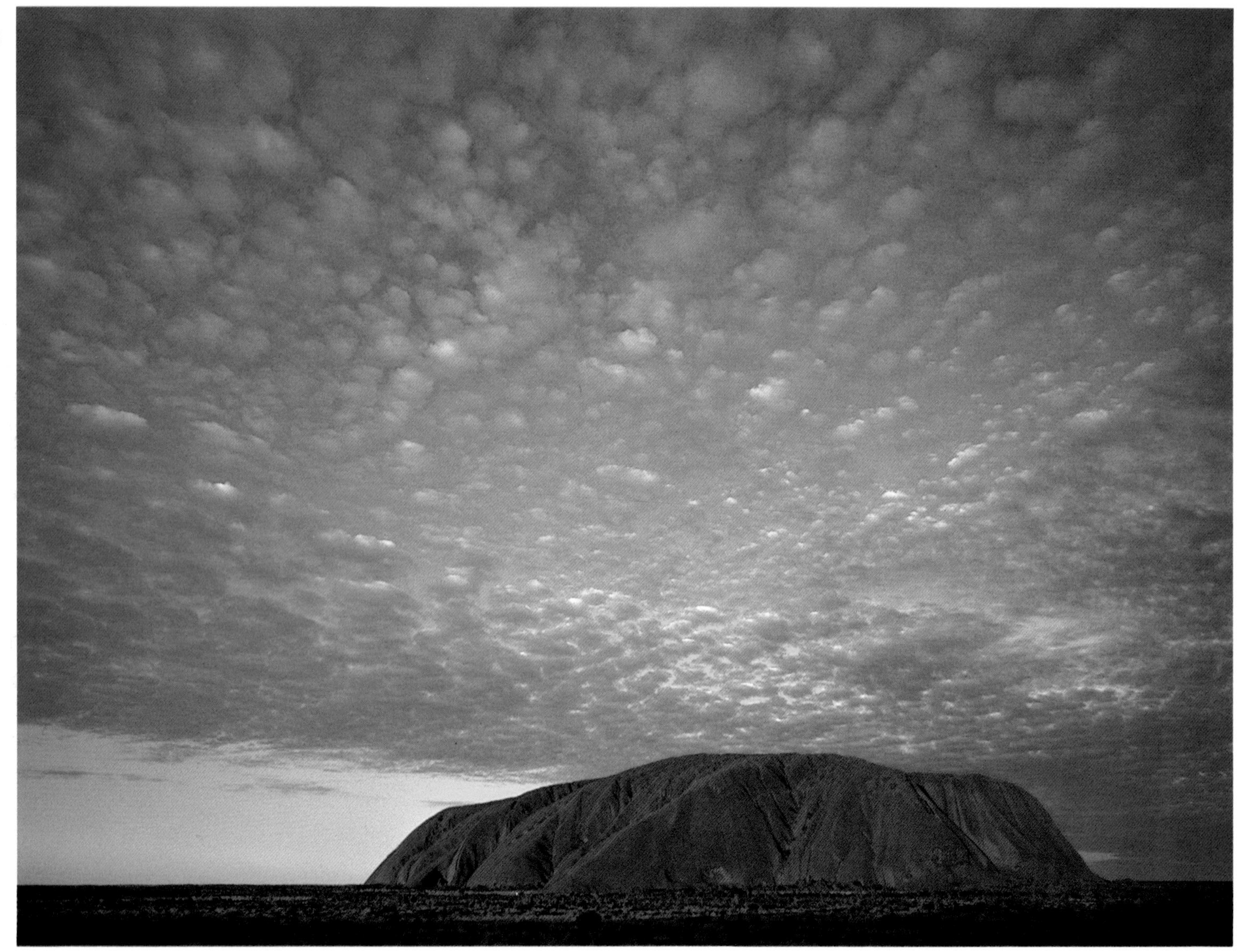

ULURU (AYERS ROCK) AT SUNSET, NORTHERN TERRITORY.
125th sec., f2.8, 24mm, 64asa.

It has been photographed millions of times, but it is still impossible to resist. I found sitting and watching the rock from the pristine desert that surrounds it absolutely awe-inspiring.

I just could not take my eyes off that great red rock floating in an endless ocean of sand. No wonder the aboriginal people hold it sacred!

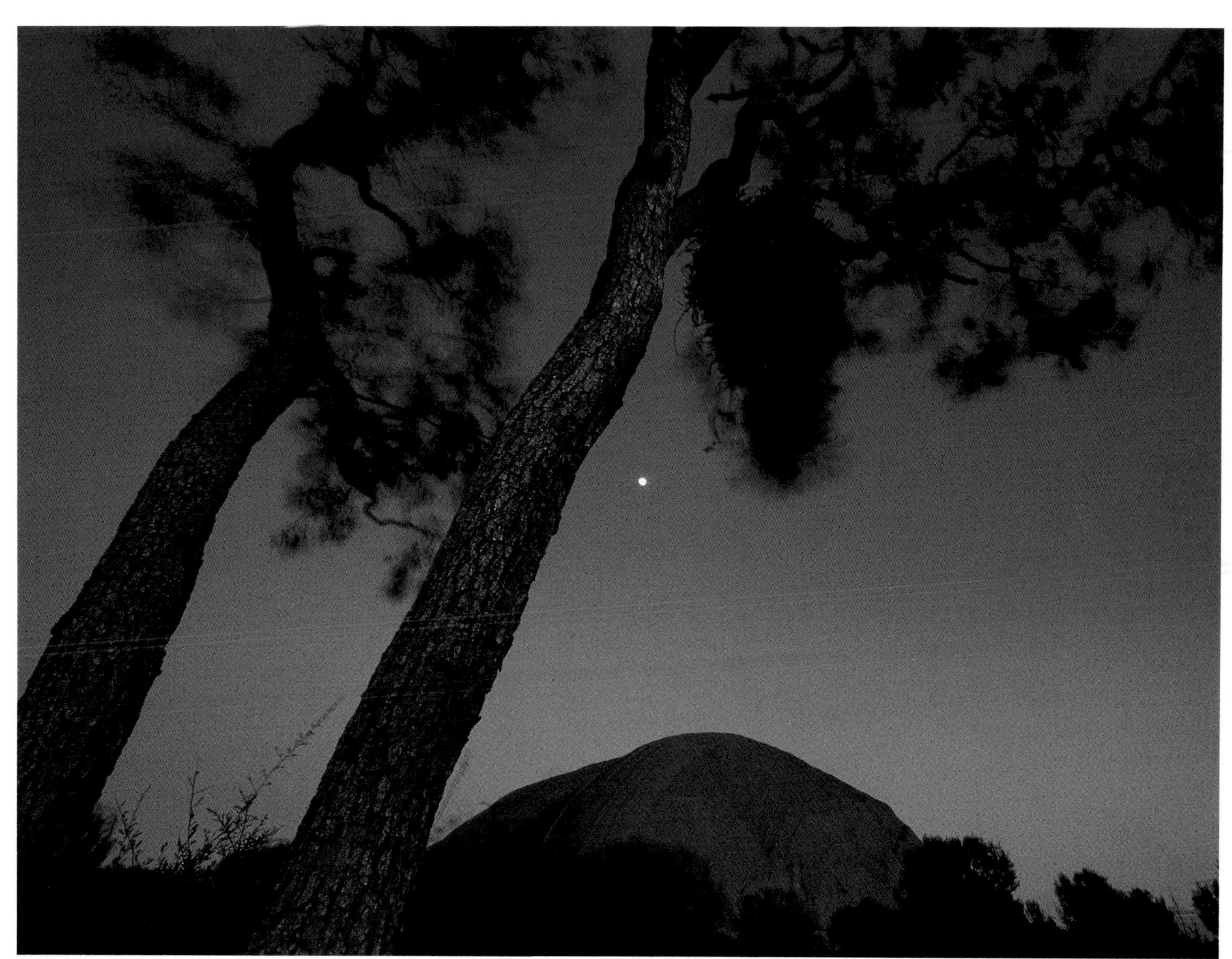

ULURU (AYERS ROCK) AFTER SUNSET, NORTHERN TERRITORY.
30th sec., f3.5, 15mm, tripod, 64asa.

Here, beneath the towering walls of Hamersley Gorge, I used a telephoto lens to 'crop out' all but the shimmering reflections in the water.

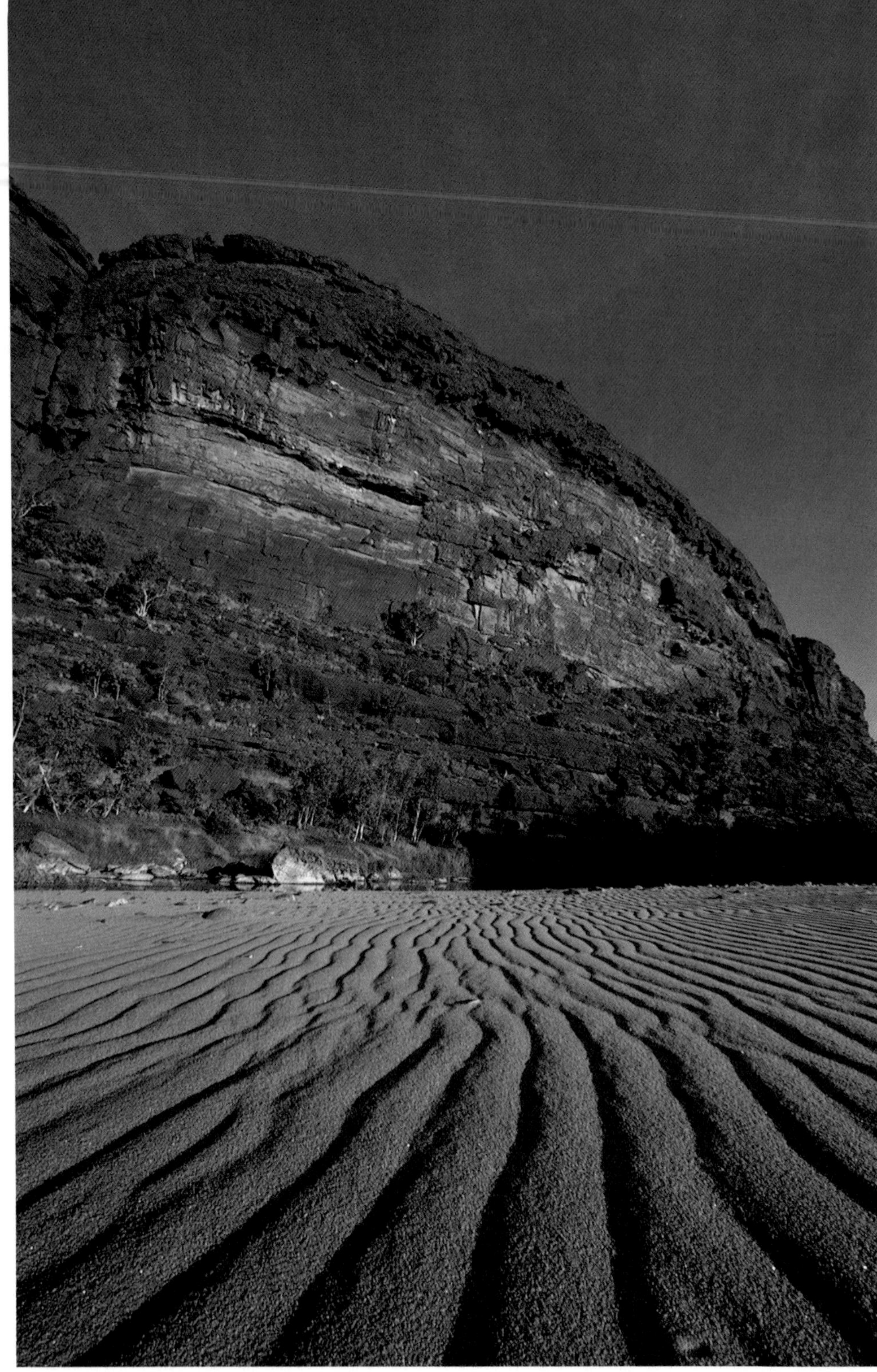

FINKE RIVER, NORTHERN TERRITORY.
30th sec., f16, 15mm, 64asa.

One of Australia's little known, but visually very inspiring places, is the Finke River. It is easy to believe that this is geologically the world's oldest river.

Here I have tried to heighten the drama of this magificent gorge by lying flat on my stomach with my wide angle lens almost touching the sand.

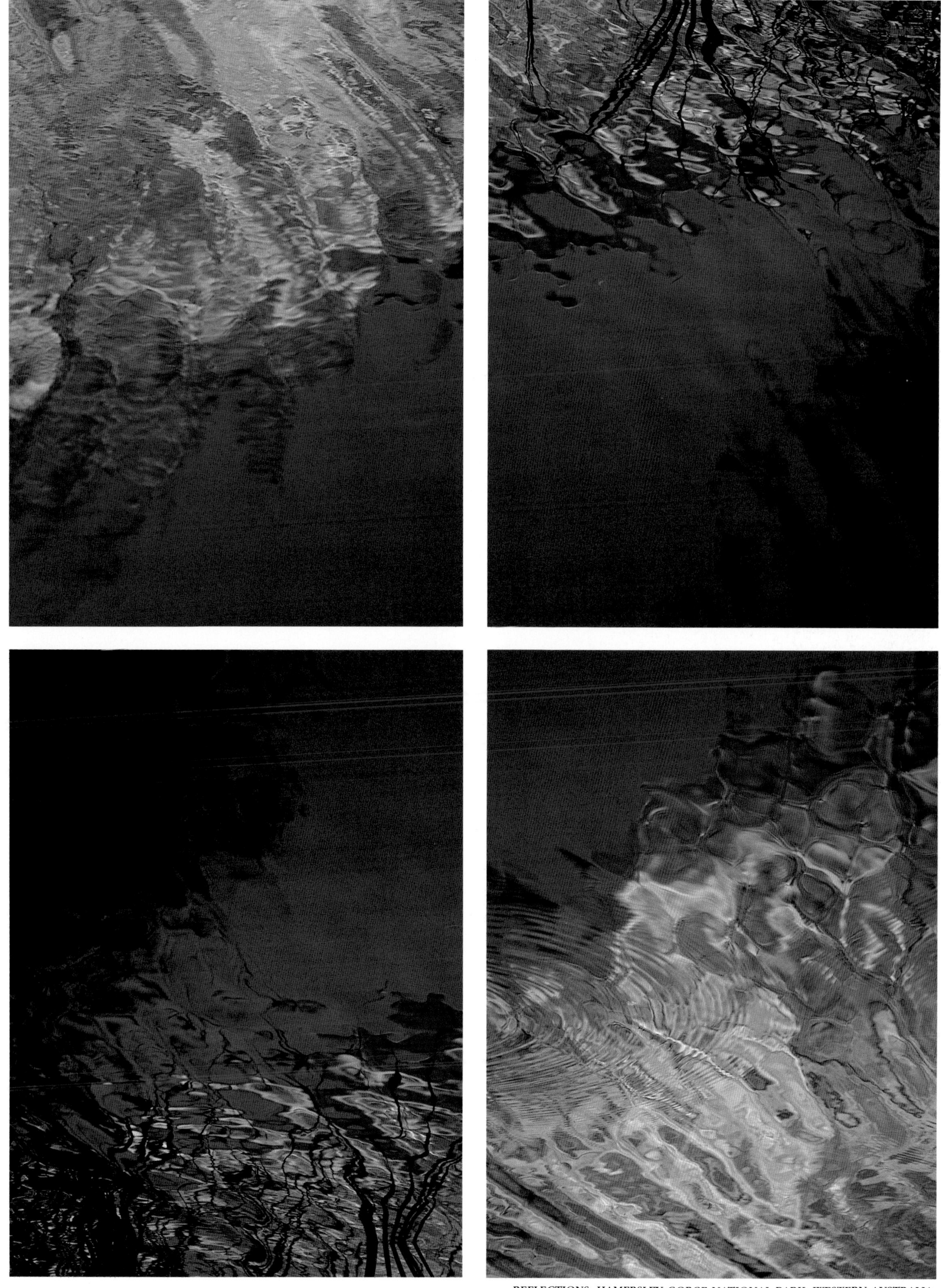

REFLECTIONS, HAMERSLEY GORGE NATIONAL PARK, WESTERN AUSTRALIA.
125th sec., f2.8, 135mm, 64asa.

RIVER RED GUM AT TWILIGHT, FLINDERS RANGES, SOUTH AUSTRALIA.
30th sec., f2.8, 24mm, tripod, 64asa.

In the soft, surreal glow of twilight, this scene offers a striking contrast with the harshness of the same landscape during a long, hot day.

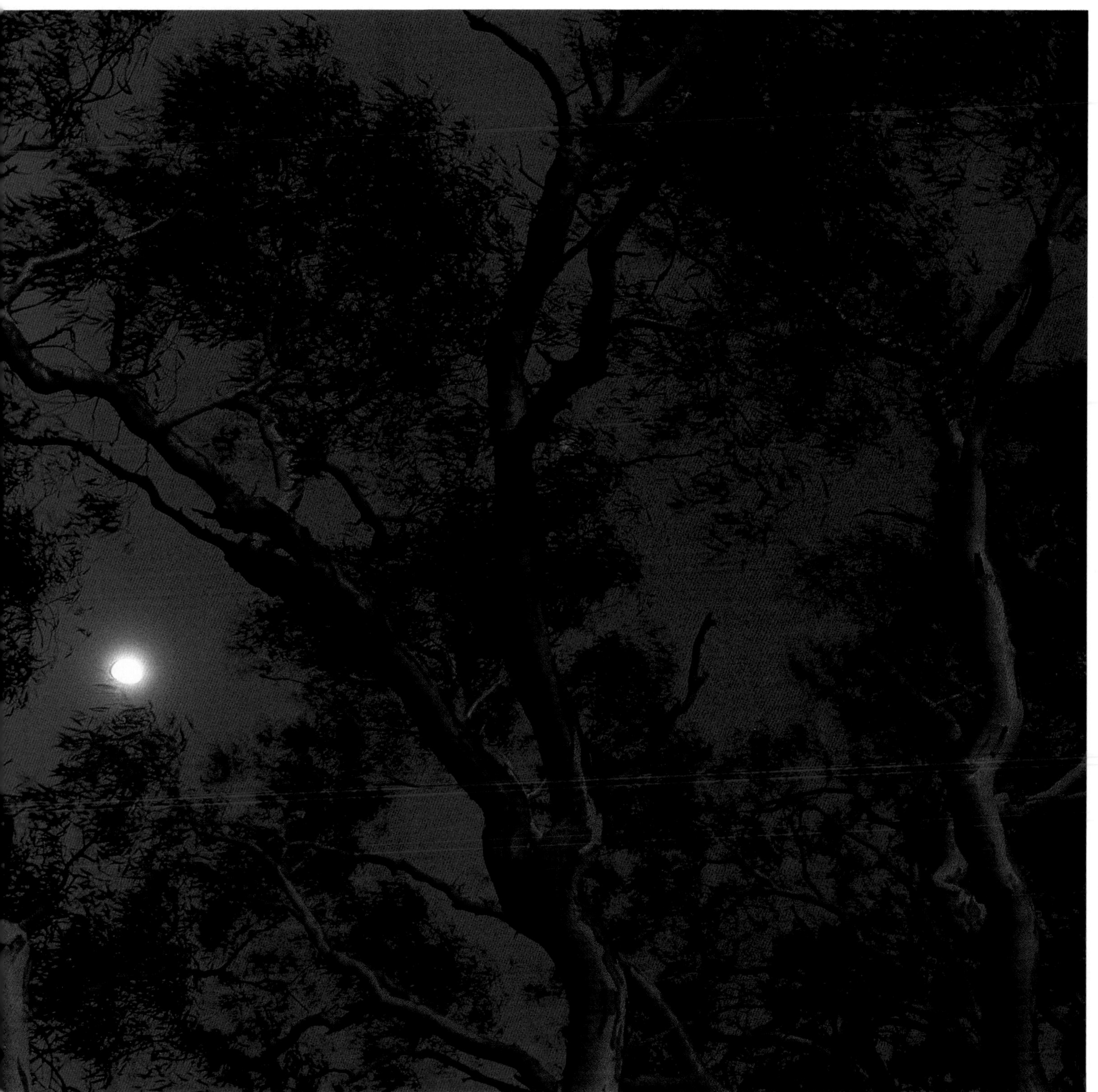

RIVER RED GUM AT TWILIGHT, FLINDERS RANGES, SOUTH AUSTRALIA.
30th sec., f2.8, 135mm, tripod, 64asa.

MITCHELL GRASS PLAINS, WESTERN QUEENSLAND.
125th sec., f5.6, 15mm, 64asa.

Space, where you can scream out loud with only the trees to hear you.

BOAB TREE, WESTERN KIMBERLEYS, NEAR THE EDGE OF THE GREAT SANDY DESERT, WESTERN AUSTRALIA.
125th sec., f5.6, 15mm, 64asa.

Space, where you can reach up and touch the sky.

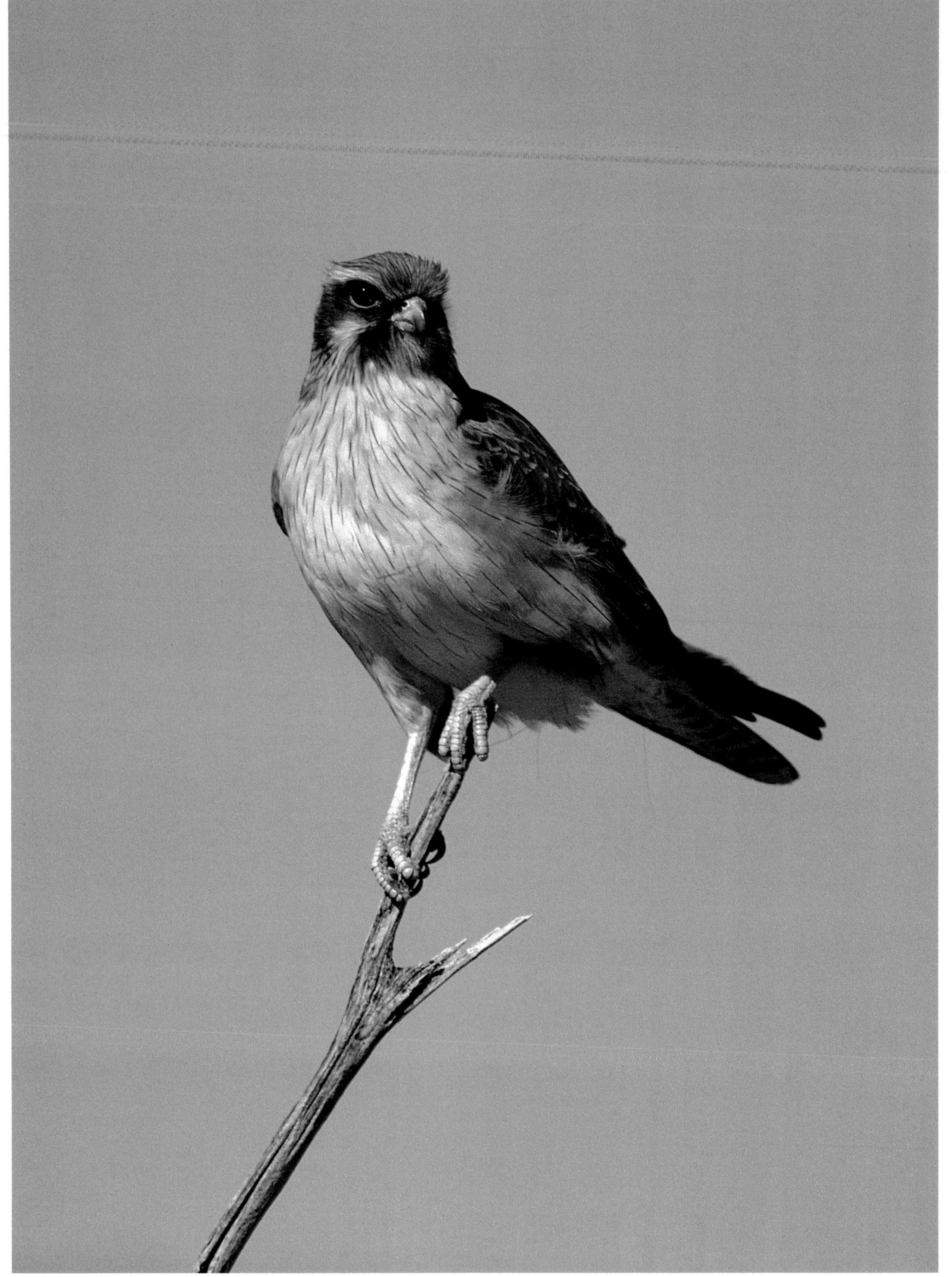

BROWN FALCON, SIMPSON DESERT, NORTHERN TERRITORY.
125th sec., f5.6, 600mm IFED, 64asa.

WILDLIFE–A ROADSIDE ENCOUNTER

T*RAVERSING A LANDSCAPE* as vast as the Australian Outback inevitably demands quite some time behind the wheel. Not being the sort of person who can waste time, I always try to travel early or late in the day. As well as providing better lighting conditions, these are the times when the wildlife is most active.

In many areas, dingos, kangaroos, birds and even some reptiles are quite used to seeing vehicles pass by. With a little driving skill and a lot of cunning, a photographer can often drive quite close to a subject.

One of the main problems with taking photos from a vehicle is the angle of view, particularly with birds in trees. The closer you get to an elevated subject the greater the angle becomes. The Brown Falcon has a good front-on perspective because it was perching quite low. The Whistling Kite was higher up, giving a less appealing angle.

WHISTLING KITE, WESTERN AUSTRALIA.
125th sec., f5.6, 600mm IFED, 64asa.

WOODSWALLOWS, ULURU NATIONAL PARK, NORTHERN TERRITORY.
125th sec., f5.6, 600mm IFED, 64asa.

With the car window wound up a few centimetres, and with a small sand bag as a telephoto rest, I watched these Black-faced Woodswallows for almost an hour as they preened each other and squabbled for perching space. Their communal roosting behaviour serves them well during a cold winter's night, and at dawn they remain together until the temperature suits them.

WEDGE-TAILED EAGLE, NEAR BROKEN HILL, NEW SOUTH WALES.
125th sec., f5.6, 600mm IFED, 64asa.

Detecting wildlife as you travel does require that you keep to a moderate speed. It is an advantage if you have company, as two pairs of eyes are always better than one. Connie, my wife and constant companion, spotted this Wedge-tailed Eagle well ahead feeding on a kangaroo road kill. We stalked it in the car as close as possible but the bird took flight before we were close enough to photograph it feeding. Here, through a hand-held 600mm lens, I was still able to 'pluck' the giant bird of prey out of the sky as it circled its prey on the ground below.

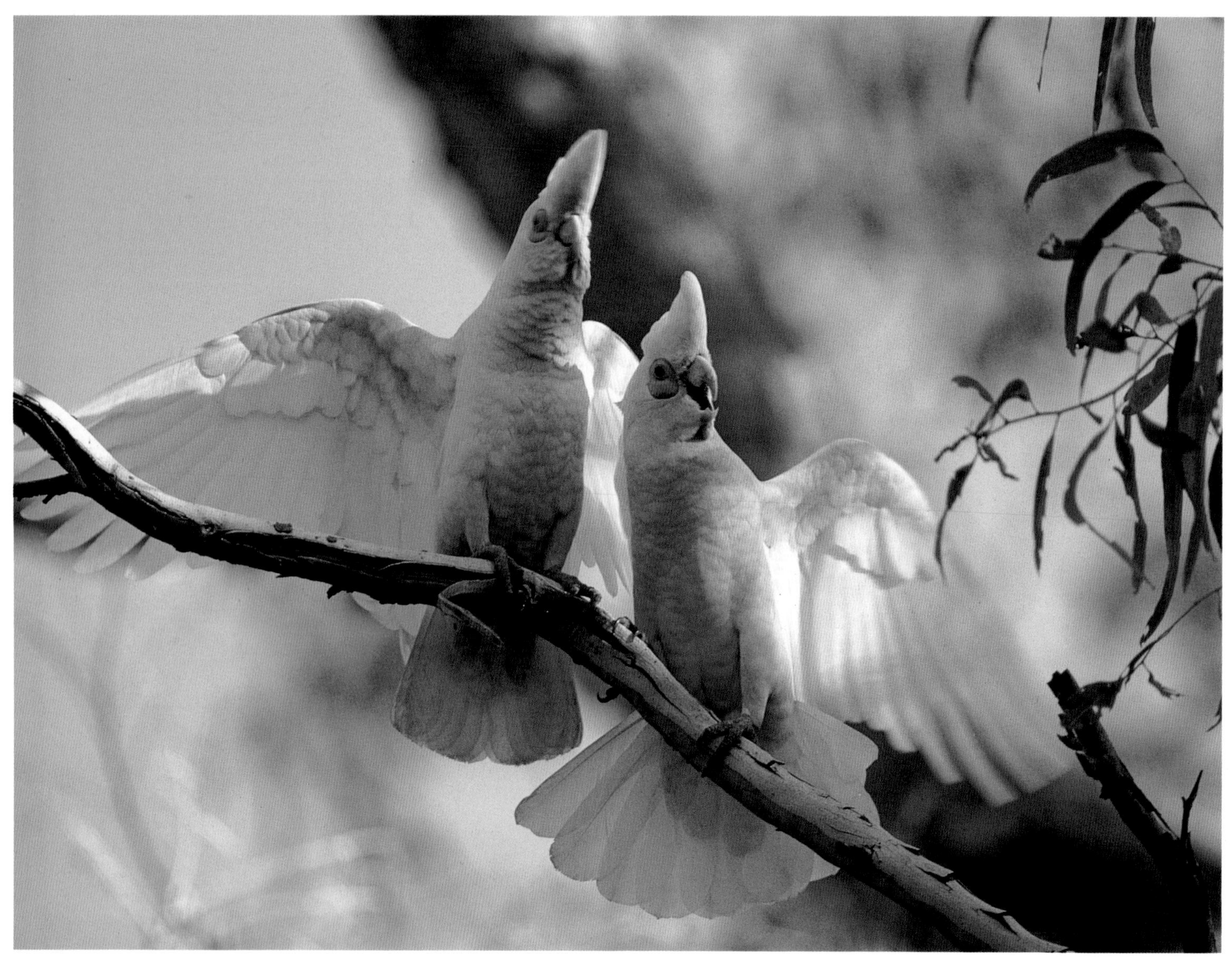

LITTLE CORELLAS, THE KIMBERLEYS, WESTERN AUSTRALIA.
125th sec., f5.6, 600mm IFED, 64asa.

One of the nicest things about wandering outback is that each evening brings a new camp site filled with adventure. Here, at an isolated billabong in the Kimberleys, we drove in to camp to a cacophony of corellas and ducks.

If the camp site is open there is little point in trying to hide. After a time however, if you quietly go about your business, the bird-life returns. If I am planning to camp, I generally do not even attempt to make pictures until everything has quietened down.

LITTLE CORELLA AND GRASS WHISTLING DUCKS, THE KIMBERLEYS, WESTERN AUSTRALIA.
125th sec., f5.6, 600mm IFED, 64asa.

PLAINS BUSTARD, PLENTY HIGHWAY, NORTHERN TERRITORY.
125th sec., f5.6, 400mm IFED, 64asa.

As a defensive tactic the Plains Bustard may either take flight or remain perfectly still, relying on its cryptic camouflage. That this animal was in an extremely photogenic pose was simply my good fortune.

Learning something about the habitats that you will pass through can be of immeasurable value. Additional information gleaned from a reference book in a matter of minutes can make your trip far more enjoyable. As your eye develops, you will detect animals previously unseen. So many people have told me that they found a locality boring as they saw no animals. In fact these people simply passed them by.

THORNY DEVIL, ULURU NATIONAL PARK, NORTHERN TERRITORY.
125th sec., f5.6, 600mm IFED, 64asa.

Thorny Devil, Star of the Desert.

I had long wanted to make the Thorny Devil famous, and in October 1983 the Daily Sun in Brisbane finally ran "Star of the Desert" as a headline.

My motive was simply that this fascinating creature was an animal which I felt people should be aware of. Few creatures survive in the hottest environments on earth, and still fewer drink by standing in water or collecting it as dew on the spines on their backs.

Like most desert dwellers, the Thorny Devil is superbly camouflaged, and I had to develop an eye for them before I could find this large individual. A long telephoto lens with a small aperture was used to give the shallow depth of field that enabled me to bring the animal out of its background in this shot.

WILD DONKEYS, THE KIMBERLEYS, WESTERN AUSTRALIA.
500th sec., f2.8, 135mm, 64asa.

Photographing both the horses and the donkeys from a car window at 35km per hour required cross country driving. This sort of shoot-on-the-run exercise can cause you to come to grief, as termite mounds and logs do have a habit of jumping up and hitting you when you least expect it. It pays to let somebody else drive while you do the shooting.

Horses and donkeys proliferate in the outback. Both are feral (domestic animals gone wild), and in some areas of Australia they are in such plague proportions that massive helicopter shoots have been organised to cull the numbers.

WILD BRUMBIES NEAR LAKE FROME, SOUTH AUSTRALIA.
500th sec., f2.8, 135mm, 64asa.

DINGO, PLENTY HIGHWAY, NORTHERN TERRITORY.
250th sec., f5.6, 600mm IFED, 64asa.

It is believed that the Dingo was introduced into Australia by nomadic aborigines some 50,000 years ago. Today, while the animal roams most parts of the continent, there is still considerable debate regarding its status: vermin or native.

In the Northern Territory, I encountered the dog on the right draped over a roadside fence deep in cattle country. The animal above was enjoying life beside a lonely country road, apparently unconcerned by what might almost have been its first encounter with man.

DINGO, BARKLY TABLELAND, NORTHERN TERRITORY.
125th sec., f8, 15mm, 64asa.

BAD VIBES, CAPE YORK, QUEENSLAND.
125th sec., f8, 135mm, 64asa.

GOOD VIBES, CAPE YORK, QUEENSLAND.
125th sec., f8, 135mm, 64asa.

LIVING OUTBACK

O*N ONE OF MY* outback wanderings I met a man in an isolated community who had been sent by his church to take up a position as resident pastor. He had come from a large church in Sydney, a situation of incredible contrast. He was sixty years old, did not drink, was a vegetarian, and did not swear as only Centralians can. At the time I met him he had convinced himself that he was doomed to be an outcast. We sat together under a star-filled sky, talking quietly. He was a sensitive, sincere man, and it was obvious that he was under great pressure.

I felt a kinship in spirit with the preacher as I had experienced some similar fears. I had found that the pressure of having to make a direct personal approach to a complete stranger for the purpose of making pictures had been a real problem. After all, I was invading privacy. As we chatted we realised that the real problem facing both of us was of our own making. What was holding us back from making contact was a fear of failure—a fear that we would not be accepted. We felt that we had to perform, that we had to change to become someone that we thought others would accept. In doing so, we did not realise that the performance, being a lie, was being rejected.

My first experience photographing people was horrific. I was petrified. As time passed I began to realise that my fellows were not very different from many of my more familiar subjects. Like so many animals, people respond to feelings. So, instead of feeling fearful, instead of expecting rejection, I simply began to approach people on my terms: as me, rather than the person I thought I should be.

If you want to experience the thrill of making people pictures, all you will need to be successful is the real you, and your camera.

STURT'S STONY DESERT, SOUTH WEST QUEENSLAND.
60th sec., f11, 15mm, 64asa.

There has been a great deal said about the hardships confronting our early settlers and explorers. I sometimes wonder if we should make comparisons based on our own expericnces.

Burke and Wills would surely turn in their graves if they could see an air-conditioned landcruiser complete with long range tanks, winches, electric fridges, gas cookers, wide wheels and stereo music floating over the very same desert that killed them.

Or perhaps they may not feel much envy for our technology. After all, the first settlers and explorers had a sense of achievement, and they were totally in touch with the landscape. I wonder how many owners of 'cruisers now leave their air-conditioned capsules to wander out there in the sun, alone with a thousand flies.

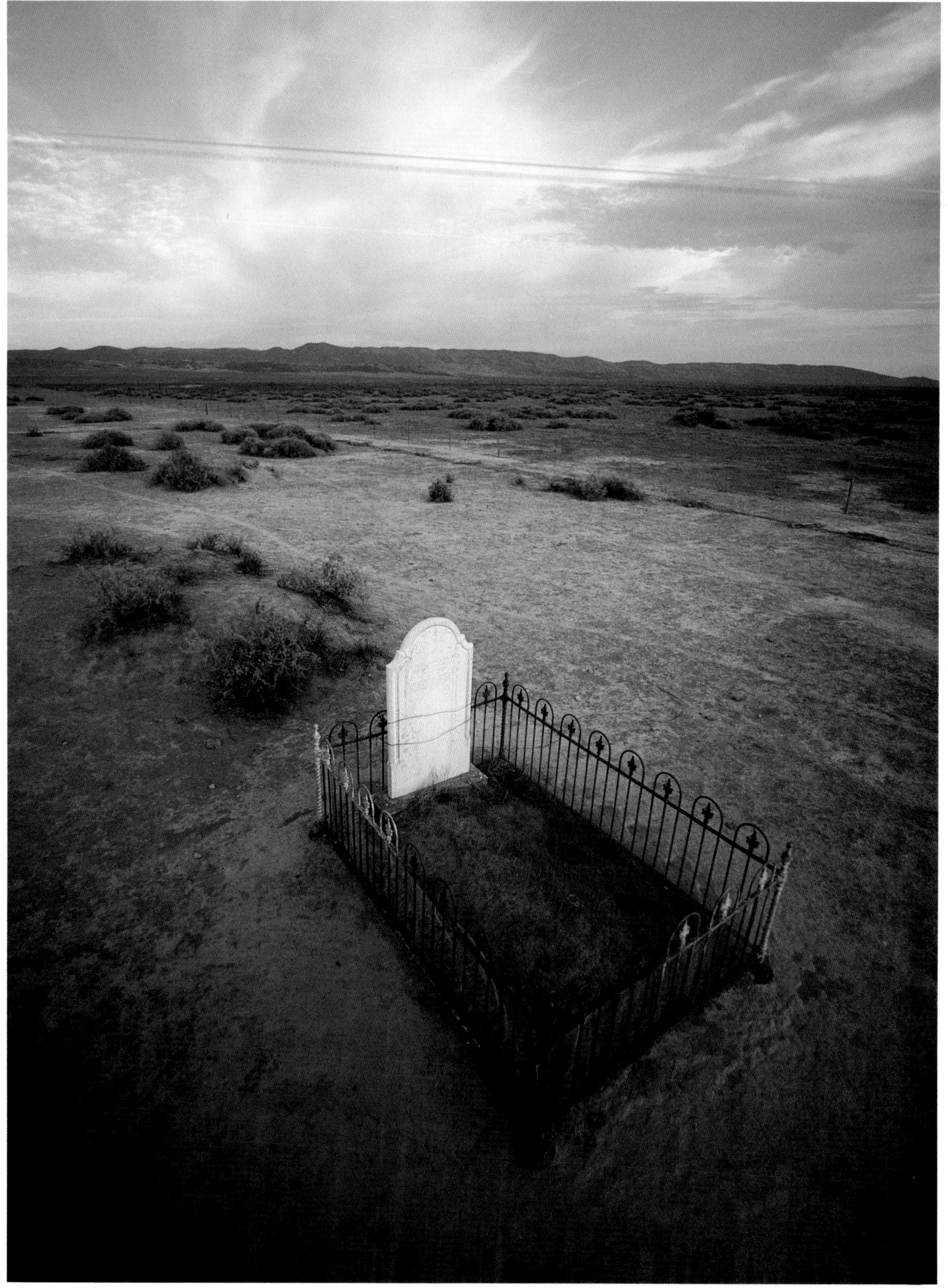

A LONELY GRAVE ON THE PLAINS EAST OF QUORN, SOUTH AUSTRALIA.
125th sec., f8, 15mm, 64asa.

Wentworth, Swan Hill and Echuca are just three of many Murray River townships that provide the photographer with a feast of historical memorabilia.

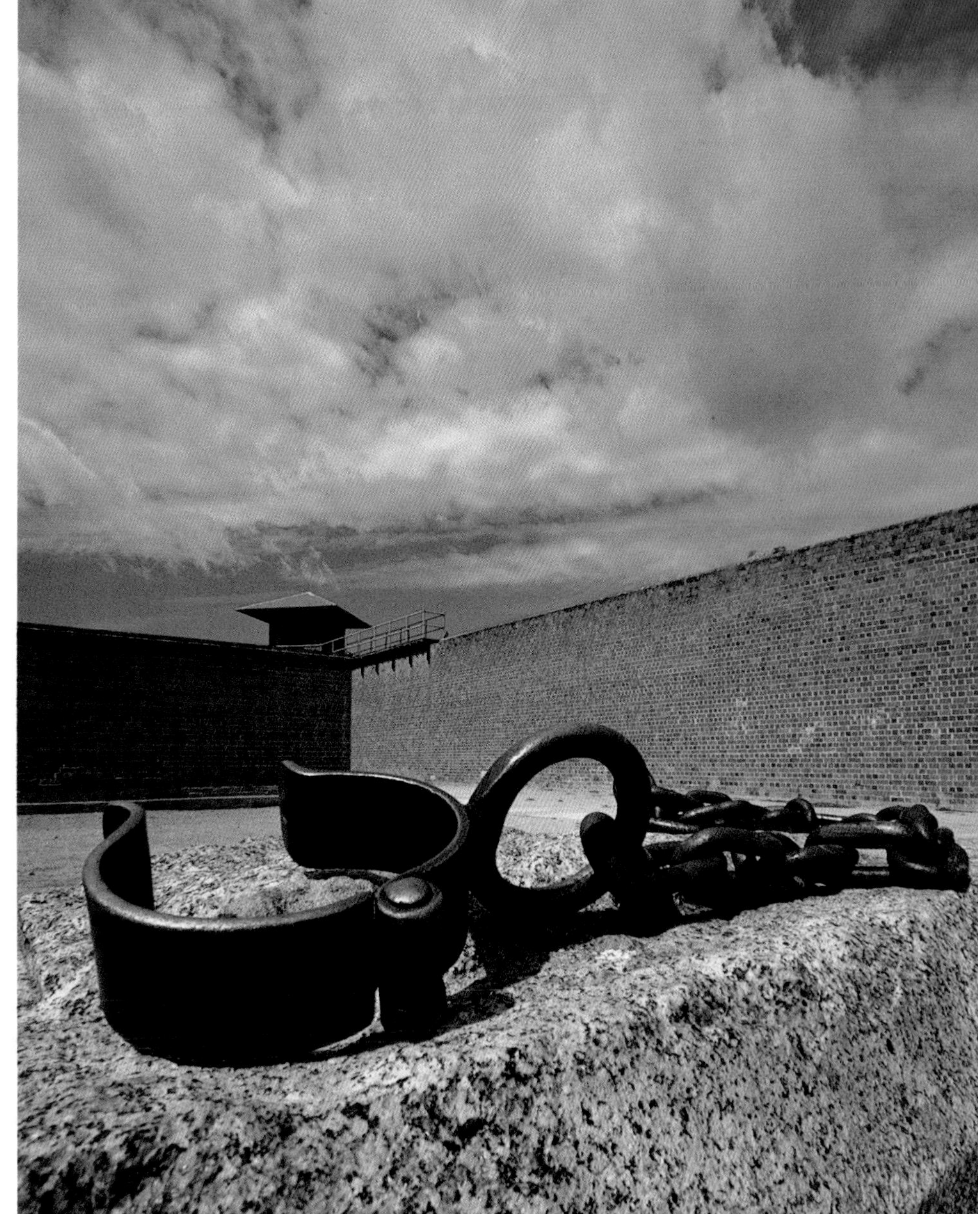

WENTWORTH GAOL, WENTWORTH, NEW SOUTH WALES.
125th sec., f8, 15mm, 64asa.

'Weep not for me my children dear
I am not alone but sleeping here
my debt is paid
my grave you see
so all prepare to follow me'

Harriet Anna Salmon
Died October 1885—
Aged 28 Years.

LAKE HARRY HOMESTEAD, BIRDSVILLE TRACK, SOUTH AUSTRALIA.
60th sec., f3.5, 15mm, tripod, 64asa.

Someone probably celebrated the day this homestead was built. It is the photographer's role to record its passing.

60

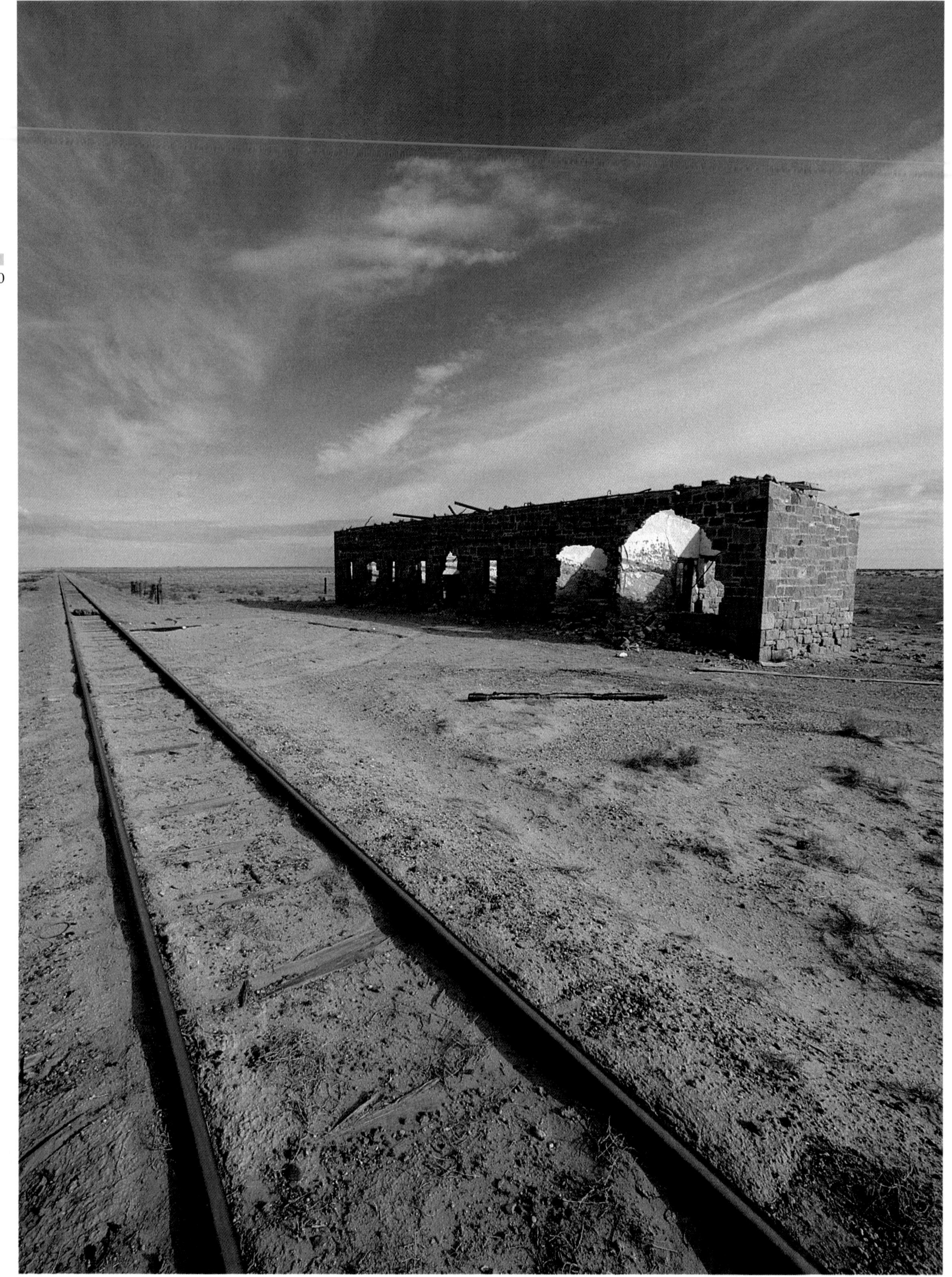

GHAN RAILWAY SIDING, SOUTH AUSTRALIA.
125th sec., f8, 15mm, 64asa.

GHAN RAILWAY FETTLERS' CAMP, SOUTH AUSTRALIA.
125th sec., f8, 15mm, 64asa.

The Ghan Railway ran from Port Augusta, north through the South Australian Outback to Alice Springs in the Northern Territory. In 1983 workers commenced removing the old line which has been replaced with a faster, wider guage several hundred kilometres to the west.

In the old days the line serviced Farina, Lyndhurst, Marree and Oodnadatta as well as numerous outback stations.

Today most of these towns lie idle, barely surviving on a scant tourist trade. In terms of ruins, graves, and a multitude of artifacts, I found the old Ghan a photographic gold mine.

TODD RIVER, ALICE SPRINGS, NORTHERN TERRITORY.
125th sec., f5.6, 15mm, 64asa.

When I discovered this old boot near an abandoned gold mine, I could almost feel the exhaustion and disappointment that I'm sure its owner experienced.

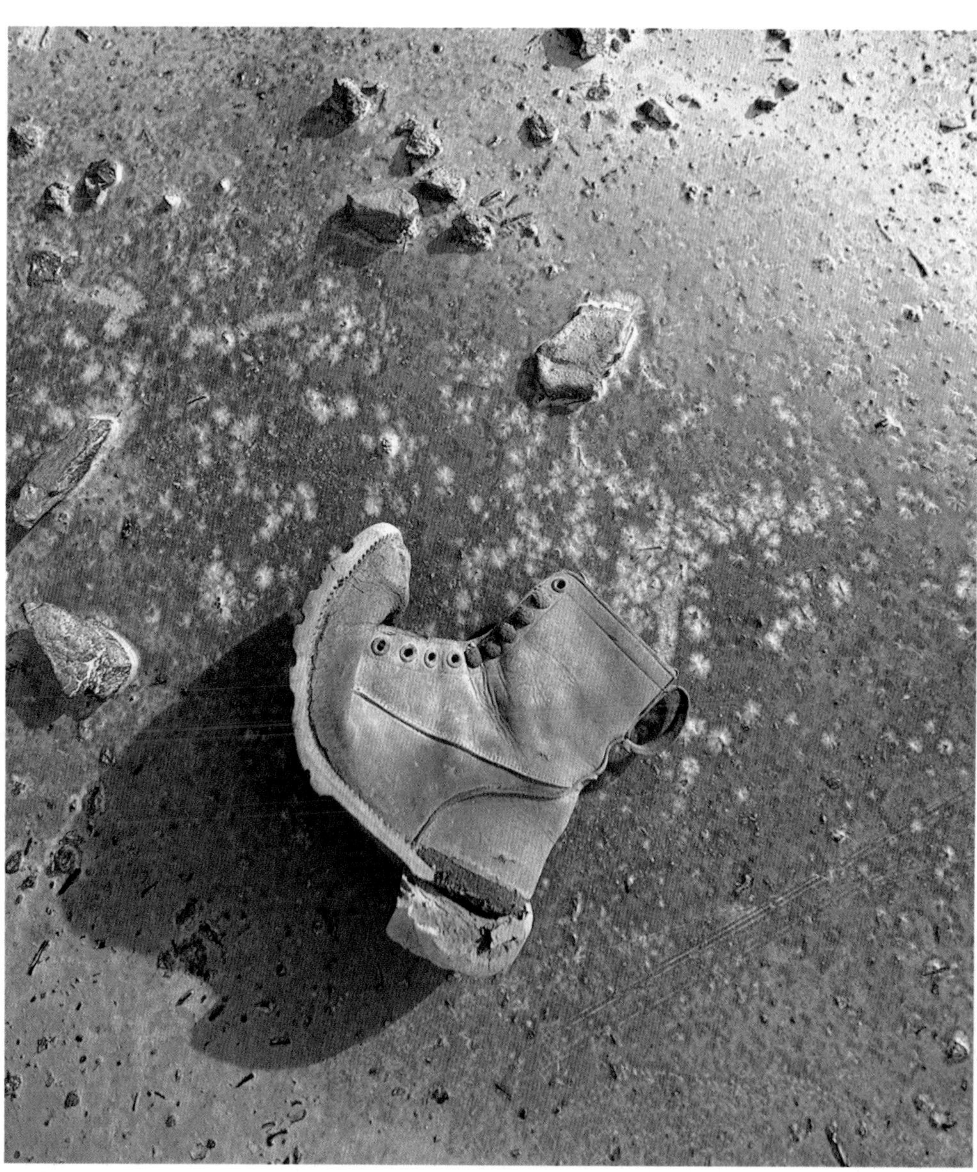

MINER'S BOOT, NORSEMAN, WESTERN AUSTRALIA.
125th sec., f5.6, 15mm, 64asa.

I made this picture after spending two weeks in one of Australia's saddest towns. It graphically portrays cultural conflict—the trolleys are used to carry booze.

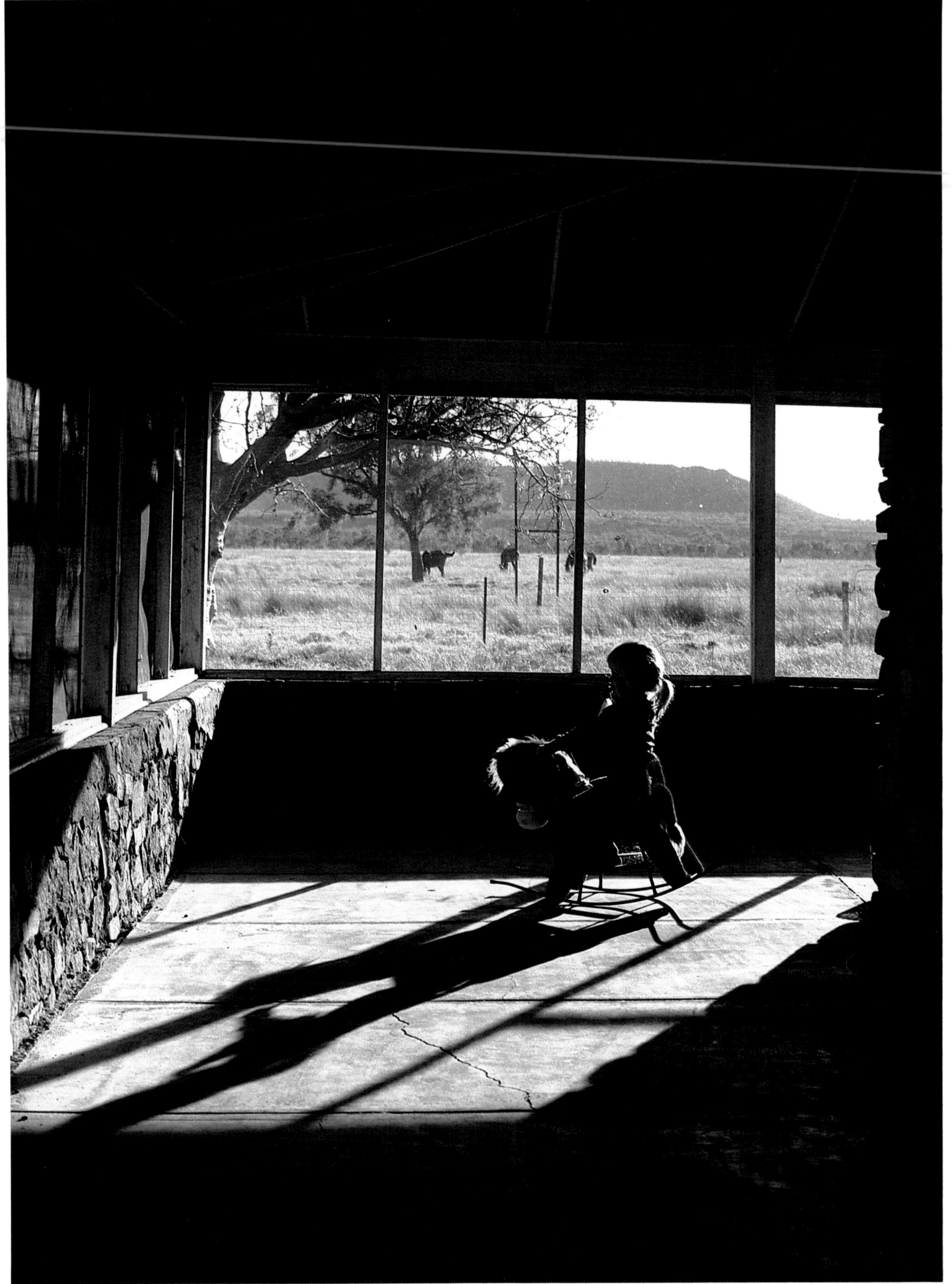

COOLIBAH HOMESTEAD, VICTORIA RIVER, NORTHERN TERRITORY,
125th sec., f8, 135mm, 64asa.

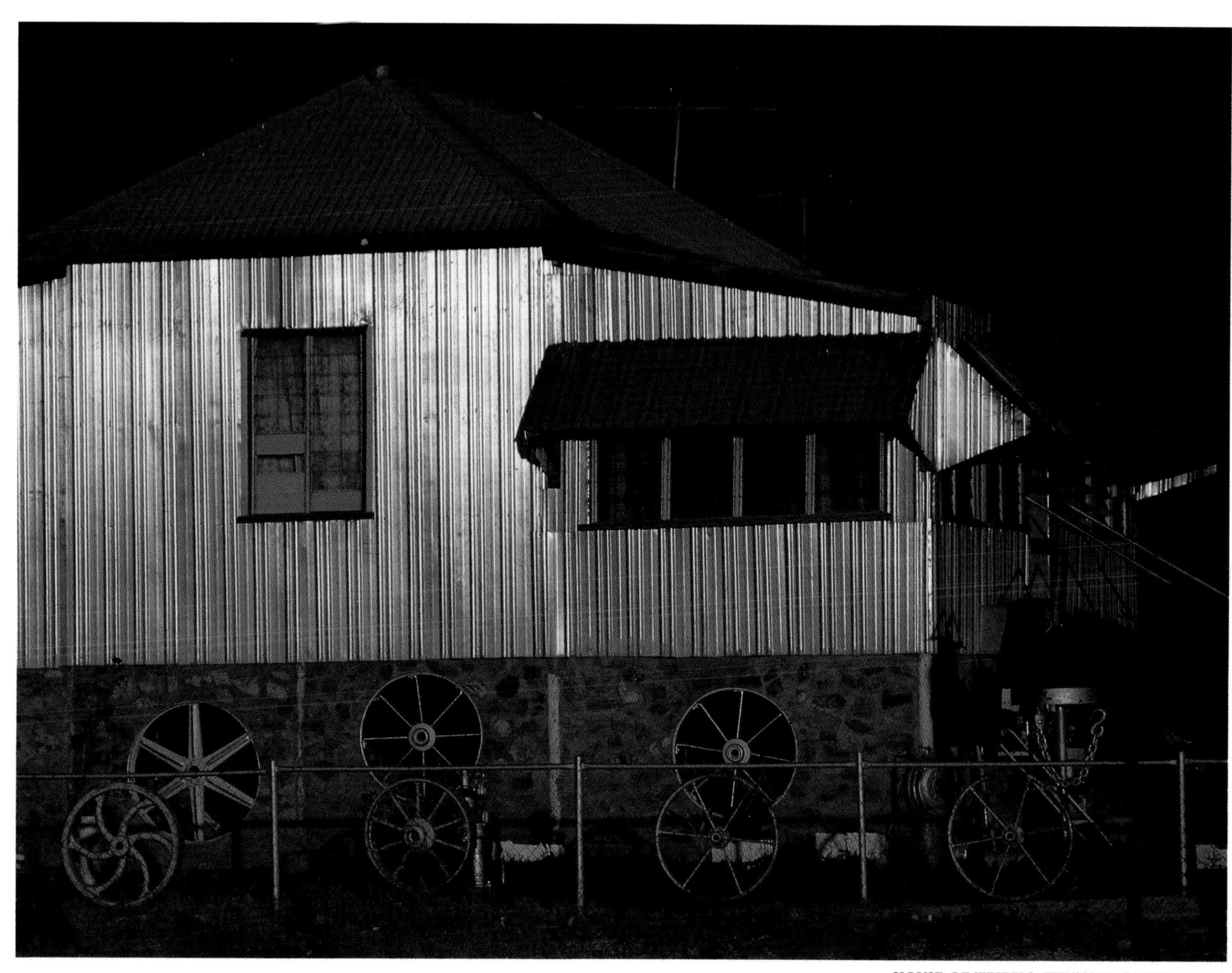

HOUSE OF WHEELS, WINTON, QUEENSLAND.
60th sec., f8, 80 - 200mm zoom, 64asa.

Coolibah is one of those delightful old homes with a huge verandah that extends around the entire house. I was sitting quietly on the verandah sipping tea when I noticed the relationship between the rocking horse and the horses in the paddock outside. I went inside to get my camera. When I returned, the rocking horse had a rider!

I am not sure whether it is simply because they have lots of time to spare, or whether it is because they have such excellent imagination, but folk of the outback certainly have a flair for creating personalised homes.

Central Queensland provides some remarkable examples—the front yards are frequently adorned with flamboyant decoration.

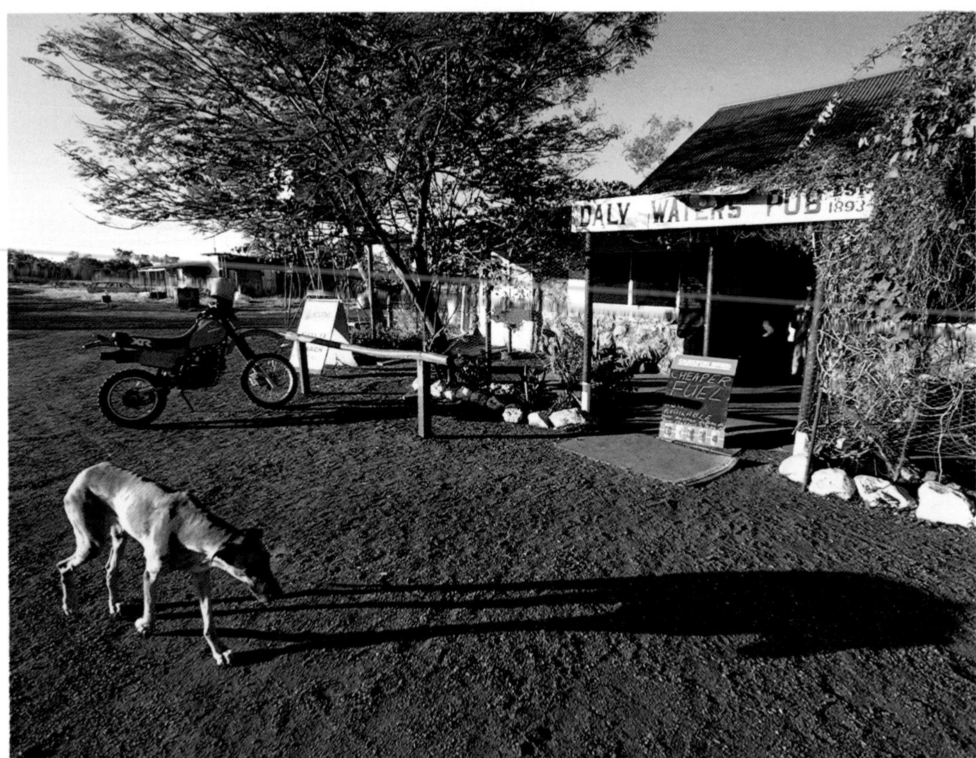

DALY WATERS HOTEL, NORTHERN TERRITORY.
125th sec., f5.6, 15mm, 64asa.

THE OLD AUSTRALIA HOTEL, KALGOORLIE, WESTERN AUSTRALIA.
125th sec., f5.6, 135mm, 64asa.

Pubs are the heart of the outback. Here you collect mail and food, have a drink and gather local information. Many 'towns' look quite large and inviting on the map, but in reality, the only building to be found might well be the pub.

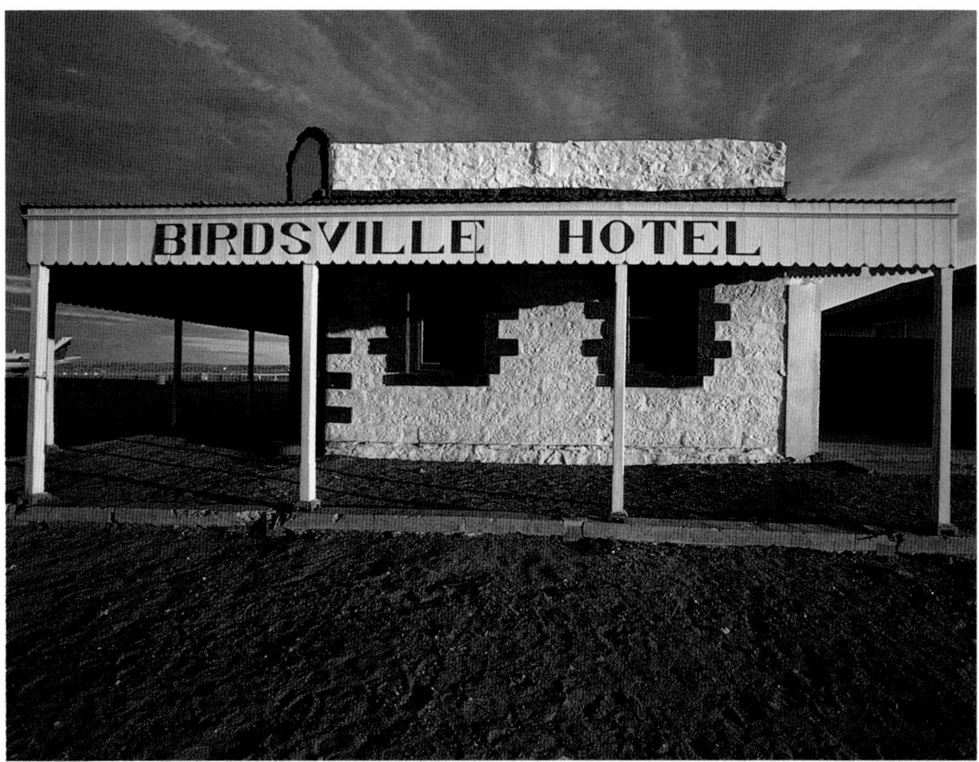

BIRDSVILLE HOTEL, SOUTH WEST QUEENSLAND.
125th sec., f5.6, 15mm, 64asa.

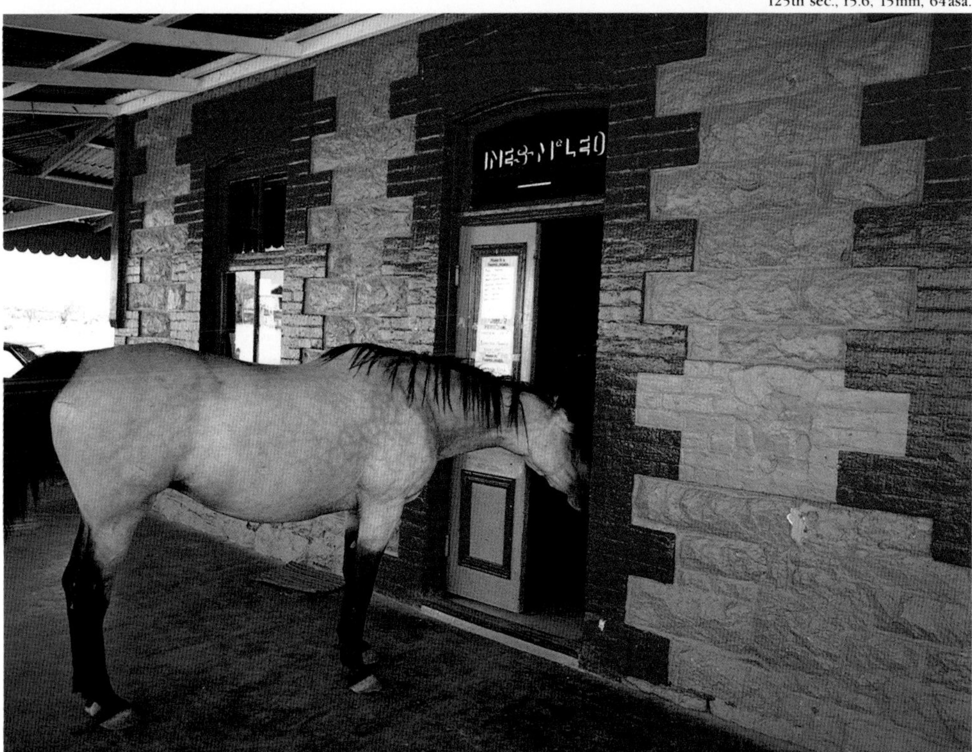

THE SILVERTON HOTEL ON A VERY HOT DAY, SILVERTON, WESTERN NEW SOUTH WALES.
125th sec., f5.6, 24mm, 64asa.

GWENYTH AND BILL OSTLING, OUTBACK PREACHERS, COOBER PEDY, SOUTH AUSTRALIA.
60th sec., f11, 35mm, tripod, 64asa.

I met Richard in the pub at Oodnadatta and was invited home for a barbecue. He had told me about his one dollar house made from remnants from the old Ghan railway line, so I made sure that I arrived before dark to make this picture.

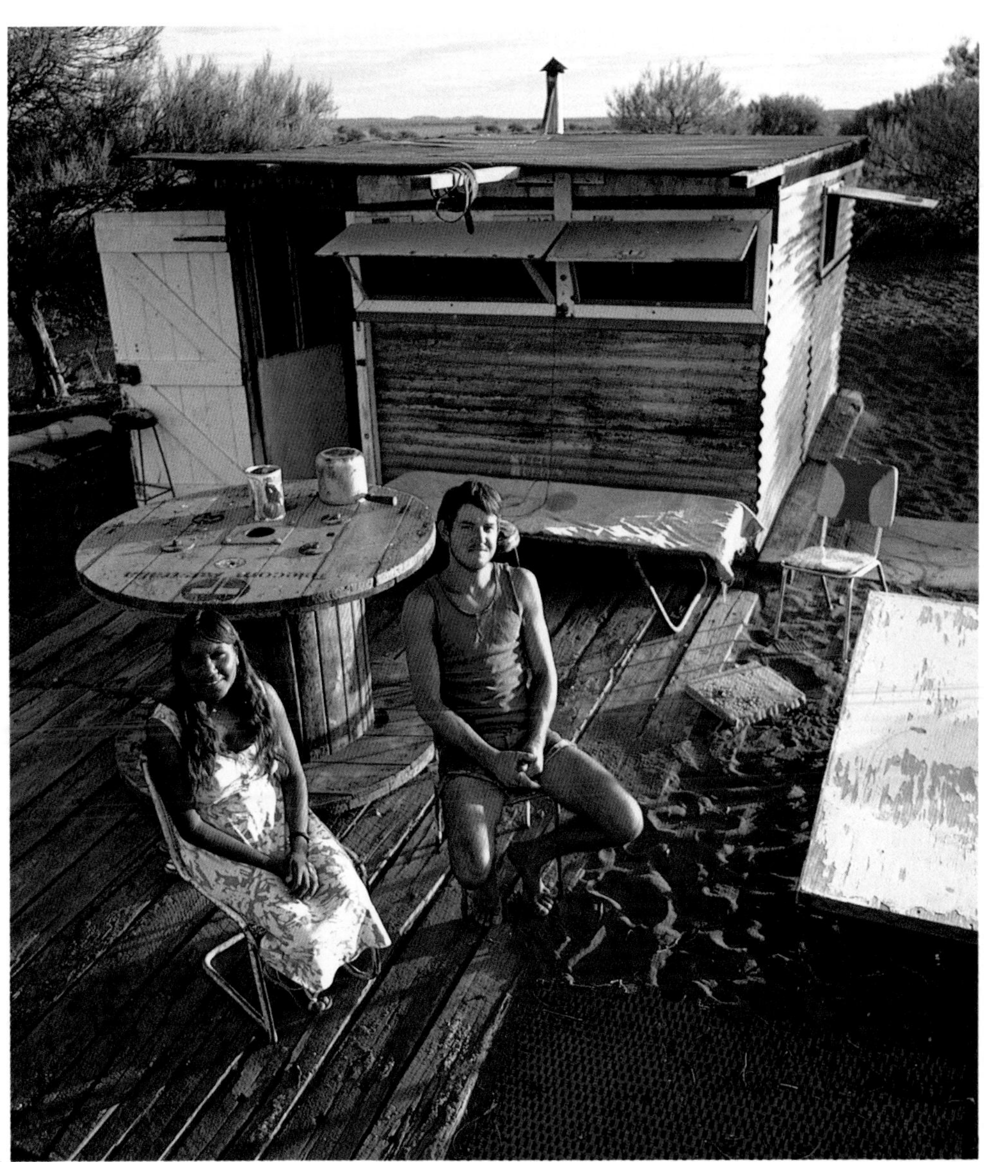

RICHARD AND CHRISTINE LODGE, OODNADATTA, SOUTH AUSTRALIA.
60th sec., f5.6, 15mm, 64asa.

Gwenyth and Bill 'picked us up' wandering around Coober Pedy just before sundown. With true outback hospitality they offered us a meal and a bed for the night. I made this portrait in the underground living room just as we were leaving.

When I rang the famous outback artist Pro Hart to ask him for a photo session he was far from enthusiastic. He had heard all the 'get in the front door' lines before; besides, it was Saturday, his day off.

When I finally did get in the door I found a man most befitting his name. Pro has a heart as big as the landscapes that he paints.

PRO HART, BROKEN HILL, NEW SOUTH WALES.
125th sec., f8, 35mm, 64asa.

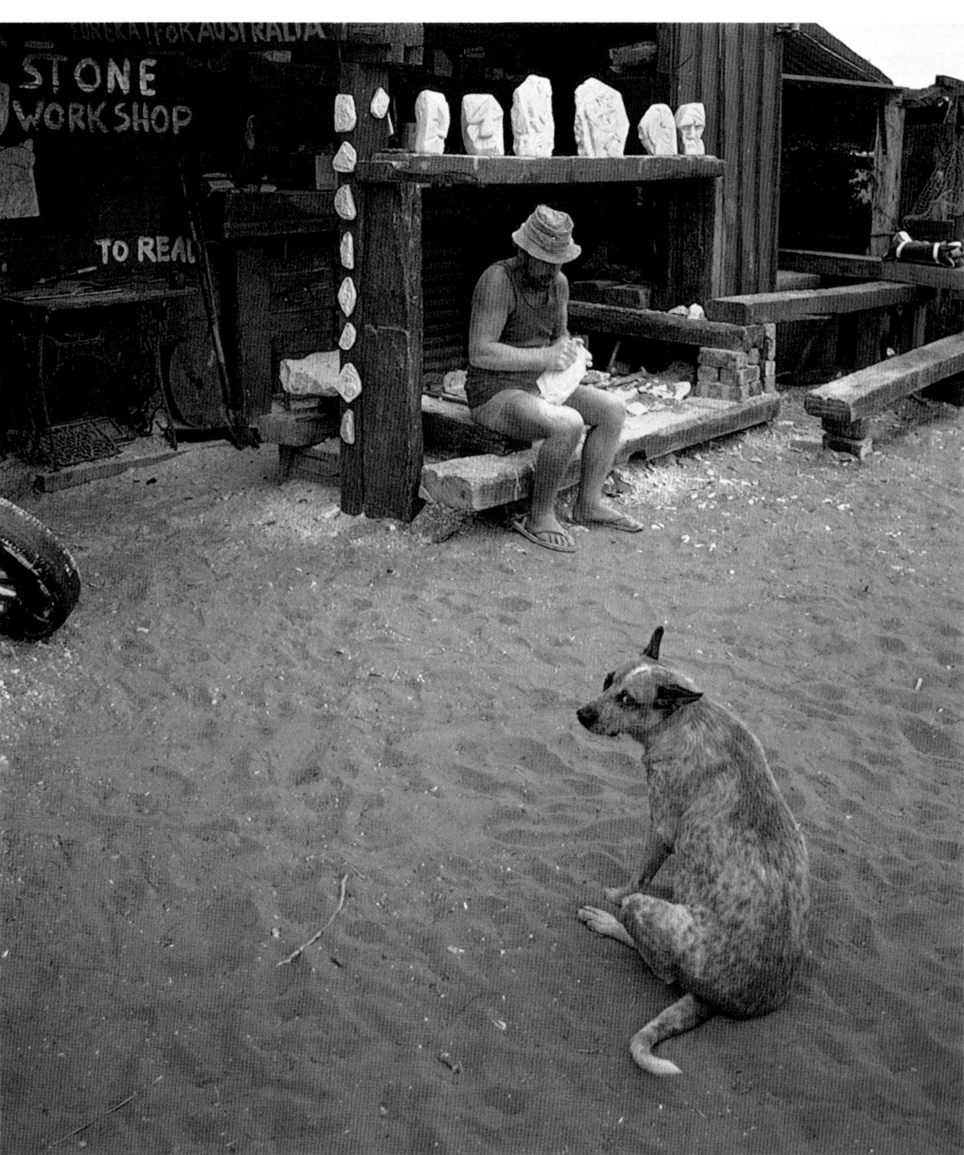

ALFRINK IN HIS STUDIO AND HOME, LYNDHURST, SOUTH AUSTRALIA.
125th sec., f5.6, 15mm, 64asa.

I asked Alfrink what motivated him to whittle away on talc stone every day.

Quick with a reply he said, "I sit down with a blank lump of talc every day and it's sort of like being the engineer, the architect and the labourer. I'm inventing something new all the time. I guess what I really like to do is to talk to people through my carvings, those with the time to listen anyway."

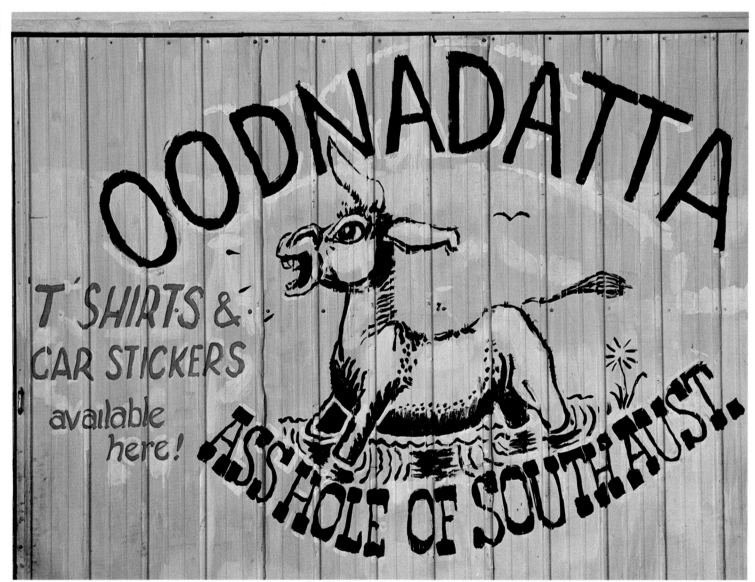

PEOPLE'S GRAPHICS, OODNADATTA, SOUTH AUSTRALIA.
125th sec., f11, 105mm, 64asa.

VITAL STATISTICS, OODNADATTA, SOUTH AUSTRALIA.
125th sec., f5.6, 15mm, 64asa.

TUCK SHOP, OODNADATTA, SOUTH AUSTRALIA.
60th sec., f8, 24mm, 64asa.

Toilet walls, old water tanks, abandoned cars, in fact anything that provides an inviting surface offers the locals an opportunity for self-expression.

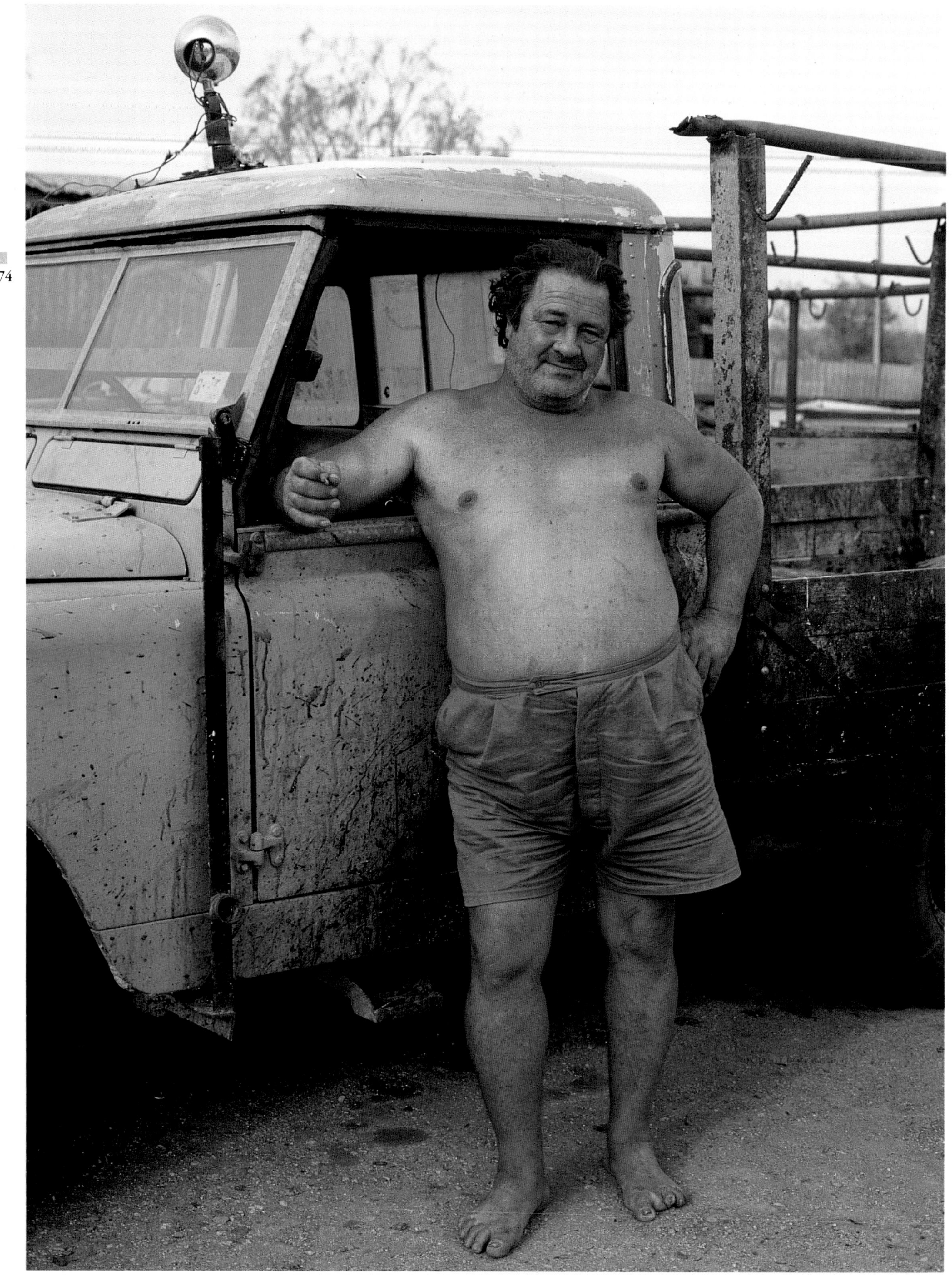

JACK MOBBS, ROO SHOOTER, MARREE, SOUTH AUSTRALIA.
125th sec., f5.6, 35mm, 64asa.

Dougal, whose mother was killed by a 'roo shooter, has a permanent desire to play. His favourite antic is to sneak up silently, as only a 'roo can do, behind his unsuspecting victims. Then, with no warning whatsoever, he lunges. He wraps his forearms around their shoulders and nibbles at their spines.

One night Doug Riley had a visitor who woke at midnight to the urgent call of nature. Not being able to find the outhouse in the dark, he headed for the fence. That was when Dougal struck!

Dougal also likes boxing.

DOUG RILEY AND DOUGAL, CHINAMAN'S CREEK, SOUTH AUSTRALIA.
250th sec., f5.6, 35mm, 64asa.

"The average conservationist from the city just never gets out into the bush to see first hand what is really happening with 'roos," says Jack Mobbs, a professional kangaroo shooter with a permit that covers some 7,000 square miles of country around Marree in South Australia.

"At the present time there is a drought on, has been for years, and the big red 'roos and euros are giving the graziers so much competition some of them are going broke. So they get me in to keep the numbers down. I have no intention of ruining my own business by shooting them out."

When we first met Jack in Marree it took us two days to convince him that we were not reporters and that we wanted his side of the story. Films like *Goodbye Joey,* and bad media coverage, have given professional shooters such a bad time that most are unapproachable.

PENNY, IAN, RODNEY AND PRUDENCE BUTTON, WELFORD DOWNS, CENTRAL QUEENSLAND.
60th sec., f8, 25mm, 64asa.

This delightful pisé-built home was created by Richard Welford in 1880 and is one of south west Queensland's first homesteads.

To make this family portrait in the right light, I had to set the alarm clock for 4am. In typical outback fashion, nobody minded.

IRIS BUNTINE, STONEHENGE, QUEENSLAND.
60th sec., f8, 35mm, 64asa.

At Stonehenge, in the heart of Queensland's Channel Country, lives Iris Buntine, postmistress and telephonist.

In recognition of service rendered to the community, Iris was made Queenslander of the Year in 1985. She provided me with all of the local historical information that I could have asked for.

JOHNNY HARRIS, VIOLET VALE, CAPE YORK.
125th sec., f5.6, 135mm, 64asa.

When I met Johnny Harris he was head stockman on Violet Vale Station. His father had recently sold the property, and it was John's responsibility to show the new owner where the cattle were.

We strolled around the homestead together late one afternoon, as he quietly reminisced about his youth. John had spent his entire life on the property; when he was three years old he sat in his father's lap on a muster.

This image was made during Johnny's last sunset.

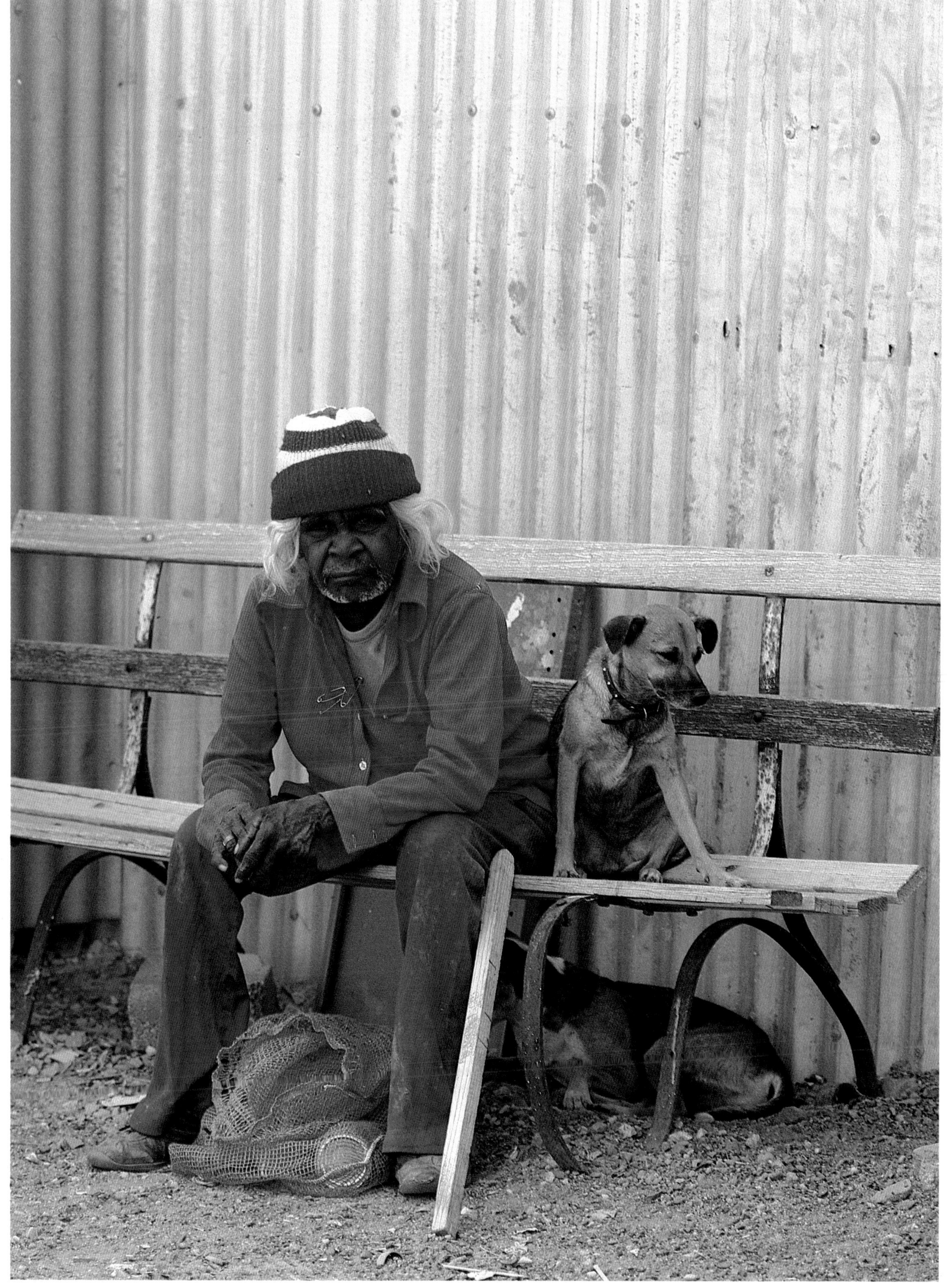

IVY RUSSELL, RETIRED JILLAROO, MARREE, SOUTH AUSTRALIA.
125th sec., f8, 135mm, 64asa.

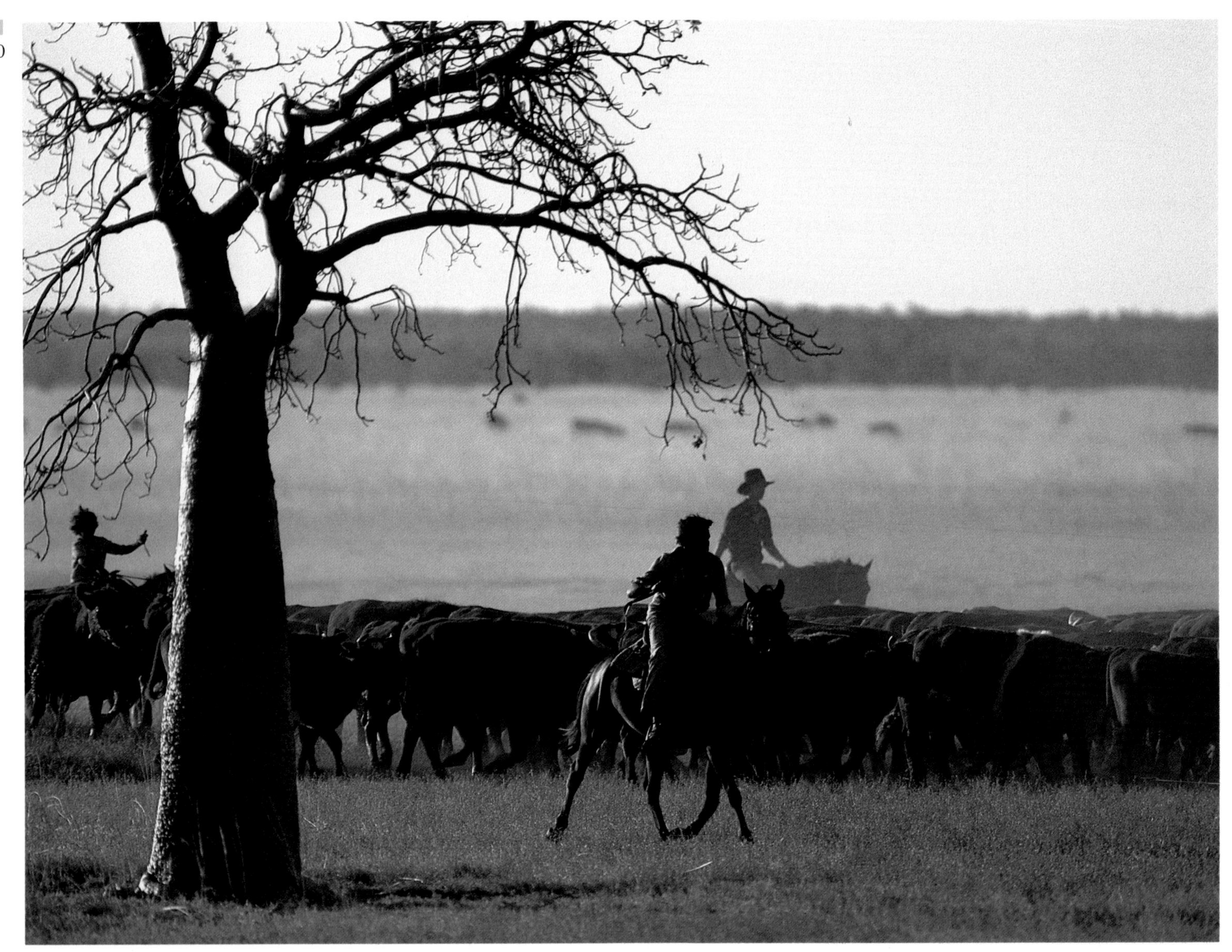

MUSTERING, THE KIMBERLEYS, WESTERN AUSTRALIA.
125th sec., f5.6, 600mm IFED, 64asa.

The vast area of north western Western Australia that is the Kimberleys, has been referred to as 'the land of bulls and boabs.'

I wanted to capture the two together, and so followed this muster all day, making pictures from afar with a 600mm lens. The boab is a most striking endemic tree.

CATTLE MUSTER, BARKLY TABLELANDS, NORTHERN TERRITORY.
125th sec., f5.6, 600mm IFED, 64asa.

Photography in and around cattle musters requires rapport with and co-operation from the ringers.

In this instance the cattle had not been handled for three years, and a mob this size was not to be trusted. As I was instructed to hide in a bush and take all my photos from 200 metres away, I used a 600mm lens.

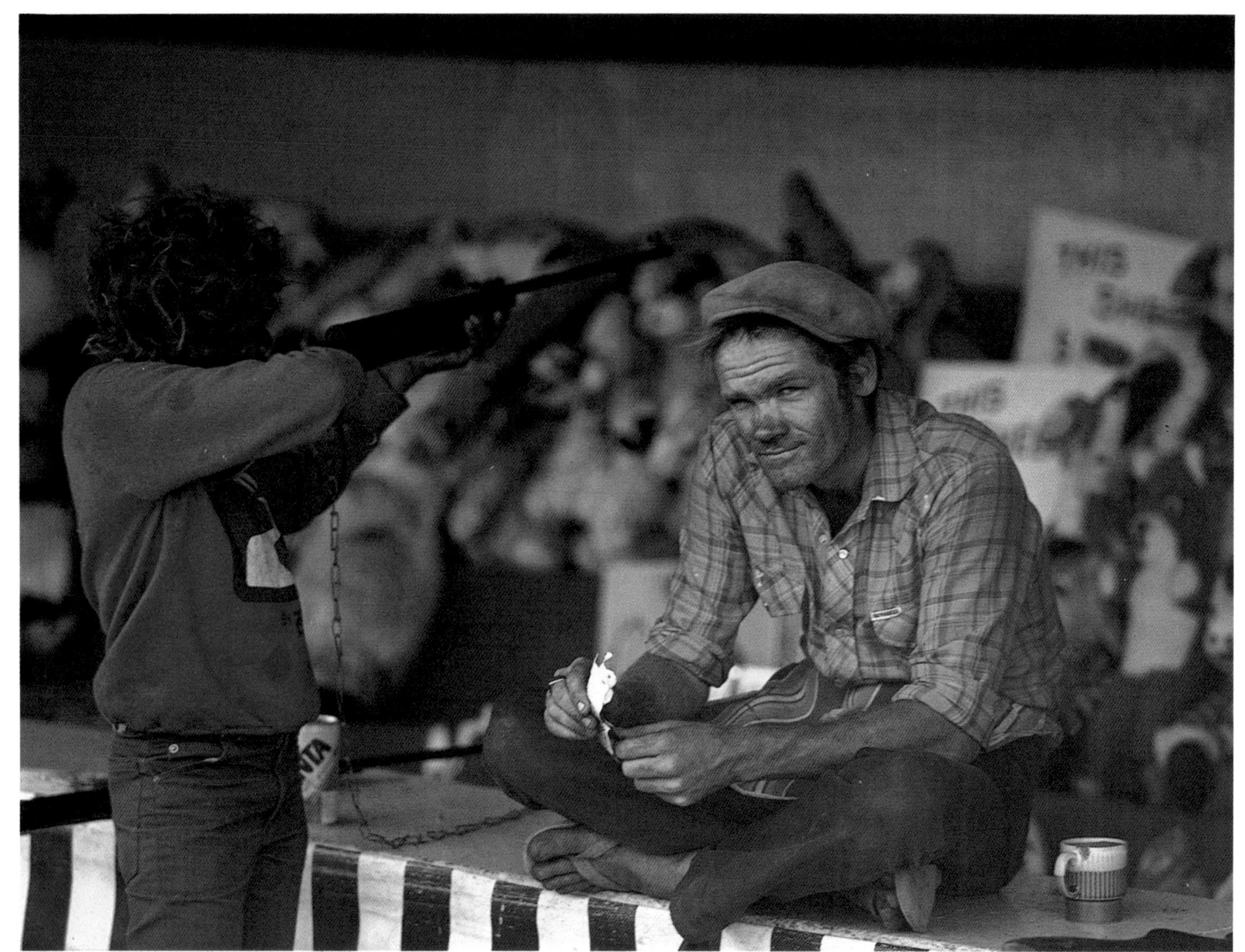

SIDESHOW MAN, ALICE SPRINGS RODEO, NORTHERN TERRITORY.
125th sec., f8, 80 - 200mm zoom, 64asa.

Occasionally all the elements just come together to make a great shot that tells a great story.

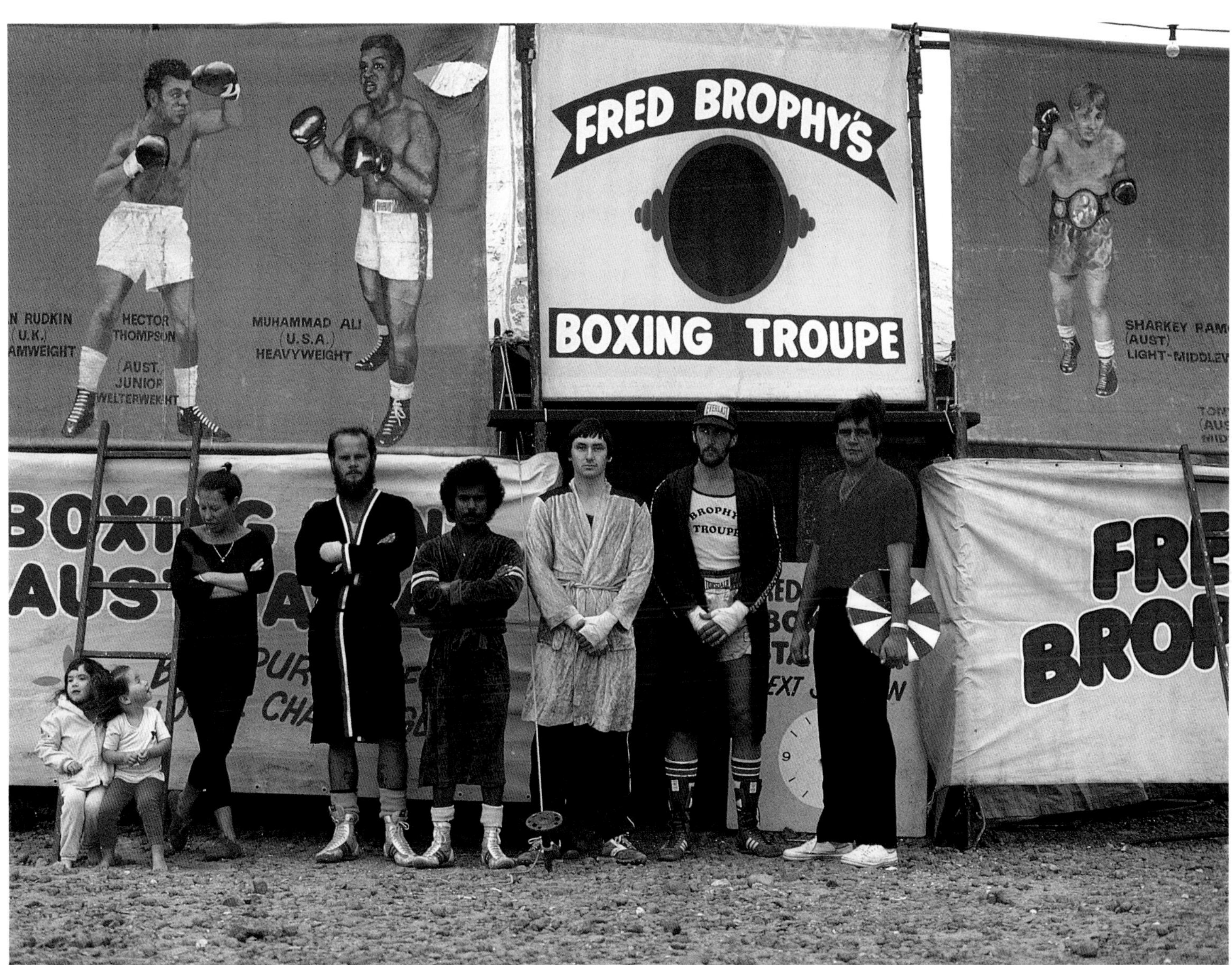

FROM LEFT TO RIGHT: JODIE, JOSIE AND SANDI. THE BIRDSVILLE MAULER, BLACK LIZARD, GENTLE JIM, THE BELGIAN BOMBER, FEARLESS FRED BROPHY. BIRDSVILLE, QUEENSLAND.
250th sec., f5.6, 80 - 200mm zoom, 64asa.

We met Fearless Fred Brophy and his boxing troupe outside the Birdsville Pub on a hot, flyblown, local race day.

Fred spoke quietly about the end of an era. His was the last of a long line of travelling shows from which many boxing greats evolved.

CRICKET IN THE OUTBACK, WILLIAM CREEK, SOUTH AUSTRALIA.
125th sec., f8, 80 - 200mm zoom, 64asa.

Gymkhanas in the outback are events which attract the locals in droves. Here at William Creek, the folk from surrounding stations began arriving 24 hours before the events began.

To while away the day, the ringers huddled together to form two cricket teams. When they withdrew it was obvious how the decision of who played who, was arrived at.

The black team won!

WILD HORSE RACE, ALICE SPRINGS RODEO, NORTHERN TERRITORY.
500th sec., f8, 80 - 200mm zoom, 64asa.

With events like the wild horse race paying purses as high as $1000, it is little wonder that entrants travel hundreds, even thousands of kilometres to take part. I am no real fan of rodeos, but I find the people who make up the audiences wonderful camera subjects.

ALICE SPRINGS, NORTHERN TERRITORY.
125th sec., f2.8, 135mm, 64asa.

What really made this picture was not discovered until after the film was processed. This element of surprise oftens adds to the excitement of photography.

TENNANT CREEK, NORTHERN TERRITORY.
125th sec., f5.6, 600mm IFED, 64asa.

Take away the 'Disco Fever,' and you could take away the picture.

COOK PRIMARY SCHOOL, NULLARBOR PLAIN, SOUTH AUSTRALIA.
125th sec., f5.6, 15mm, 64asa.

MORGAN STATE SCHOOL, MORGAN, SOUTH AUSTRALIA.
125th sec., f8, 15mm, 64asa.

Being in the right place at the right time is something that every photographer prays for.

Here at Cook, a tiny fettler's outpost on the east-west railway line, I arrived on the one day of the year that the kids leave their classroom. Smack in the middle of the world's biggest theatre, the South Australian Community Arts Team performed their musical story-telling magic.

The kids were playing in the school yard when I arrived. I saw the giant hamburger mural and just had to get the kids and their creation together.

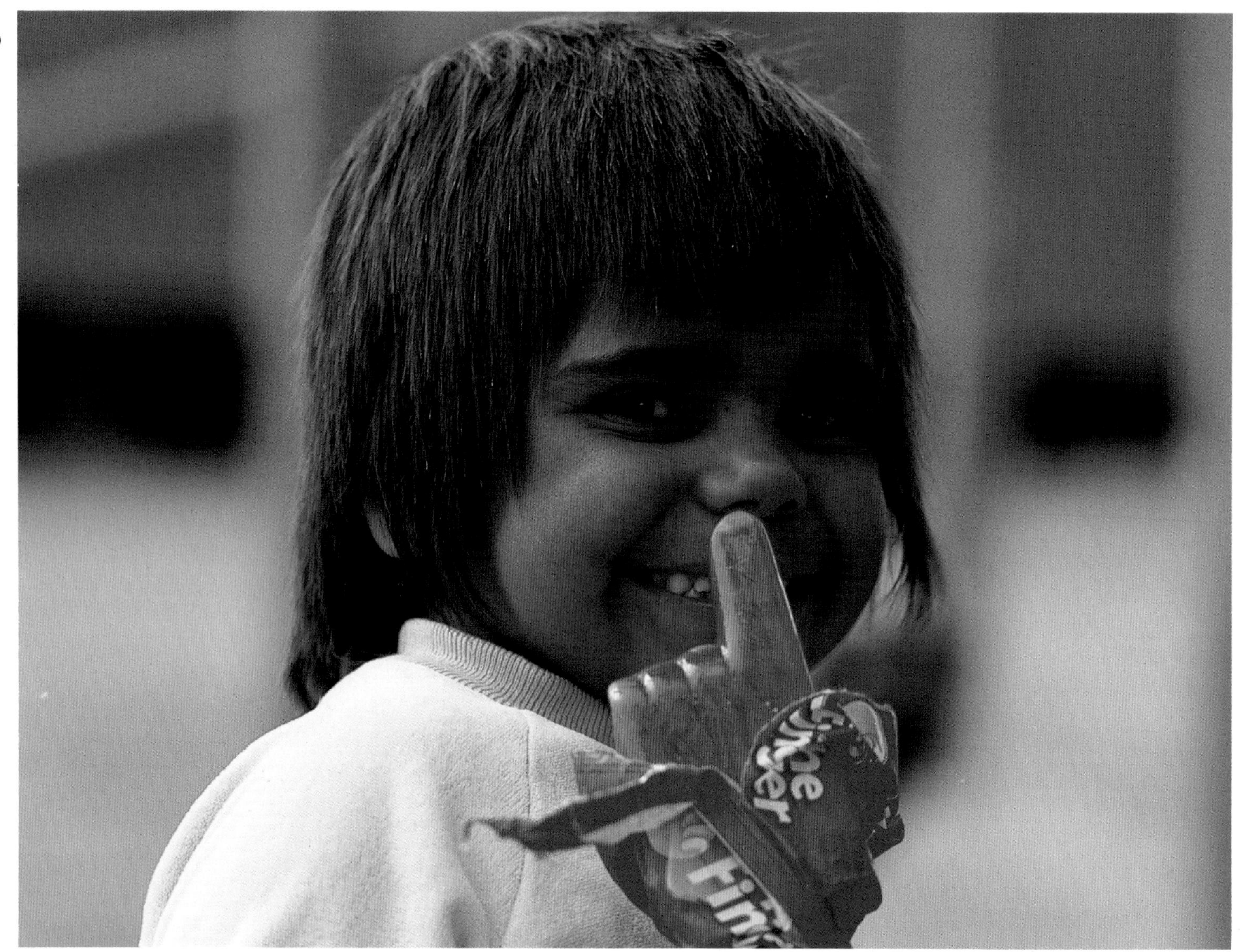

Before I could make pictures of the kids at Nepabunna Aboriginal Settlement, I had to apply for permission. My application was duly heard, and two weeks later I was given the O.K.

Outback people, and particularly aboriginal people, have a whole different concept of time. If you are in a hurry outback, don't bother the locals.

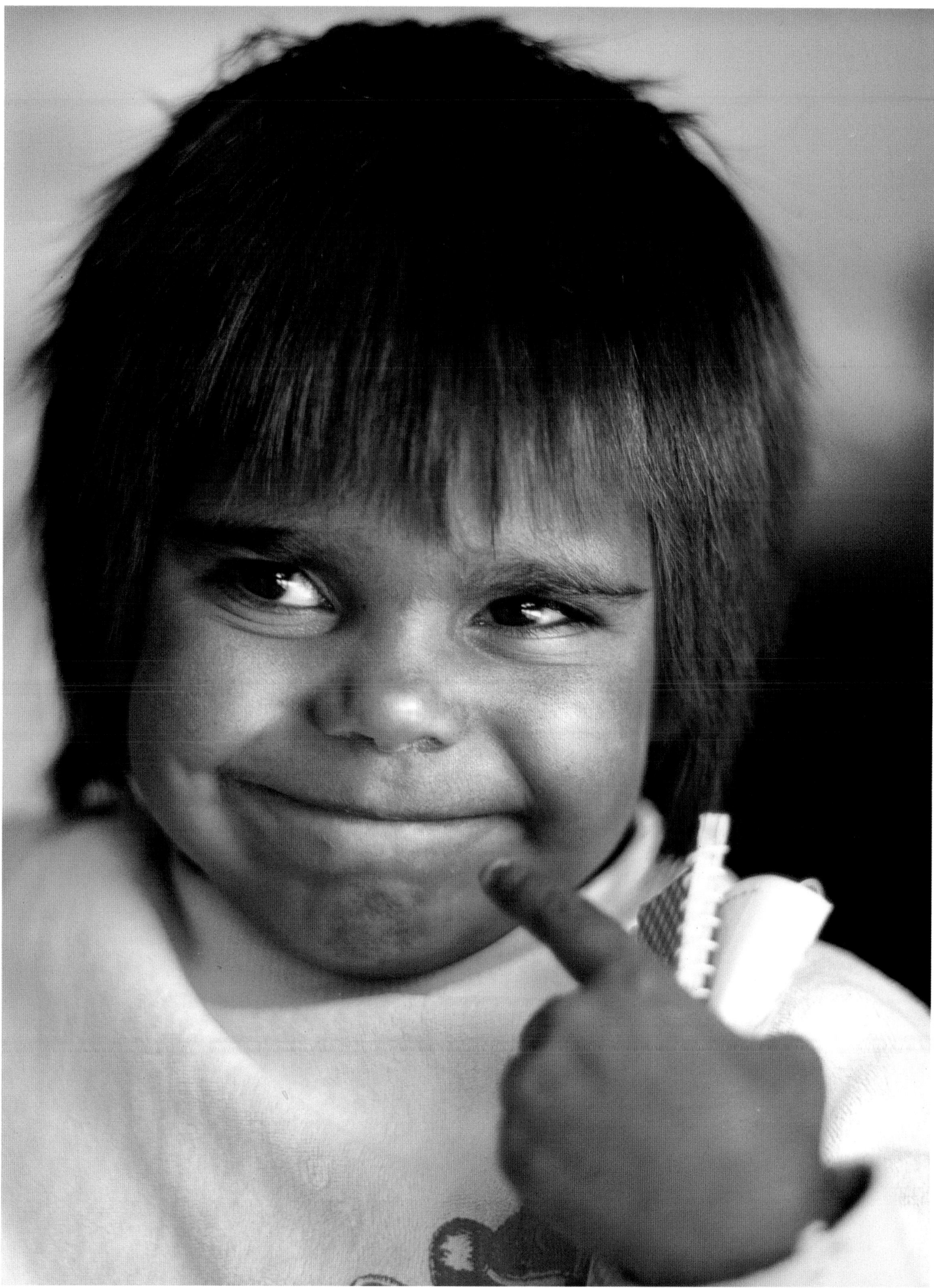

NEPABUNNA SETTLEMENT, SOUTH AUSTRALIA.
125th sec., f8, 135mm, 64asa.

APOSTLE BIRDS, MOOTWINGEE, WESTERN NEW SOUTH WALES.
250th sec., f8, 600mm IFED, 64asa.

The 1983 drought had a devastating effect on both native animals and domestic livestock. Here, a group of Apostle Birds spent the entire day in the hot sun squabbling over the infrequent drips that fell from a leaking tap at the Mootwingee National Park camp site.

During drought, millions of dollars worth of livestock might perish.

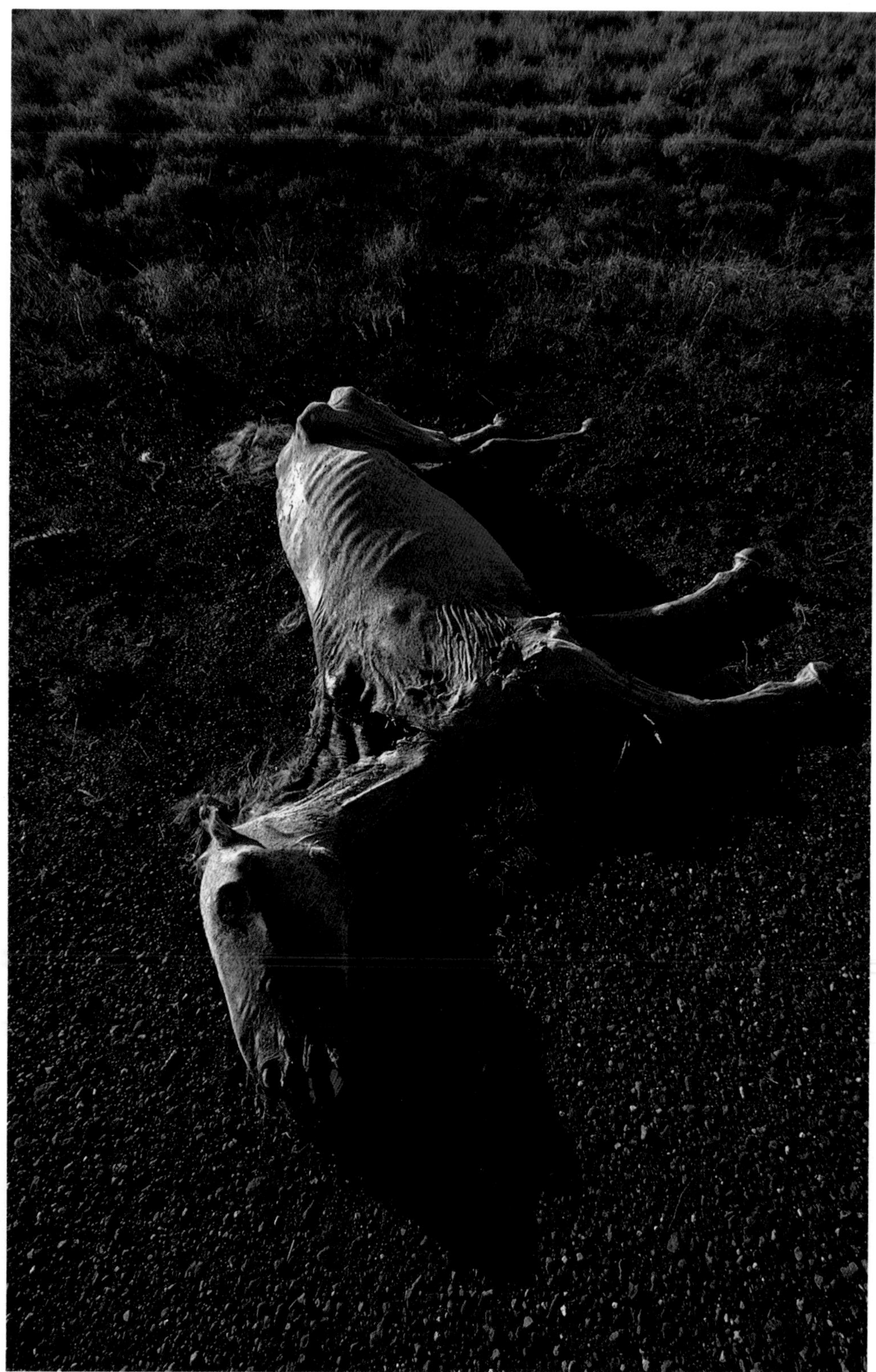

DEAD HORSE, WESTERN NEW SOUTH WALES.
250th sec., f11, 15mm, 64asa.

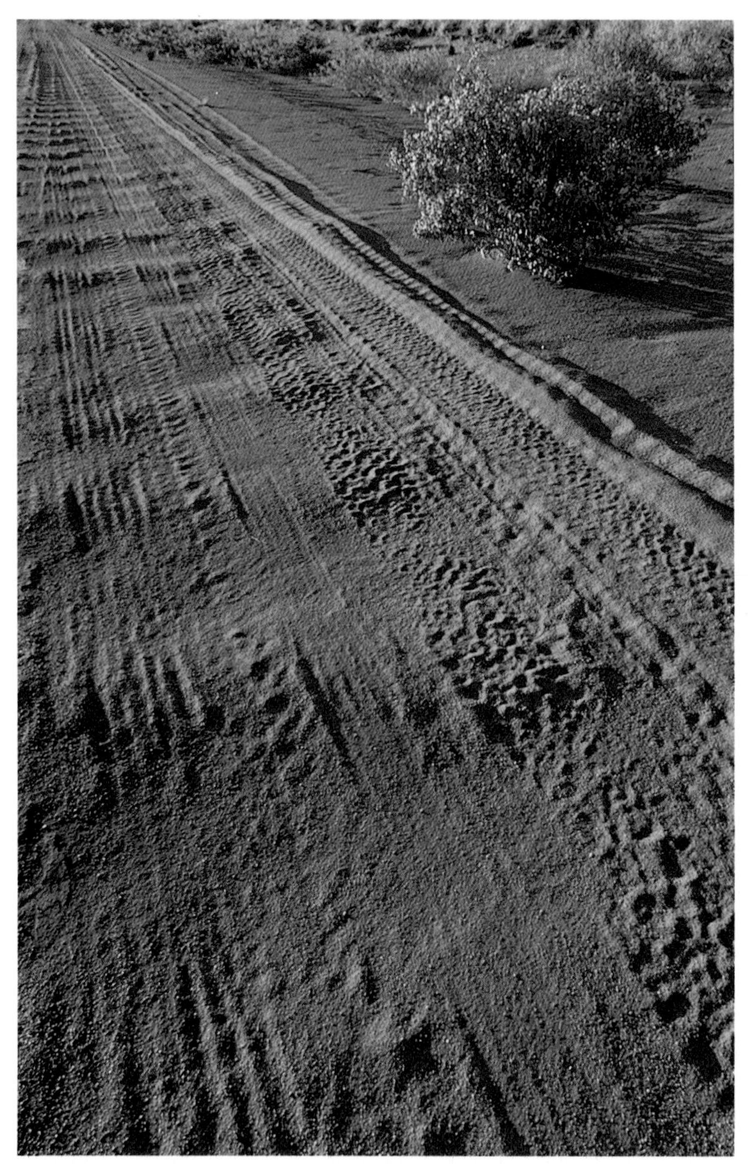

A ROAD TO NOWHERE, NORTHERN TERRITORY.
125th sec., f5.6, 15mm, 64asa.

CROW TRACKS, NORTHERN TERRITORY.
125th sec., f8, 55mm micro, 64asa.

CROW AND SAND-DUNE, SOUTH AUSTRALIA.
125th sec., f5.6, 600mm IFED, 64asa.

I feel greatly saddened when I look at the impact we have made on the outback. Roads that go nowhere, fragile dune systems devastated by cattle and the mass removal of vegetation to feed livestock in times of drought. Then there are feral pigs, donkeys, horses, cattle, rabbits, camels and goats.

I was feeling rather depressed when I made this picture of a crow climbing a sand dune. I wrote in my diary, *Crows' tracks are gone with the first wind. Man's tracks go in and on forever.*

EXPLORING MOUNTAINS

O*OZING GREEN RAINFORESTS* glisten in the summer rain. Deep palm-filled gorges in which to hide from the hot sun and enjoy the sound of trickling water, while dozing on a smooth, flat rock. Shade dappled mountain slopes to stroll, bespeckled with giant gums all swathed in story-board scribbled bark to ponder.

At dawn, the sparkling, icicle-edged creeks with snowy banks, and frozen ice-art pools, can entertain for hours. Garden heathlands, white snow covered, with chilly mountain winds remind me of my altitude. Enveloping mist on a late walk spells out a warning.

Mountains offer creatures too. Secretive, silent wallabies whose long shadows erupt from forest edges in the dawn light. Vibrant flocks of scarlet parrots wheeling like circus acrobats through tangled forests where vines loop and curl through giant trees. Grasslands filled with dancing butterflies, and woodlands wrapped in spiders' webs to stick and tangle.

These are the rewards of patience.

PORCUPINE GORGE NATIONAL PARK, QUEENSLAND.
125th sec., f5.6, 135mm, 64asa.

PRECIPITOUS BLUFF, TASMANIA.
500th sec., f2, 135mm, air, 64asa.

I was on a photographic assignment in Tasmania for one month, and was keen to photograph the south west wilderness area from the air. I particularly wanted drama: storm clouds, sea mist, afternoon light . . . the whole effect.

I rang several pilots explaining what I was after. I finally found one who knew exactly what I wanted, and he told me to ring daily at 2pm.

For three weeks I made these calls. Finally, one rainy, wet and very bleak Hobart day, we took off. Within 45 minutes, I was amongst it . . . 38 rolls of film later, I landed!

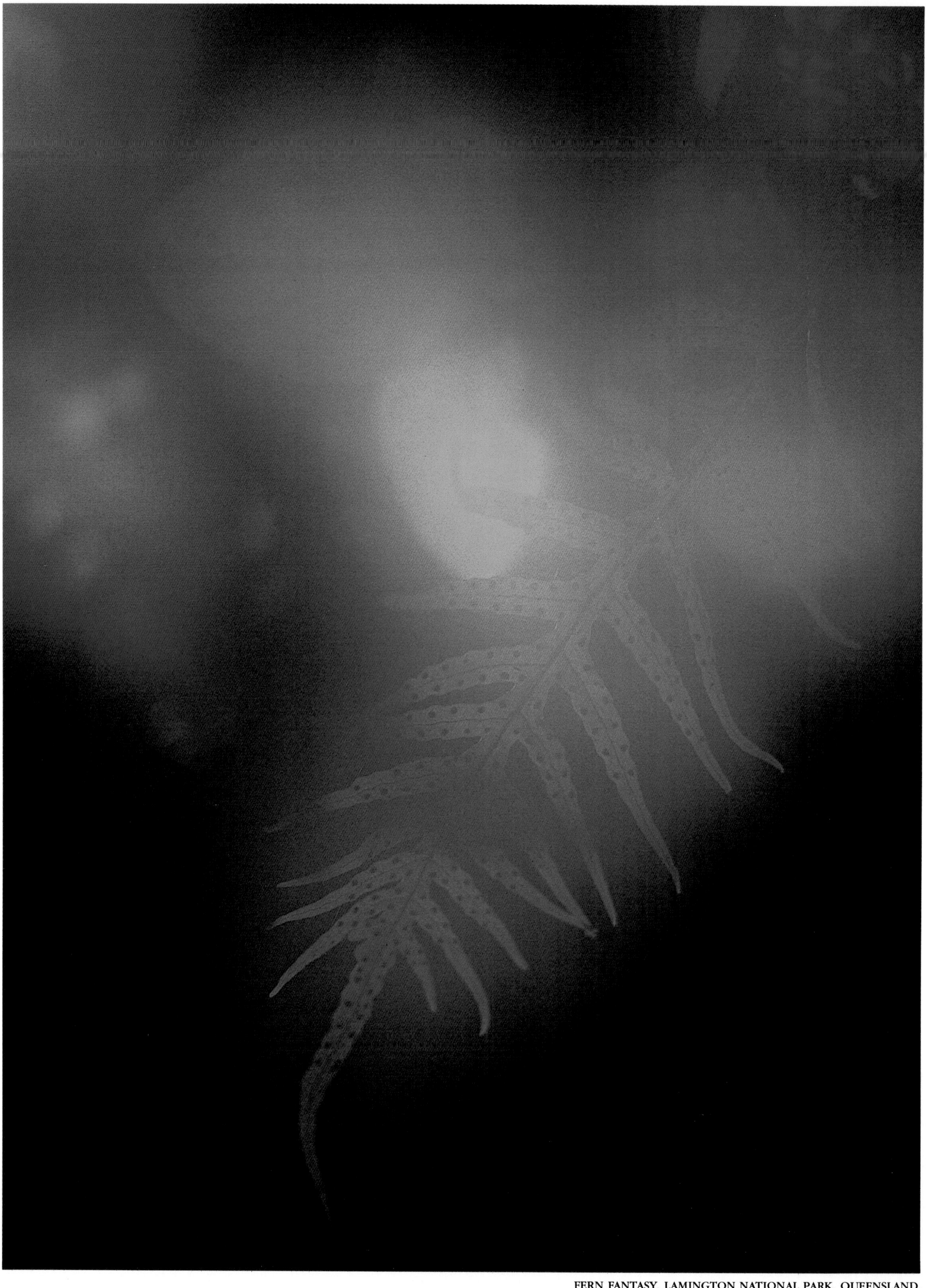

FERN FANTASY, LAMINGTON NATIONAL PARK, QUEENSLAND.
60th sec., f8, 15mm, 64asa.

COLOUR IT GREEN

I *LIKE TO THINK* of cameras as toys rather than working tools. To me they are play things for my imagination; I cannot let them take over and control me.

I had been walking all day in the rainforest at Lamington National Park with a group of students. It was near the end of a ten day workshop, and they were as high as kites. It was pure joy to watch them enthusiastically taking photos.

The forest was wet and misty and, being in a fanciful mood, I breathed on my 15mm lens causing it to fog over. I then made this picture just for fun!

MAKING PICTURES,
LAMINGTON NATIONAL PARK, QUEENSLAND.
125th sec., f2.8, 24mm, 64asa.

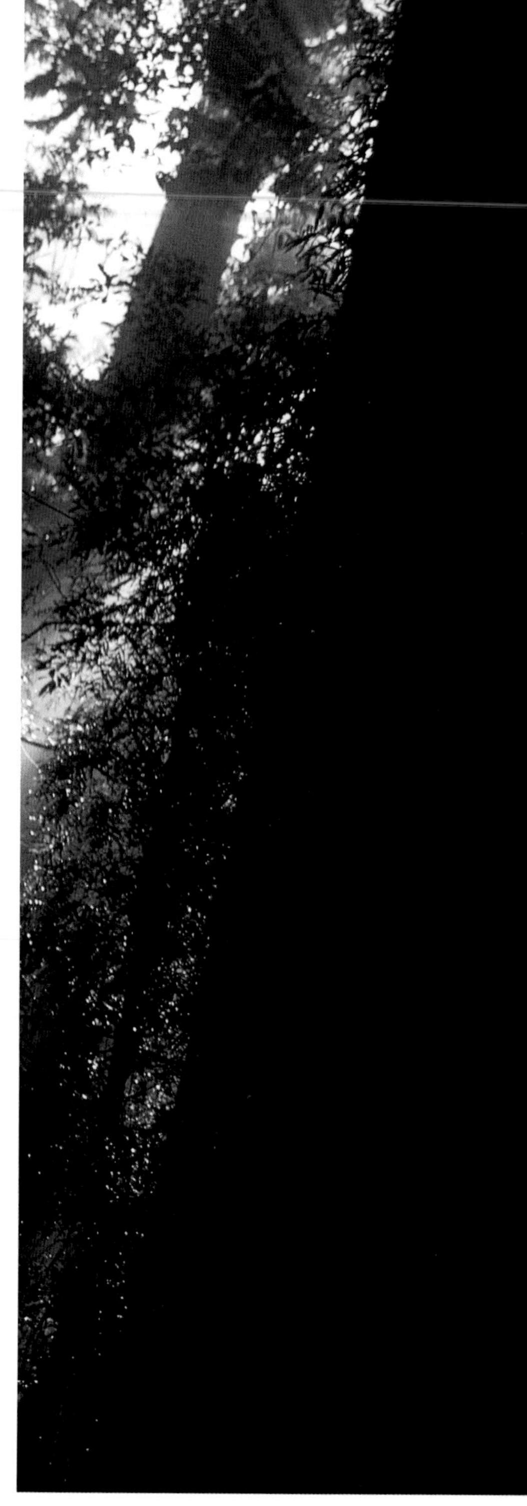

RAINFOREST DURING A STORM, LAMINGTON NATIONAL PARK, QUEENSLAND.
30th sec., f8, 24mm, tripod, 64asa.

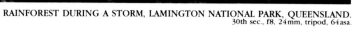

The very best times to visit and photograph rainforests are either during or after heavy rain. At these times the diffuse light helps create an atmosphere that, on a sunny day, would be lost in dark shadow and high contrast.

Apart from your camera, all you'll need is a tripod and cable release for long exposures. A raincoat, umbrella, strong shoes and some leech repellent won't go astray.

RAINFOREST JUST AFTER RAIN, LAMINGTON NATIONAL PARK, QUEENSLAND.
125th sec., f5.6, 15mm, 64asa.

LOOKING OUT THROUGH A WATERFALL, TAMBORINE MOUNTAIN, QUEENSLAND.
125th sec., f5.6, 15mm, 64asa.

RAINDROPS ON PALM LEAVES, MOUNT WARNING NATIONAL PARK, NEW SOUTH WALES.
60th sec., f11, 135mm, tripod, 64asa.

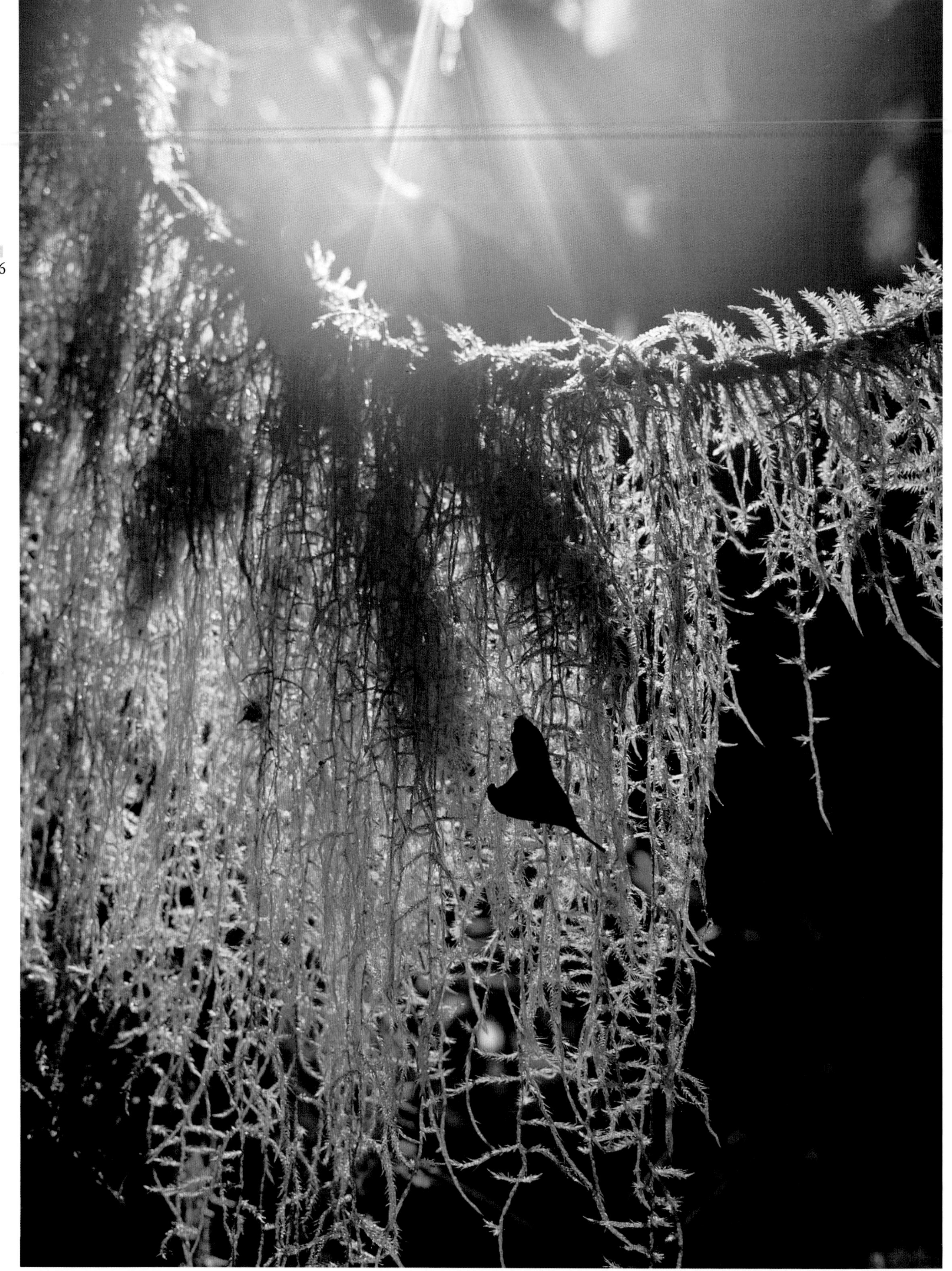

LICHEN, LAMINGTON NATIONAL PARK, QUEENSLAND.
250th sec., f11, 15mm, 64asa.

RAINFOREST FUNGUS, LAMINGTON NATIONAL PARK, QUEENSLAND.
60th sec., f8, 105mm micro, tripod, 64asa.

Here, I wanted to draw the relationship between the sun and a green forest plant, two of life's essential elements.

I positioned the camera to allow the sun to play directly onto the lens, and used my hand as a sun shield to control the light.

The intricacy of this fungus, is heightened through soft, natural back-lighting. Sometimes it is necessary to get down on your hands and knees to make pictures. When you do, the discoveries that you make are amazing.

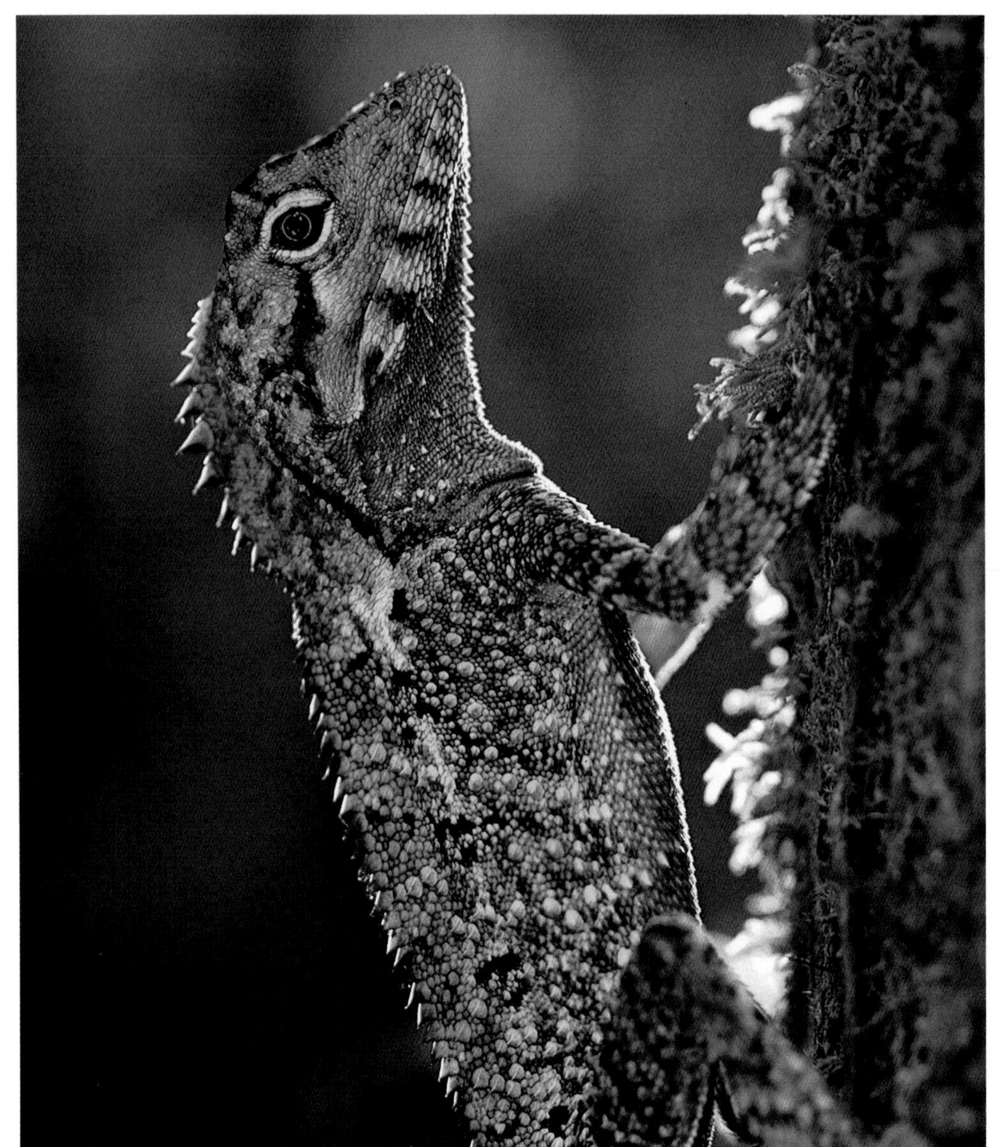

FOREST DRAGON, LAMINGTON NATIONAL PARK, QUEENSLAND.
8 secs., f8, 105mm micro, 64asa.

The Rainforest Dragon is one of the few animals that will remain absolutely motionless for long periods. I discovered this small individual on a tree trunk in almost total darkness. I set up my tripod and, exposing for the background, made the picture.

During the long shutter release, I artificially illuminated the dragon twice by using a small electronic flash. What I wanted was the effect of sunshine. By using the flash, once from in front and once from behind, I was able to achieve this.

I rarely carry a flash, preferring to make all of my pictures with natural light. This is the only time I have used this method.

To highlight this Green Tree Snake, I used a 135mm lens on an aperture of f2. This creates a very short depth of field which isolates the subject. This technique does require very careful focus, so I usually make lots of exposures to be sure of getting a sharp image.

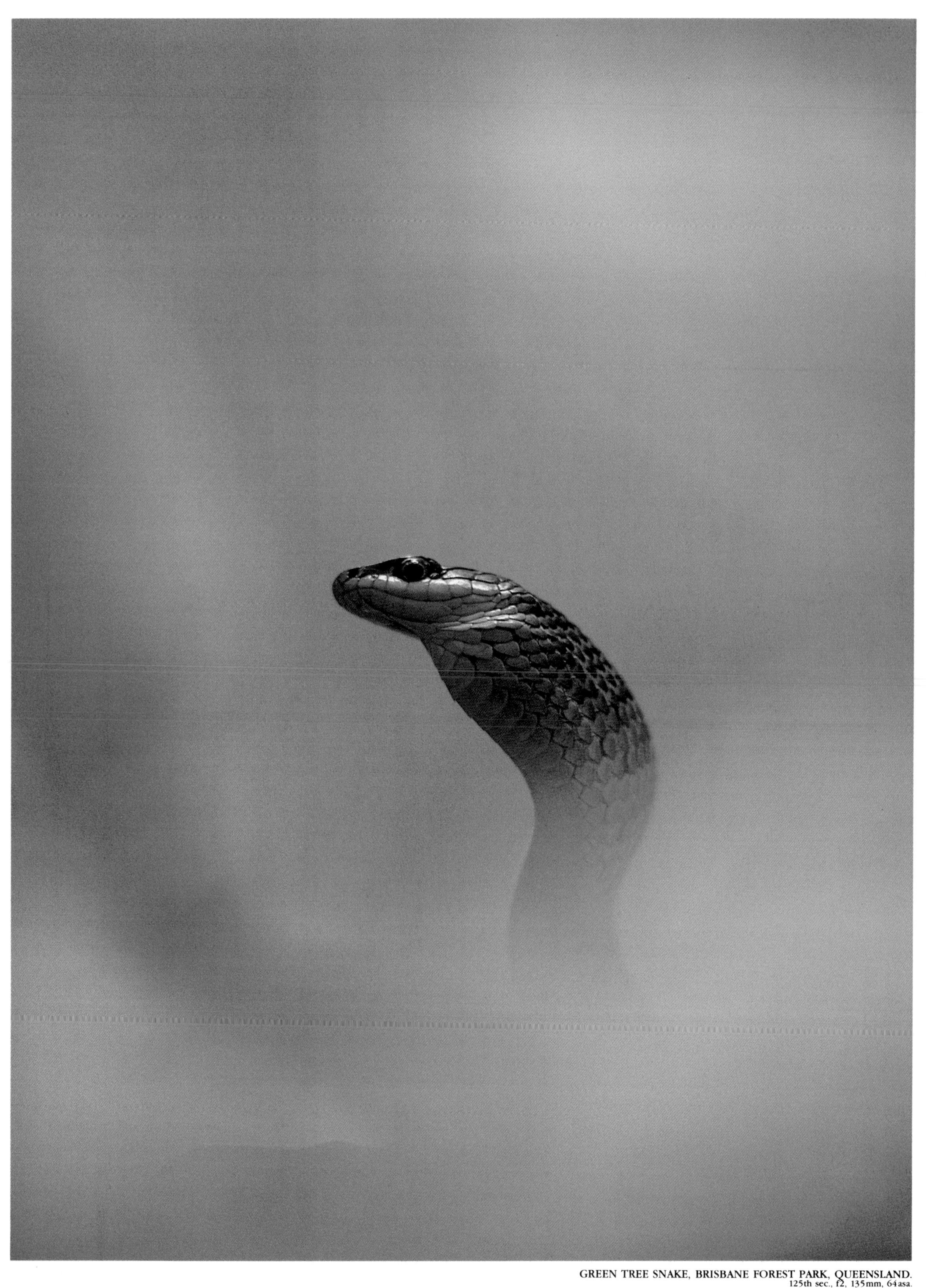

GREEN TREE SNAKE, BRISBANE FOREST PARK, QUEENSLAND.
125th sec., f2, 135mm, 64asa.

MALE KING PARROT, BUNYA MOUNTAINS NATIONAL PARK, QUEENSLAND.
125th sec., f2, 135mm, 64asa.

FEMALE KING PARROT, BUNYA MOUNTAINS NATIONAL PARK, QUEENSLAND.
60th sec., f5.6, 600mm IFED, tripod, 64asa.

NEW SOUTH WALES ALPS AT SUNSET.
500th sec., f2, 135mm, air, 64asa.

SNOW AND ICE

MY PILOT HAD twenty-three years flying experience around the New South Wales Alps and he oozed enthusiasm and confidence. It was the only occasion on which I did not need to give detailed instructions for aerial photography. This pilot was inside my head!

We took off from Cooma, and within minutes we were soaring with the eagles over craggy mountain peaks. The door was off and the air was icy, but sometimes you just don't feel a thing . . .

All of the alpine pictures in this book were made during the 1983 drought when the snow coverage in the alps was very light. This may not have enthused the skiers, but a total blanket coverage of snow makes fairly boring pictures.

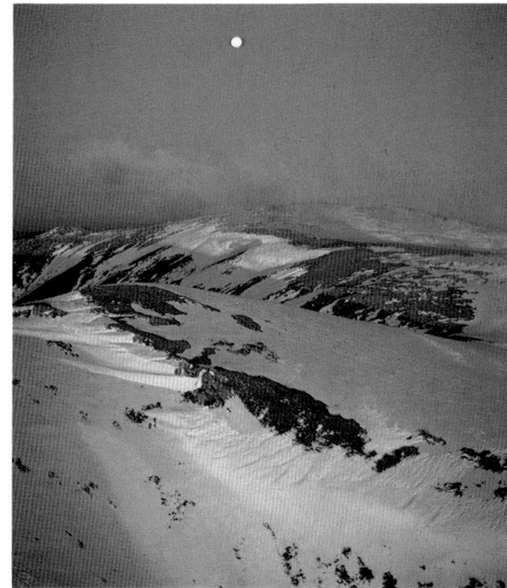

TWILIGHT OVER NEW SOUTH WALES ALPS.
250th sec., f2.8, 35mm, air, 64asa.

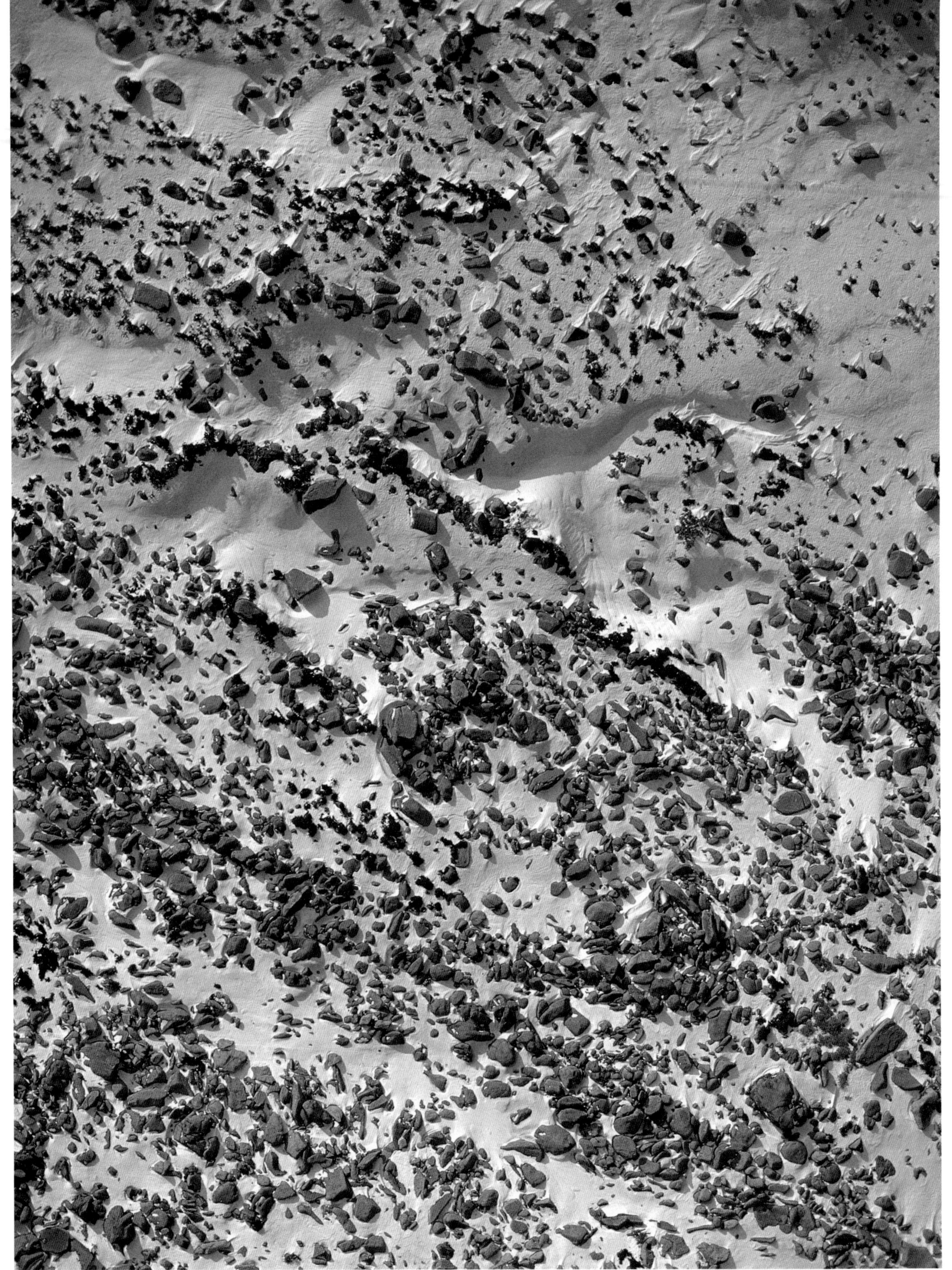

SCREE SLOPE FROM THE AIR, THE ALPS, NEW SOUTH WALES.
250th sec., f2, 135mm, 64asa.

SNOW STORM, THE ALPS, NEW SOUTH WALES.
125th sec., f2.8, 135mm, 64asa.

Photography is largely about creating illusions. In many cases it could even be called 'telling lies.' There are two very different kinds of illusions here.

Giant boulders, some as big as a house, cover a scree slope on the side of a mountain. The photograph was taken from an aircraft, but without that information one might imagine that the boulders were pebbled sized.

The second image gives the impression that the photographer must have suffered hardship to make it. It was actually made from my heated Toyota while I was caught in a traffic jam at Kosciusko National Park.

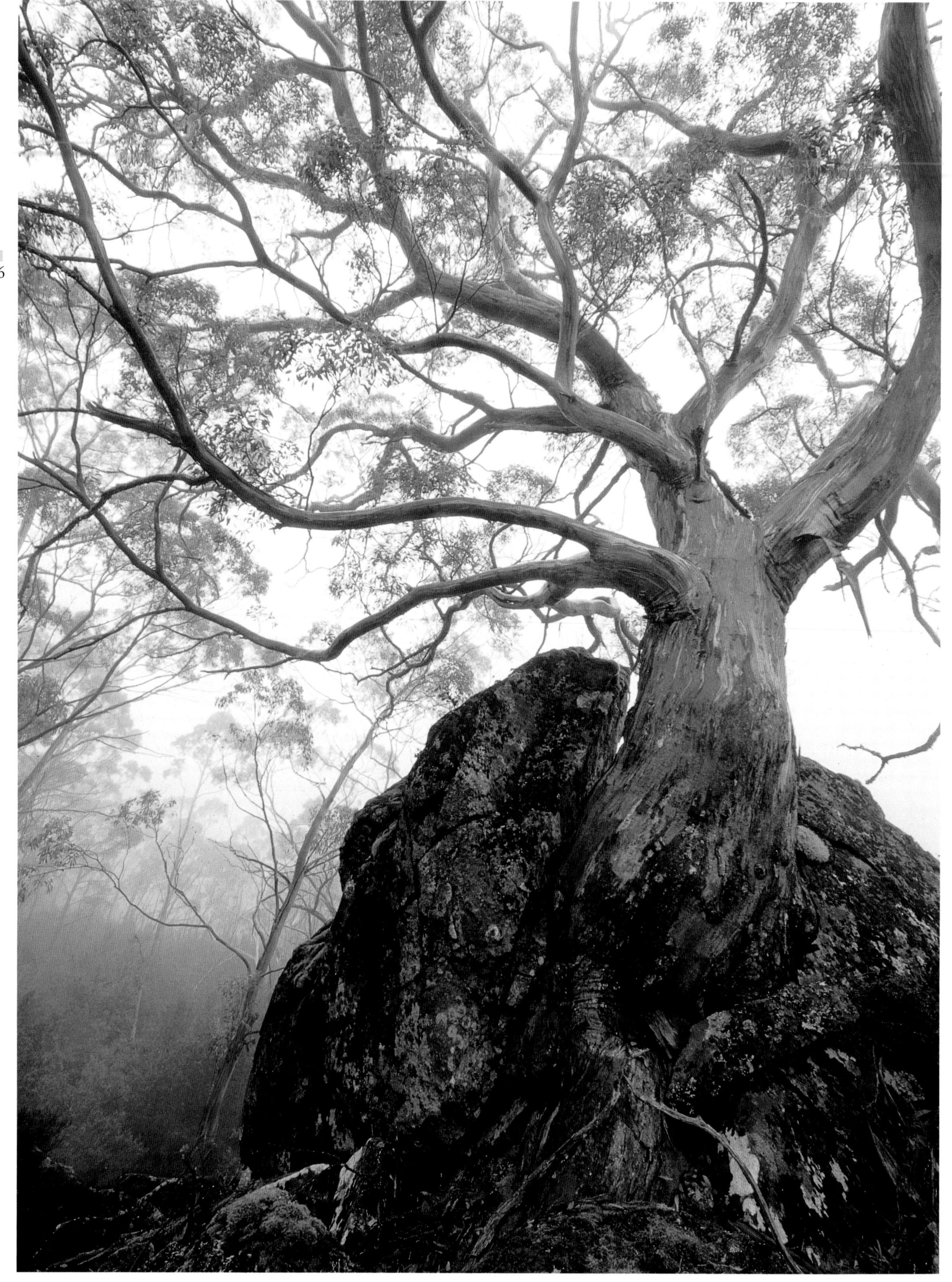

SNOW GUM, MOUNT FIELD NATIONAL PARK, TASMANIA.
30th sec., f8, 15mm, tripod, 64asa.

A wide angle lens positioned close to the tree and angled towards the sun achieved this dramatic effect. I wanted the image to portray a feeling of hopelessness.

SNOW GUM, THE ALPS, NEW SOUTH WALES.
125th sec., f8, 15mm, 64asa.

It was getting dark and I was hopelessly confused in the mist. Even with the concern that I might have to spend a freezing night in the open, I could not resist this magnificent Snow Gum. It always makes me feel that anything is possible.

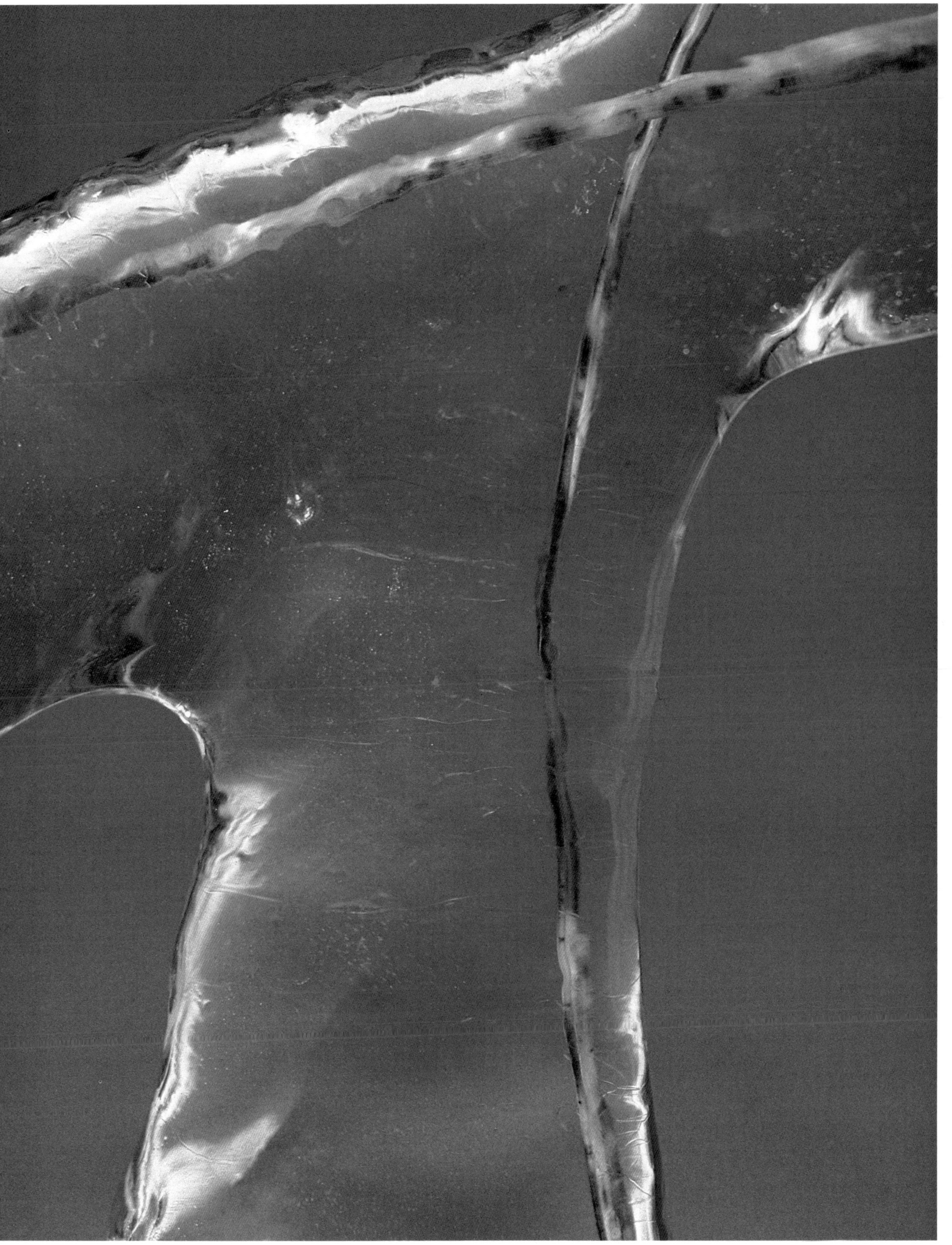

ICE ART FROM THE ALPS, NEW SOUTH WALES.
250th sec., f11, 55mm micro, 64asa.

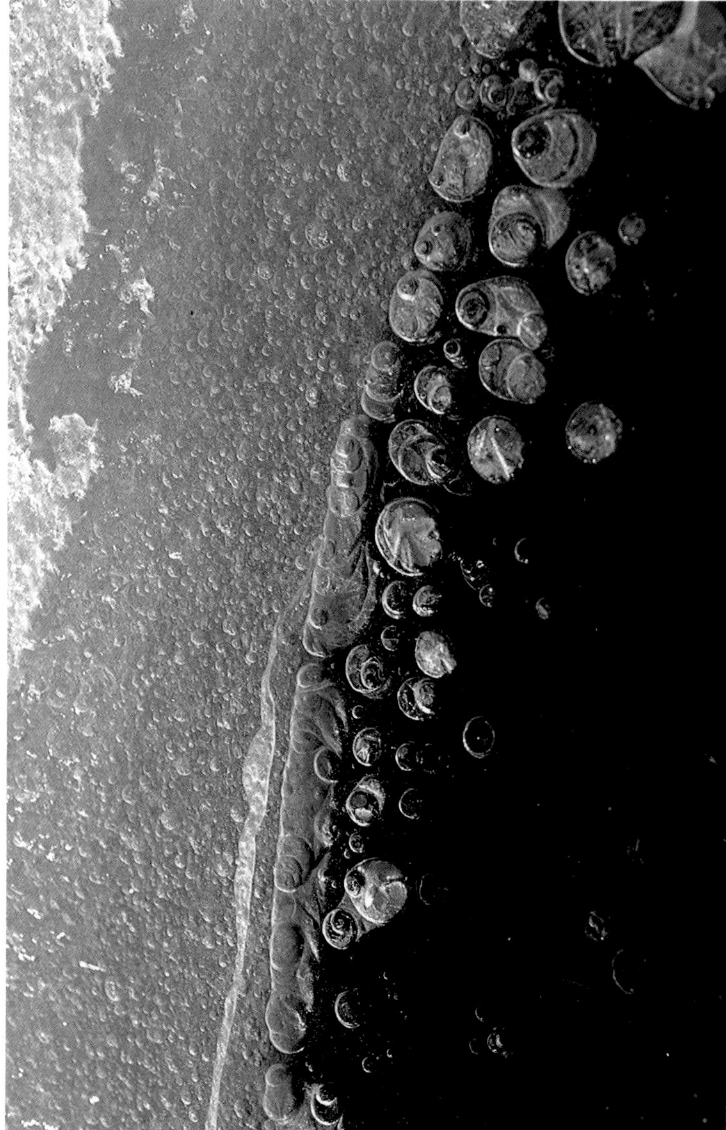

ICE ART FROM THE ALPS, NEW SOUTH WALES.
125th sec., f8, 55mm micro, 64asa.

It had been cold, wet and very windy for almost a week. My time had run out, and I was packing up to go when the sun broke through. I drove to the summit, left the car and struggled through thigh-deep snow to a creek flat. There I found a fantasy-land in ice! I extended my deadline and settled down to expose twelve rolls of film in a single hour.

Making a picture can be likened to an artist making a final drawing. The artist builds the image through a series of marks on paper. Finally, when he is satisfied, the drawing is complete. The photographer may make many images, often using a variety of lenses and photo techniques applicable to focus, lighting and composition. Later, when the film has been processed, final decisions are made.

The secrets of successful image-making are film and time. Use them freely.

PERISHER VALLEY, THE ALPS, NEW SOUTH WALES.
250th sec., f8, 15mm, 64asa.

NEW SOUTH WALES ALPS.
250th sec., f8, 15mm, 64asa.

In a snow-white environment colour is striking. Here, at Perisher Valley Ski School, two dozen gaily coloured youngsters waited patiently for their class to begin.

The Twins Club of New South Wales posing for a portrait.

The composition was not mine—
I simply shot over dad's shoulder
while he arranged the picture.

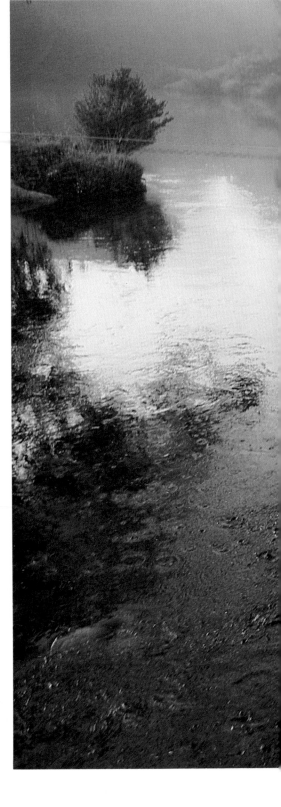

SANDY, TOM GROGGIN STATION MANAGER, NEW SOUTH WALES.
125th sec., f8, 24mm, 64asa.

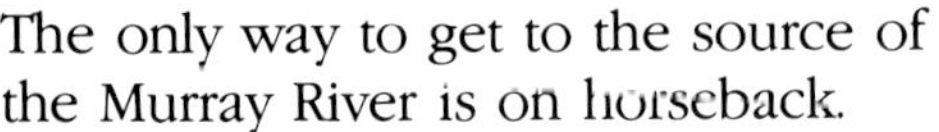
The only way to get to the source of the Murray River is on horseback.

I had made a date with Sandy, head stockman at Tom Groggin Station, and we were to start at 4am. Sandy had been on horseback all his life, and could have been the *Man from Snowy River* re-incarnate.

In this country only the best survive. It was with some fear and trepidation that I surveyed our mounts as they emerged from the mist with fiery eyes and flaring nostrils. I decided it was time to announce my lack of riding skill, but Sandy, a man of few words, replied in his quiet Irish Brogue: "Me lud, I could tell. Doon't wurry I'll be puck'n oot Barney fur yer. He'll be gett'n yer there and back in one piece."

I learned a great deal on that day, but mostly I learned that being a cattleman in the high country requires a great deal of practice and as much patience. Barney grew tired of me after four hours and decided that he would simply throw me off a cliff. I guess the real alarm was that Barney came too, and horse and rider fell in a mess. I broke two ribs and went out like a light.

MURRAY RIVER CROSSING, TOM GROGGIN STATION, NEW SOUTH WALES.
125th sec., f5.6, 15mm, 64asa.

BLACK SWAN AT SUNSET, LAKE DAYLESFORD, VICTORIA.
250th sec., f8, 80 - 200mm zoom, 64asa.

These two photos were taken thirty minutes apart; the first during sunset and the second in twilight, that magic time when the sun has set but the afterglow remains.

These images are a perfect example of how the same source material can be used to communicate quite different messages. A knowledge of subject, light and lenses is all that is required.

The sunset shot was a comparatively easy picture to make because of the amount of light available. The more subdued image required a fast lens and a steady hand. It also required many shots to capture the exact moment a drop of water fell from the swan's bill.

BLACK SWAN IN TWILIGHT, LAKE DAYLESFORD, VICTORIA.
60th sec., f1.2, 135mm, 64asa.

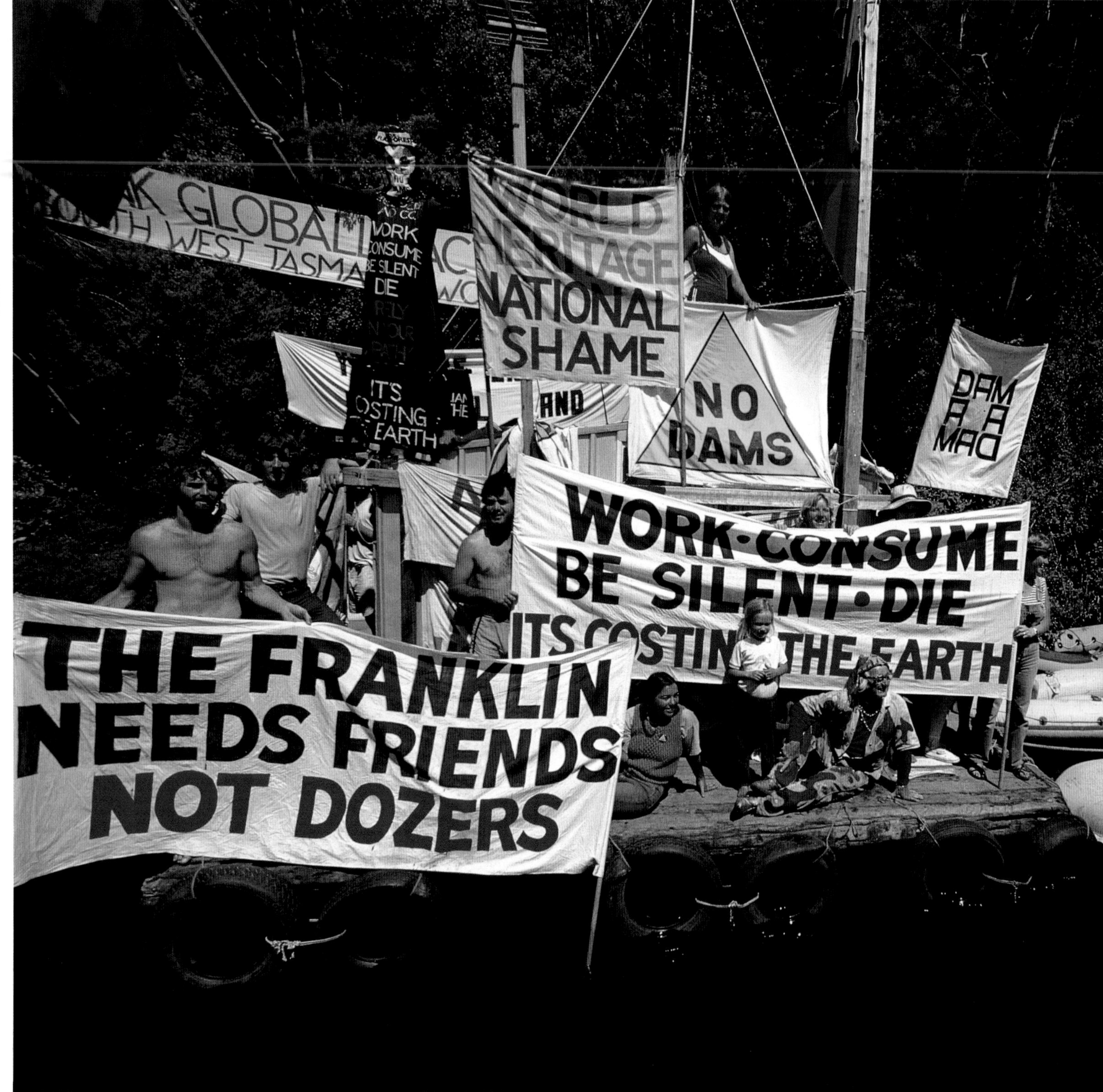

I went to Tasmania during the 1982 83 anti dam crusade to photograph the blockade from both the dam builders' and the protestors' points of view.

Near the dam site on the Gordon River the protestors, known as the 'greenies,' had set up base camp. Part of the task was to construct protest banners to hang from boats, barges and river-side trees.

Here, among a great deal of comings and goings, we met the chief banner painter, *Harold The Kangaroo—The Greatest Genius That Ever Lived.* Believe it or not, that was his real name!

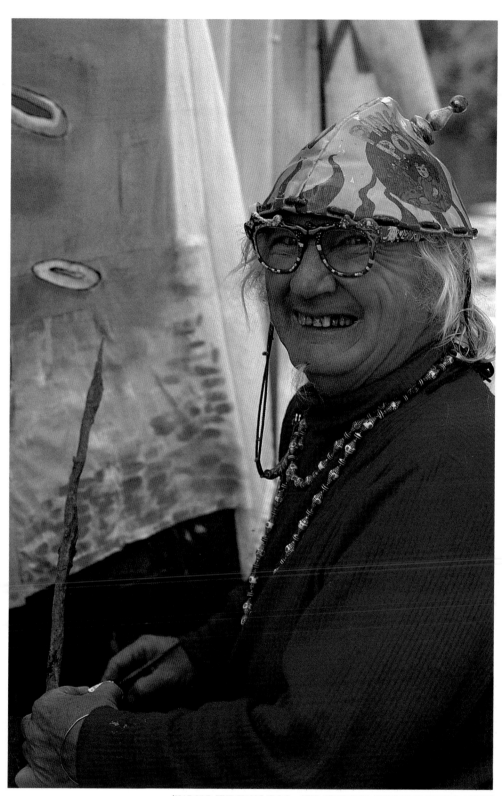

THE GREENIES, GORDON RIVER BASE CAMP, TASMANIA.
125th sec., f8, 15mm, 64asa.

'HAROLD THE KANGAROO - THE GREATEST GENIUS THAT EVER LIVED',
GORDON RIVER, TASMANIA.
125th sec., f8, 135mm, 64asa.

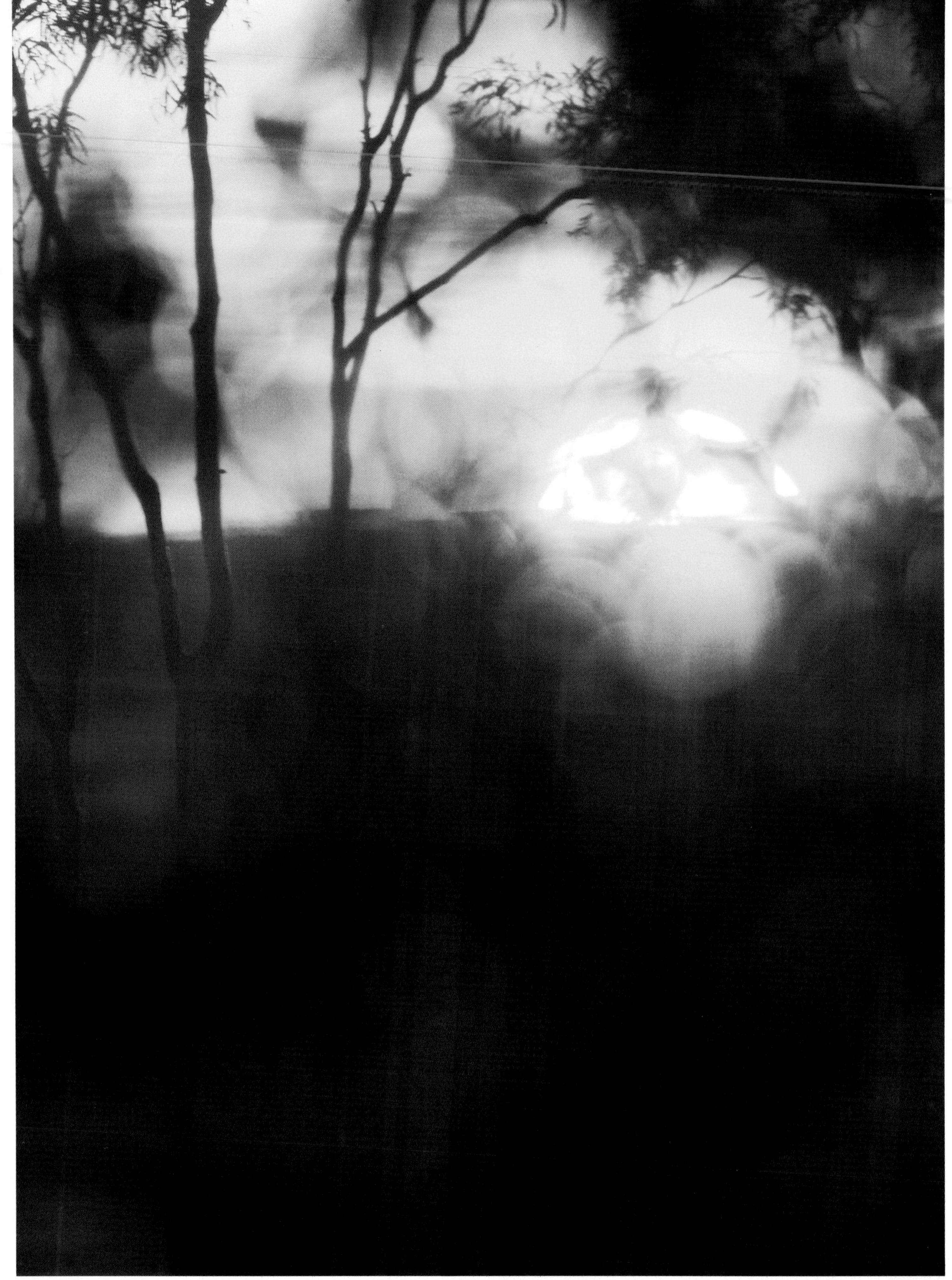

THE BUSH AT SUNSET, QUEENSLAND.
250th sec., f5.6, 600mm IFED, tripod, 64asa.

BUSH MAGIC

EXPLORING THE BUSH has become a national pastime in Australia. In fact 'going bush' has become so popular that city-bound folk have developed a new fanaticism which compels them to create bushlands on their urban blocks.

The photograph on the left was taken from a friend's lounge room window. I was illustrating to him the lovely soft, abstract effect that can be obtained with long telephoto lenses when the point of focus is interrupted by out of focus leaves and branches.

The image to the right was made at a native plant exhibition on the Darling Downs. Here, bush fanatics from all over Australia come to show off their latest garden creations.

It is not important to know the names of every plant you encounter. What is important is that you see the colours, textures, patterns and shapes; these are the things that make pictures powerful.

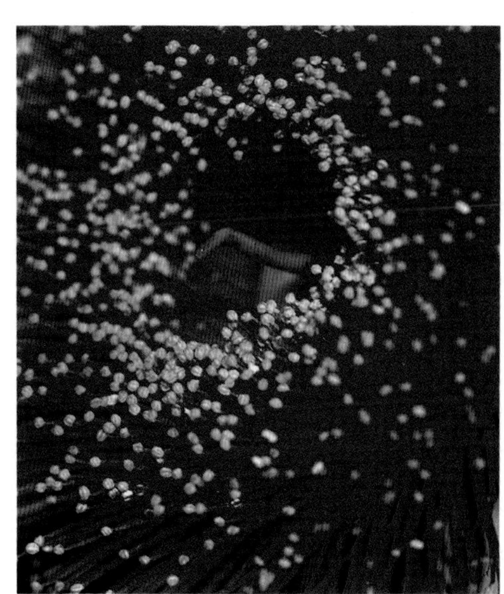

GUM BLOSSOM, QUEENSLAND.
125th sec., f4, 105mm micro, 64asa.

GUM LEAVES, CARNARVON GORGE, QUEENSLAND.
125th sec., f5.6, 600mm IFED, tripod, 64asa.

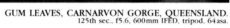

Drooping gum leaves, golden light playing through peeling gum bark, a magpie roosting after a long day in the Australian bush. As a photographer, I am always on the lookout for images that epitomise this country's character.

MAGPIE, BUNYA MOUNTAINS, QUEENSLAND.
125th sec., f5.6, 600mm IFED, tripod, 64asa.

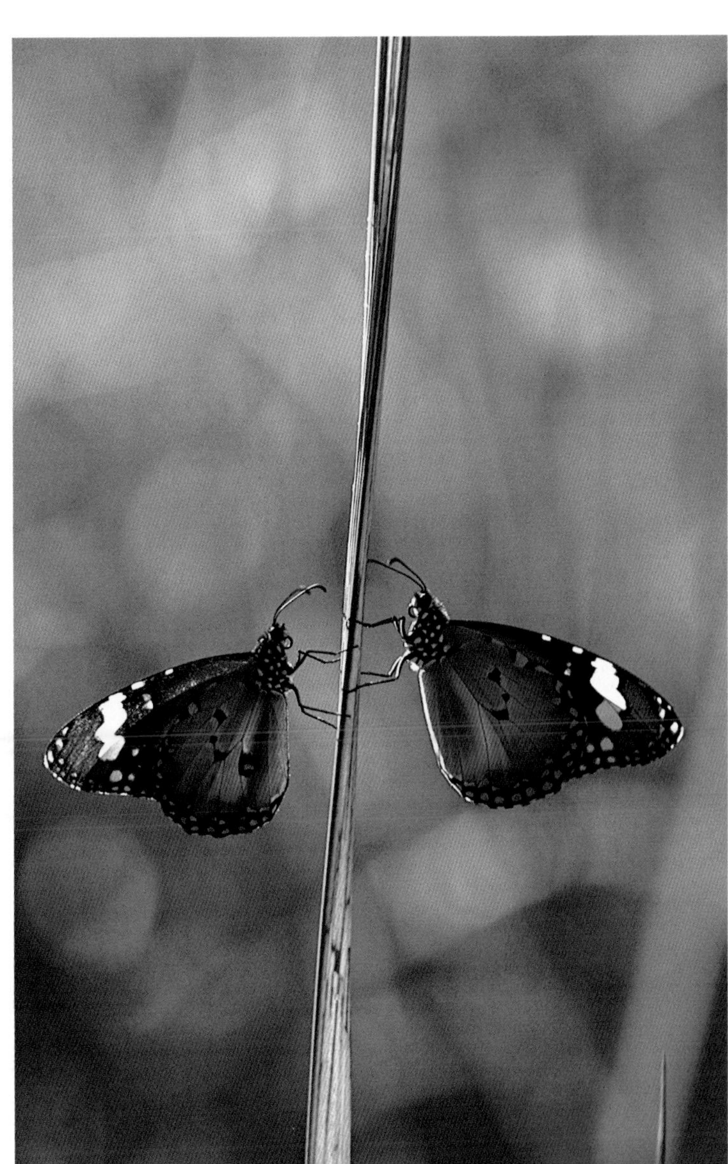

BUTTERFLIES, CARNARVON GORGE, QUEENSLAND.
250th sec., f4, 105mm micro, 64asa.

WILDFLOWERS, THE GRAMPIANS NATIONAL PARK, VICTORIA.
125th sec., f4, 105mm micro, 64asa.

PALM FRONDS, CARNARVON GORGE, QUEENSLAND.
125th sec., f5.6, 600mm IFED, tripod, 64asa.

MOON OVER BOTTLE TREE, CENTRAL QUEENSLAND.
125th sec., f5.6, 600mm IFED, 64asa (superimposed).

BUSH FEELINGS, GIRRAWEEN NATIONAL PARK, QUEENSLAND.
125th sec., f8, 105mm micro, 64asa (superimposed).

Sometimes I feel that I must say more in an image than is possible with a single exposure. Here, I wanted to draw a relationship between earth and moon, so I made two exposures, one on top of the other, both with a 600mm lens. All that stood in that totally devastated landscape was this one Bottle Tree. I looked up at the moon and wondered if we would ever clear our planet completely.

Three exposures made this single image. The first was the tree bark, the second gum leaves, and the third was the sun. In this instance I made no attempt to previsualise the picture.

THE CLOSER YOU LOOK, THE FURTHER YOU SEE, GREVILLEA, QUEENSLAND.
250th sec., f4, 105mm micro, 64asa.

BENNETT'S WALLABY, TASMANIA.
125th sec., f2, 135mm, 64asa.

Patiently watching and waiting for the right moment is what wildlife photography is largely about.

At the edge of the forest I encountered shy, secretive wallabies. The animals had come to the forest's edge at dawn to bask in the sunshine. In National Parks, where wallabies are familiar with people, I have been able to approach quite close and remain with the animals for hours at a time.

This photograph of a Koala is an example of how a little extra touch can make a picture really work. Without the pouched baby, this would be just another Koala picture.

The side of Hanging Rock is a particularly good place from which to photograph Koalas. I was sitting there watching mum sleep through my 600mm lens when a tiny head appeared. I was able to make three pictures before the baby withdrew, and although I waited for more than an hour, the young one showed no sign of reappearing.

KOALA, HANGING ROCK, VICTORIA.
125th sec., f5.6, 600mm IFED, tripod, 64asa.

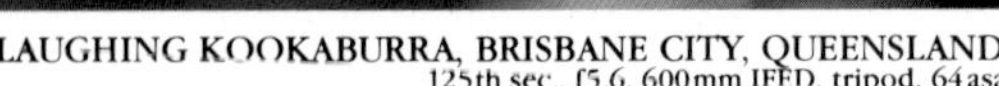

LAUGHING KOOKABURRA, BRISBANE CITY, QUEENSLAND.
125th sec., f5.6, 600mm IFED, tripod, 64asa.

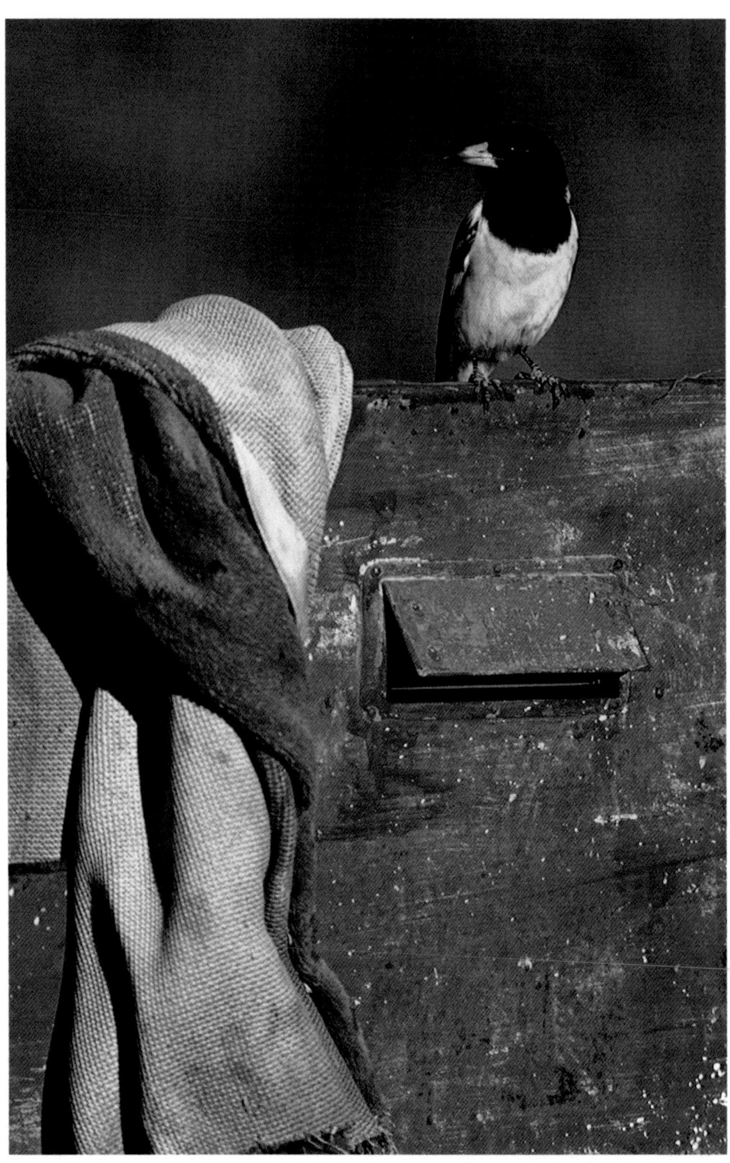

PIED BUTCHER BIRD, JERICHO, QUEENSLAND.
125th sec., f5.6, 600mm IFED, tripod, 64asa.

One of the main excuses I hear from people wanting to make pictures is that they simply do not have time. There is one sure way of making time and that is to have a habitat for wildlife in your own garden. Lots of shrubs, trees, rocks and perhaps a pond or a bird bath will attract an assortment of birds, insects, reptiles and even the odd mammal.

This Kookaburra was photographed with a 600mm lens in my front yard in Brisbane. I did not really need such a long telephoto lens, but the short depth of field enabled me to blur out the side fence!

This portrait of Australia's finest songster was made in the back yard of a friend's house in central Queensland. Like many bush birds, this Pied Butcher Bird was always hanging around looking for a hand out. When it landed, I couldn't resist the monochromatic simplicity of the bird against the strong textural arrangement of the hessian bag and the backboard of the old truck.

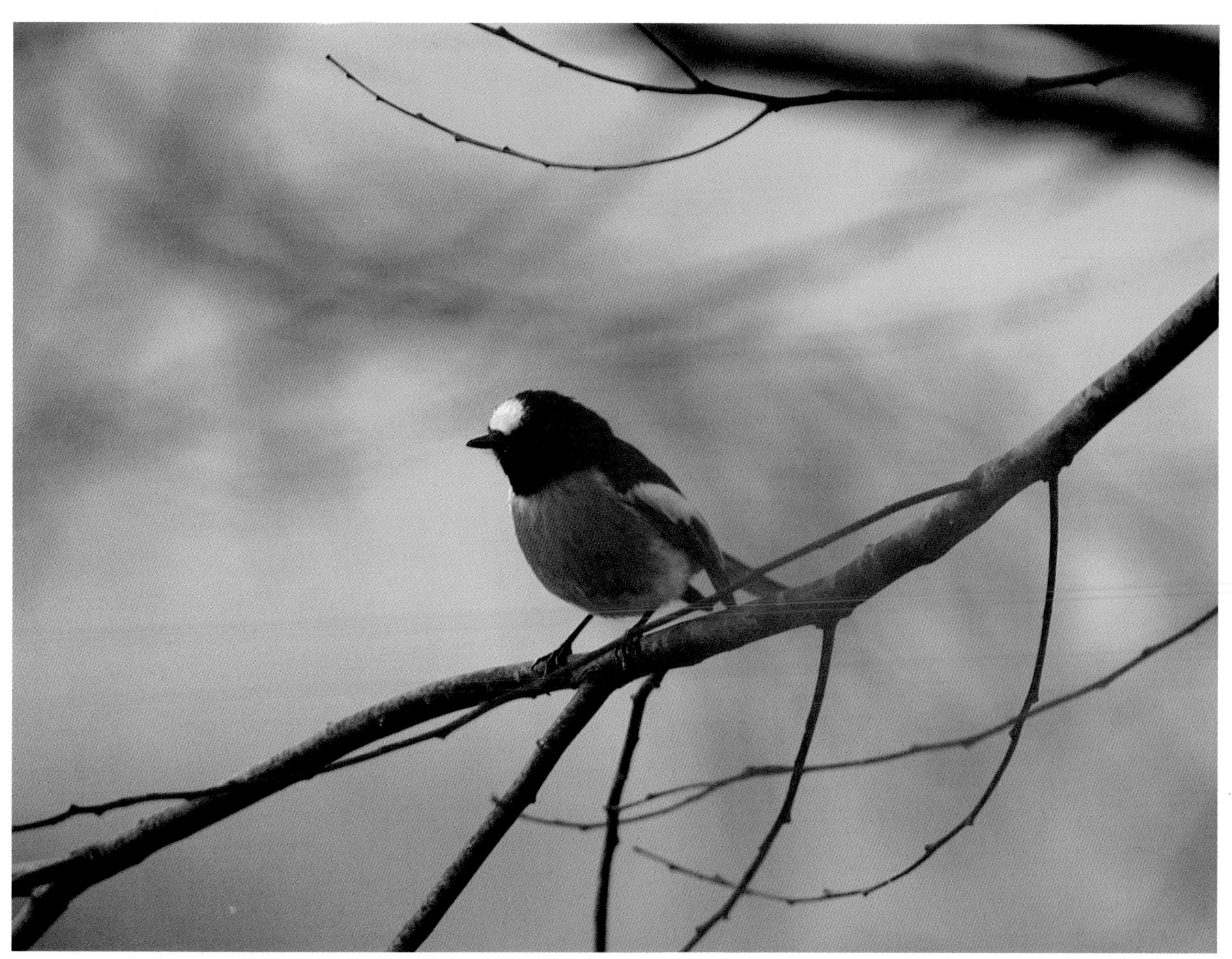

ROBIN, GIRRAWEEN NATIONAL PARK, QUEENSLAND.
125th sec., f5.6, 600mm IFED, tripod, 64asa.

Small, highly active bush birds often require that you have quick reflexes both for composition and shutter release timing.

There is rarely time to check the background. As a result, most images do have obtrusive sticks, branches, and light and dark areas to spoil them. The only solution is to take lots of pictures.

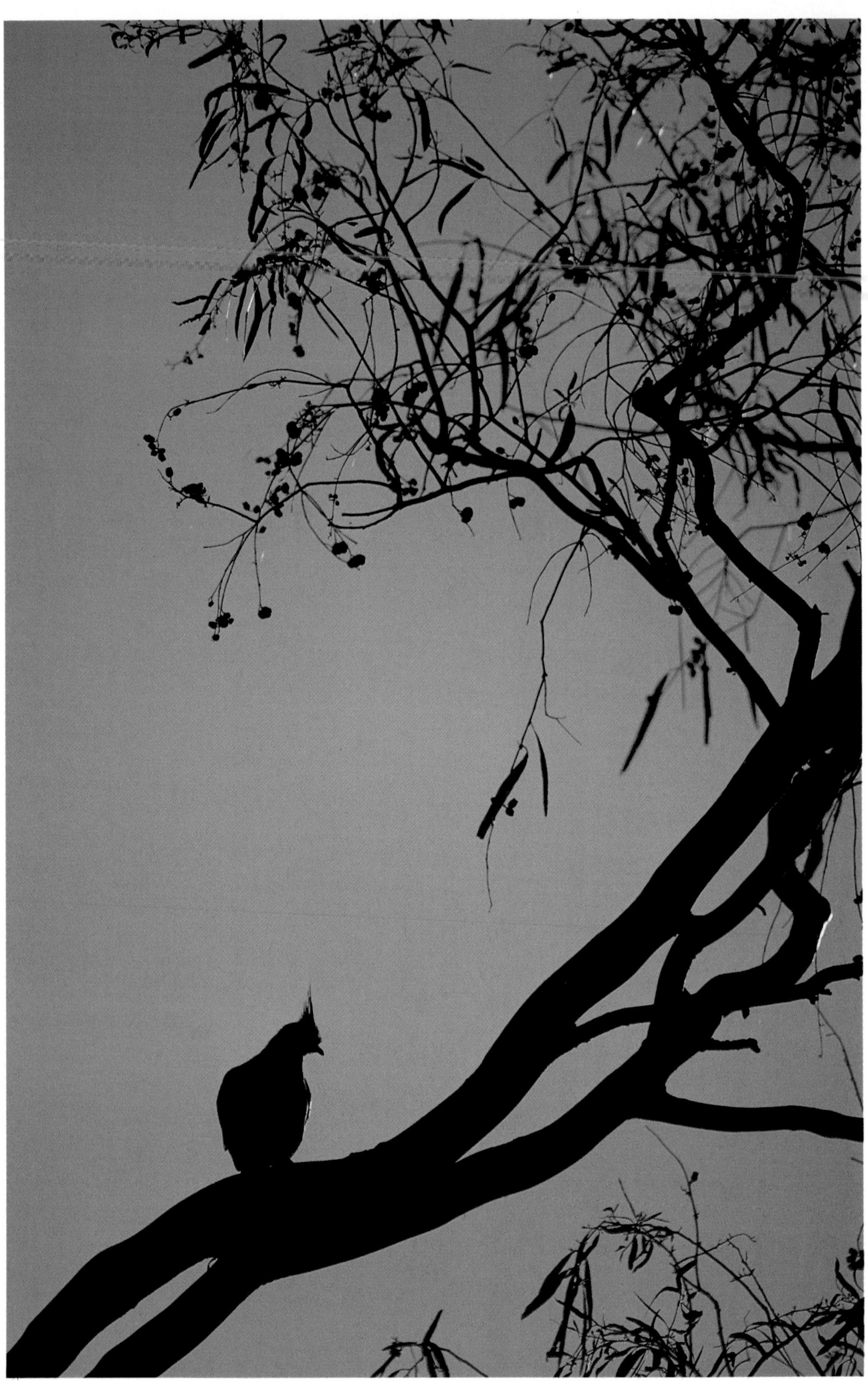

PIGEON SHAPE, DARLING DOWNS, QUEENSLAND.
125th sec., f5.6, 600mm IFED, tripod, 64asa.

Not intended as bird studies, these two pictures are more about the elements of shape and composition. They are also about simplicity, and they remind me to look at the space between the branches rather than just at the tree.

PIGEON SHAPE, LAMINGTON NATIONAL PARK, QUEENSLAND.
125th sec., f5.6, 600mm IFED, tripod, 64asa.

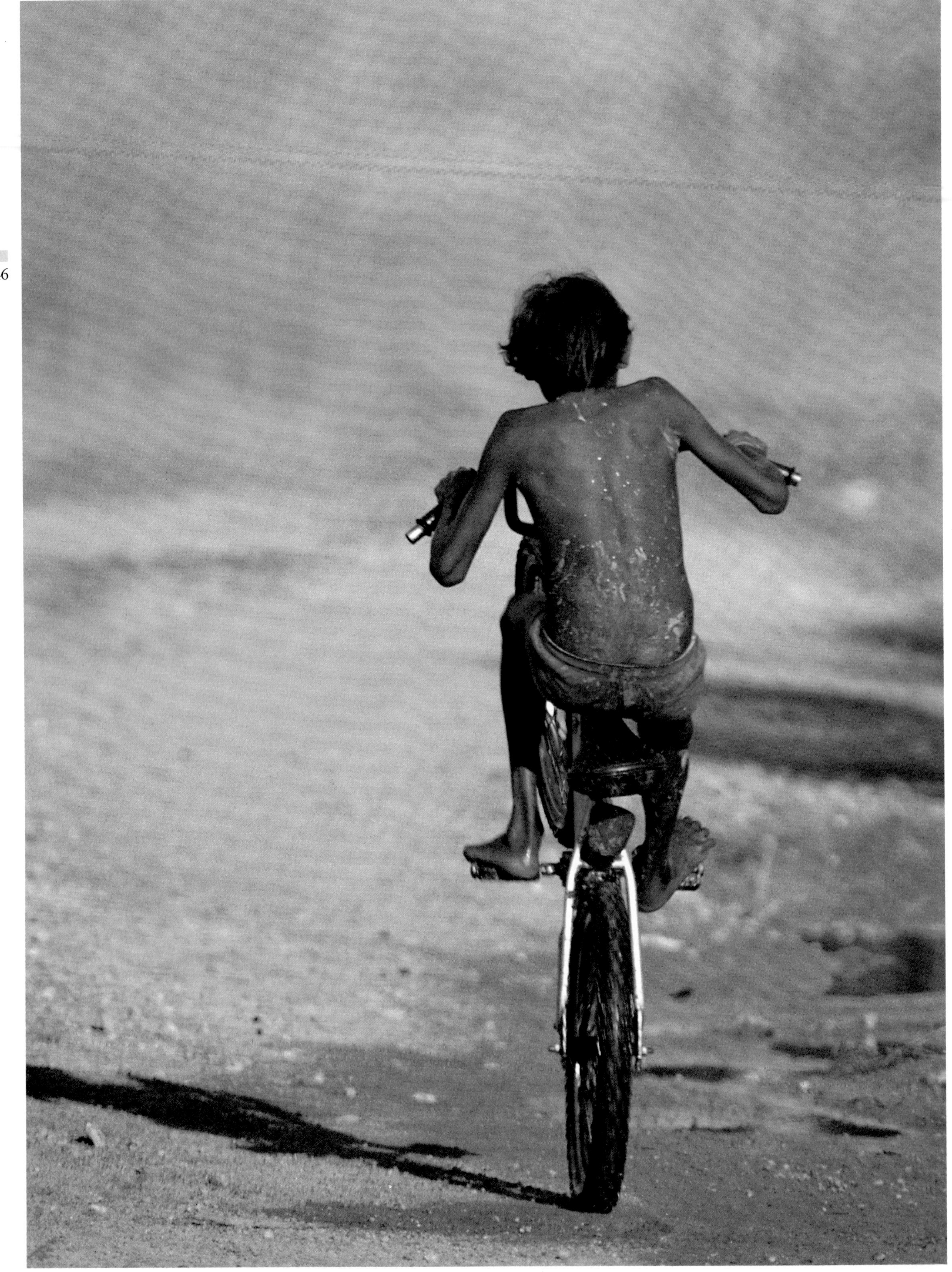

ROADSTER, NORTH QUEENSLAND.
250th sec., f5.6, 80 - 200mm zoom, 64asa.

CRUISING COUNTRY ROADS

C*OUNTRY ROADS.* The slopes and plateaus of the Great Divide have endless kilometres of them. Early in the morning or late in the afternoon there are few things more relaxing than cruising down the track with a little country music for company.

In 1982 I set out for six months to photograph the entire length of the Great Divide from the tip of Cape York to the Grampians in Victoria. Apart from the Cape, sections of the Great Divide in Queensland, and the Alps in New South Wales, most of this vast mountain range has been cleared for pasture and could quite aptly be referred to as 'country', or settled land.

I might have two or three lenses beside me as I drive. There are always images everywhere. A grazing cow, some backlit sheep, neat picket fences and the inevitable isolated gums, standing tall.

Travelling the backroads, one meets the country folk too. Tiny verandahed pubs present colourful publicans; there are shearers, drovers and ringers to pass the time of day with, and country kids, whose pranks and off-hand comments I always find entertaining.

COUNTRY ROAD, NORTH QUEENSLAND.
125th sec., f4.5, 80 - 200mm zoom, 64asa.

BARN OWL DURING MOUSE PLAGUE, ATHERTON TABLELAND, NORTH QUEENSLAND.
125th sec., f4.5, 80 - 200mm zoom, flash, 64asa.

ALF WRIGHT, PUBLICAN, DORA DORA HOTEL, NEW SOUTH WALES.
125th sec., f11, 35mm, flash, 64asa.

GREAT DIVIDING RANGE, VICTORIA.
125th sec., f5.6, 600mm IFED, tripod, 64asa.

A distant mountain range can become a graphic art piece with a long telephoto lens and fading light. I have photographed hundreds of such scenes while cruising country roads, but as subjects they still pose great compositional challenges.

STIRLING RANGE, WESTERN AUSTRALIA.
125th sec., f5.6, 600mm IFED, tripod, 64asa.

LAWSON RANGE, TASMANIA.
125th sec., f5.6, 600mm IFED, tripod, 64asa.

GREAT DIVIDING RANGE, QUEENSLAND.
125th sec., f5.6, 600mm IFED, tripod, 64asa.

FRANKLAND RANGE, TASMANIA.
125th sec., f5.6, 600mm IFED, tripod, 64asa.

DROVER, RIVER MURRAY FLATS, KHANCOBAN VALLEY, NEW SOUTH WALES.
125th sec., f8, 80 - 200mm zoom, 64asa.

They used to say that Australia rode on the sheep's back, and I'm sure they're right. If you spend any time at all cruising country roads, you are sure to encounter scenes like this.

DROVER, CAPE ARID, WESTERN AUSTRALIA.
125th sec., f8, 80 - 200mm zoom, 64asa.

SHEPHERDS NEAR WALCHA, NEW SOUTH WALES.
125th sec., f8, 80 - 200mm zoom, 64asa.

The subjects of these two pictures were complete opposites. When I asked the shepherds above whether they objected to my photographing them they replied, "sure, s'long as we don't have to talk to yer."
The shepherd in the picture on the right, had superb oral skills. He did not stop talking for over an hour!

SHEPHERD, CAPTAINS FLAT, NEW SOUTH WALES.
125th sec., f11, 24mm, 64asa.

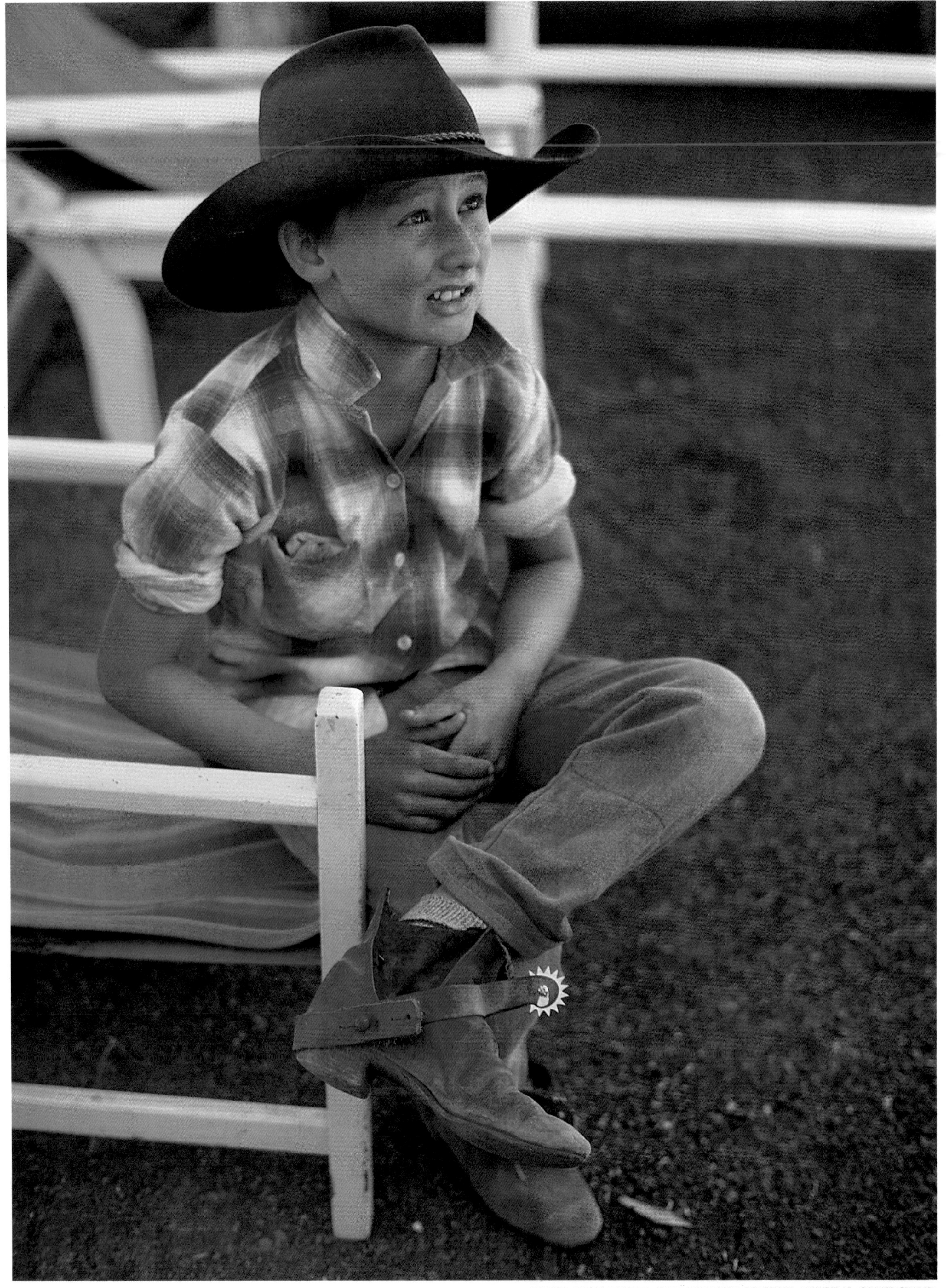

KEVIN JOHN HEROD, YARROWMERE STATION, CENTRAL QUEENSLAND.
125th sec., f2, 50mm, 64asa.

I had been sitting on the cow rail for over an hour trying to make an interesting picture out of a black cow going into a black milking shed.

Suddenly John Marriott appeared. I started our conversation with, "Hey, its Monday, why aren't you at school." With a dry, slow drawl, and with no hesitation whatsoever, John replied, " 'cause, you'd have to be a mug, wouldn't yer. Yer don't get paid for do'n that!"

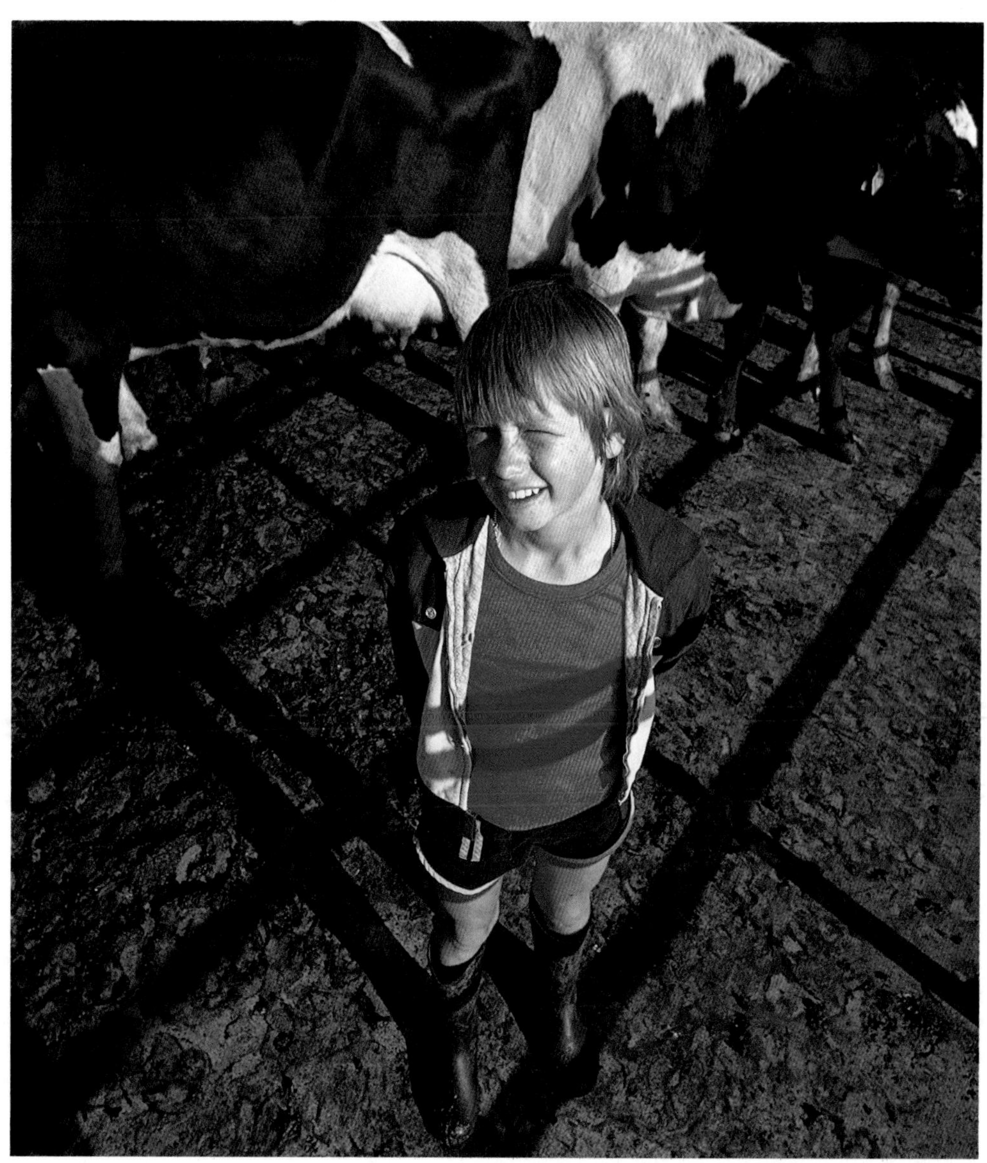

JOHN MARRIOTT, ATHERTON TABLELAND, QUEENSLAND.
125th sec., f2.8, 35mm, 64asa.

Young Kevin John Herod had just spent the day helping his dad muster on Yarrowmere Station. He had come inside for a cool drink. His mum, in a casual off-hand sort of manner, looked him in the eye, then cast a glance at his spurs. He immediately sat down and swung the spurs to the front of his boots. I guess mum was telling her son not to dig holes in the lino.

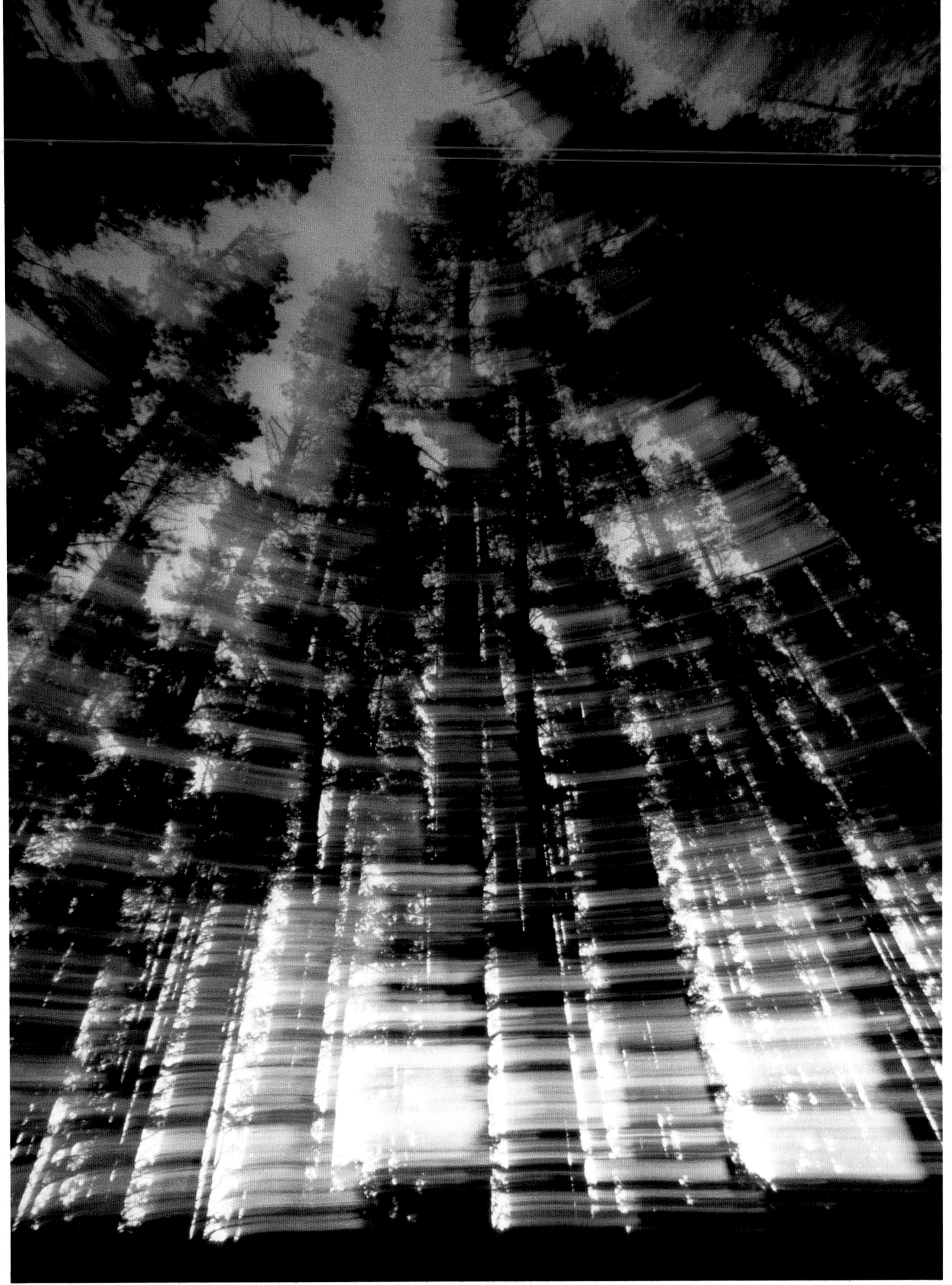

PINE PLANTATION, VICTORIA.
8th sec., f5.6, 15mm, 64asa.

NEW ENGLAND TABLELAND, NEW SOUTH WALES.
125th sec., f5.6, 35mm, 64asa.

I had been driving for hours through endless pine plantations and was dead tired when I decided to take a walk to see what I could find. I was in a pine forest, and about a hundred metres away there was a patch of natural bush.

Standing alone in the forest and looking up gave me a strange, giddy, empty feeling. There were birds calling, not close by, but outside the forest. For a moment I felt as though I was inside a cage, so I slowed the shutter speed down to a 15th of a second to record that feeling on film.

Going, going, gone. The Australian bush is disappearing at an alarming rate. Here, two of the causes, a mysterious tree disease called die-back, and clearing to raise sheep and cattle, have a devastating combined effect.

DISCOVERING SEASHORES

H*ARD, WET, SQUEAKY* sand beneath bare feet on long moonlit walks where watery sounds seem to follow everywhere. Lumbering turtles whose tractor-tread tracks always intrigue at daybreak. Startled crabs that dart from underfoot in the dark. The incoming tide floats armadas of boat-shaped leaves amongst tangled mangrove forest roots, and warm, wet, oozing mud squelches between the toes.

At noon the stillness is broken by giant wheeling flocks of white birds that fill blue skies beneath a hot sun. There are giant waves of sand to climb, heathland garden fantasies to explore, and rocky pools to gaze into.

And then to leave this world for another where fanciful blue-green shapes, patterns and textures create illusions that no drug can imitate.

Discovering seashores. The very words make sibilant sea-sounds, and smell of salty air!

ESPERANCE, WESTERN AUSTRALIA.
125th sec., f5.6, 135mm, 64asa.

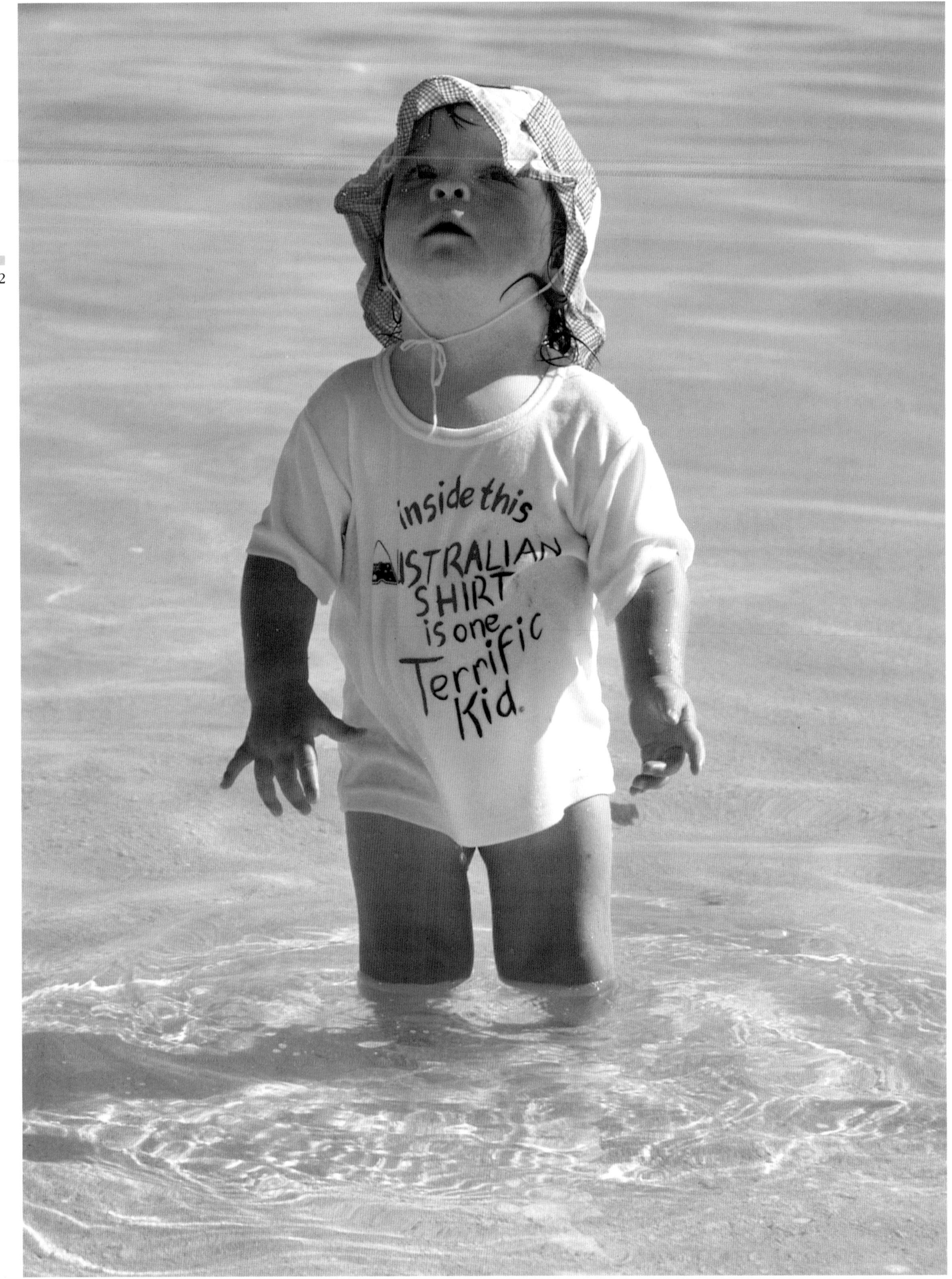
inside this
ISTRALIAN
SHIRT
is one
Terrific
Kid.

MELISSA MANN, HERON ISLAND, QUEENSLAND.
250th sec., f11, 135mm, 64asa.

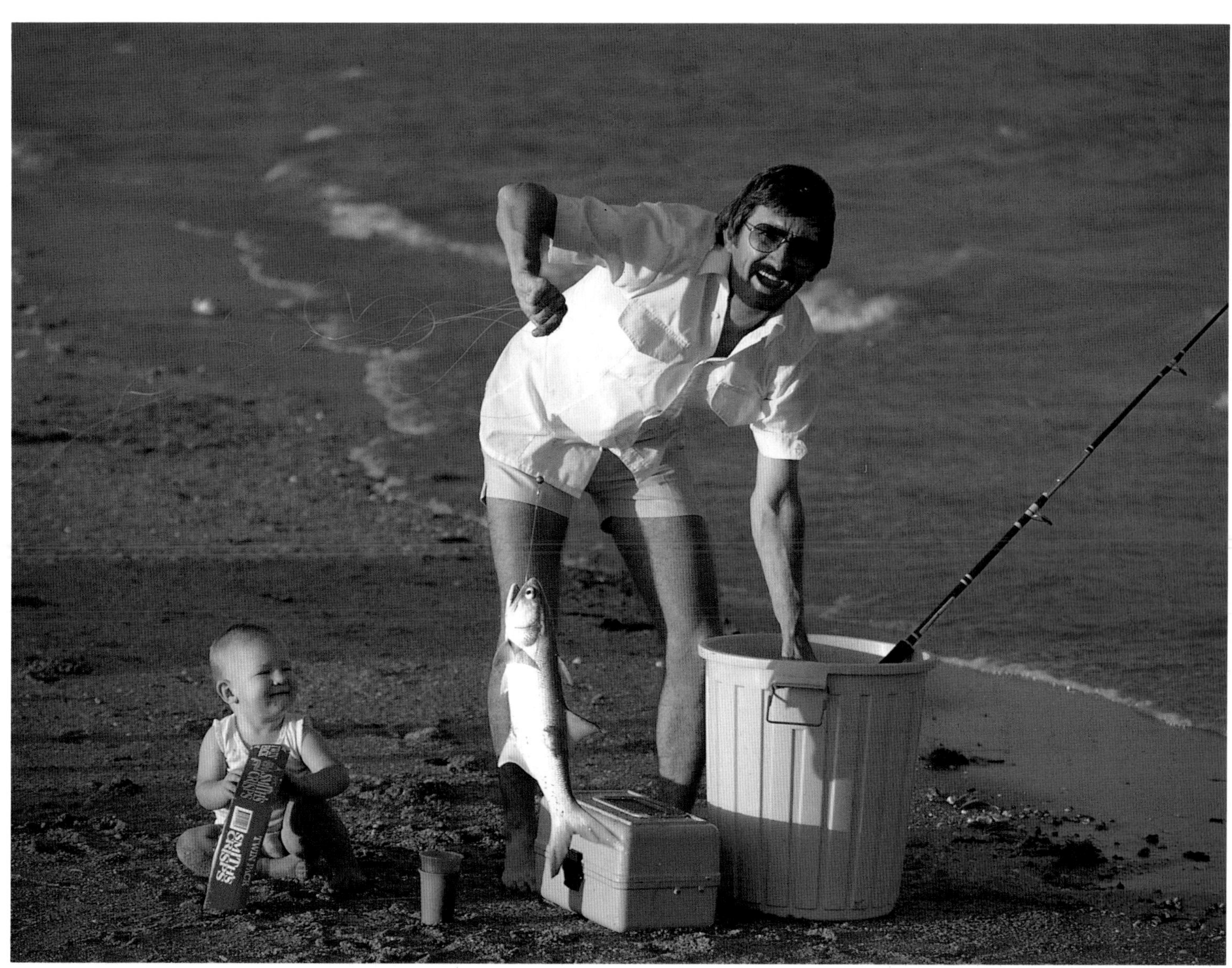

SHARING HAPPINESS, CAPE YORK, QUEENSLAND.
125th sec., f8. 80 - 200mm zoom. 64asa.

When this image was made, Melissa Mann had just made first contact with the Coral Sea. At seventeen months of age, she had probably forgotten the incident by tea-time. The experience will no doubt remain with her for life.

A moment of joy for father and daughter, captured on film forever. This is what the true magic of making pictures is all about, and where better to practise than beside the sea.

DUNE AND ROCKS, CAPE ARID NATIONAL PARK, WESTERN AUSTRALIA.
125th sec., f8, 15mm, 64asa.

Each image is a story, and when a story is short and simple it has more power.

Wandering among the dunes at Cape Arid, I was impressed by the graphic simplicity of the landscape. In many ways, the white sand reminded me of the alps.

To capture something of this feeling, I arranged my photographic compositions to present the least possible number of elements.

The majority of the pictures in this book apply this concept.

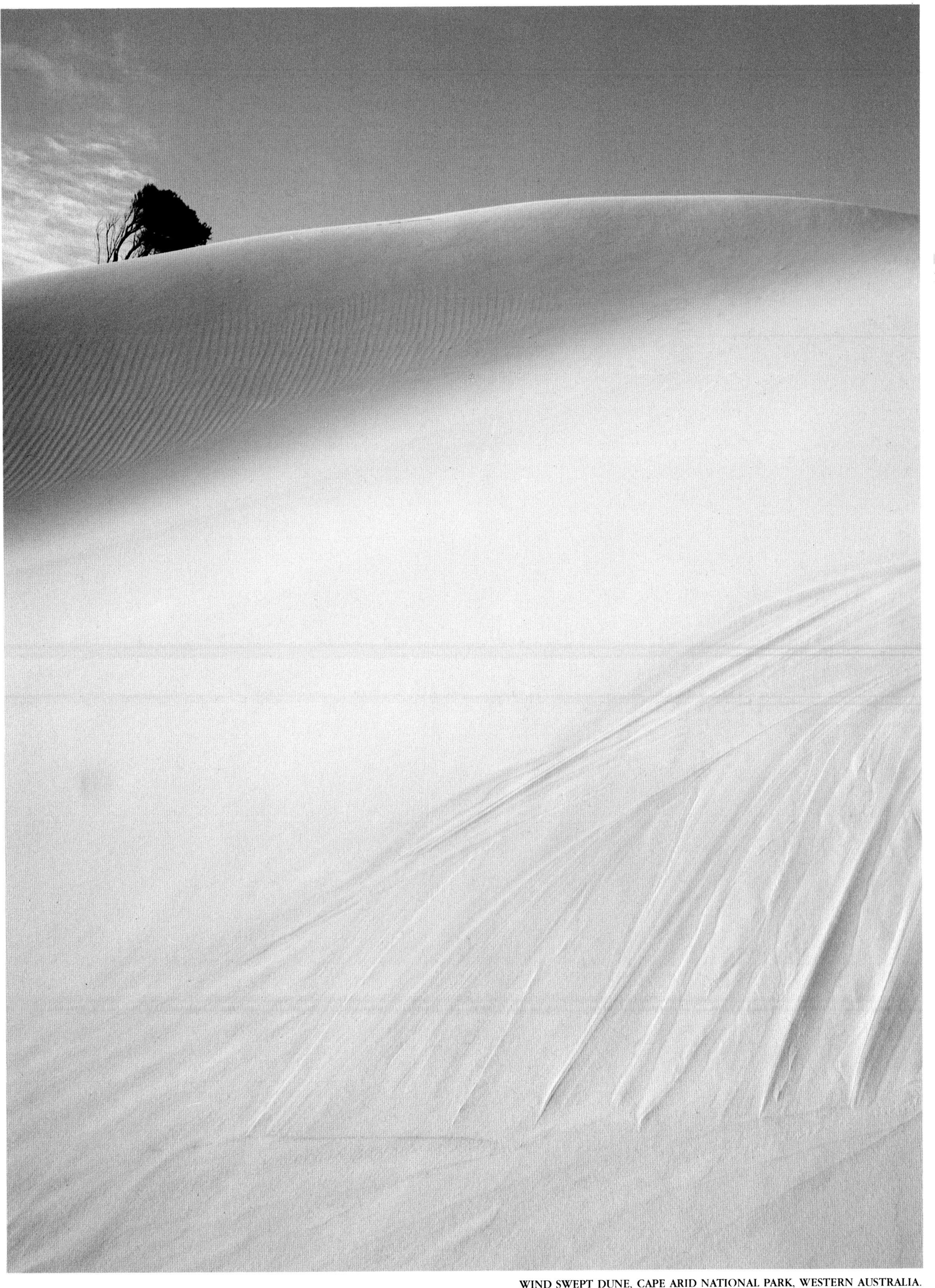

WIND SWEPT DUNE, CAPE ARID NATIONAL PARK, WESTERN AUSTRALIA.
125th sec., f11, 15mm, 64asa.

RAINDROPS ON A FEATHER, GANNET CAY, SWAIN REEFS, QUEENSLAND.
30th sec., f4, 105mm micro, tripod, 64asa.

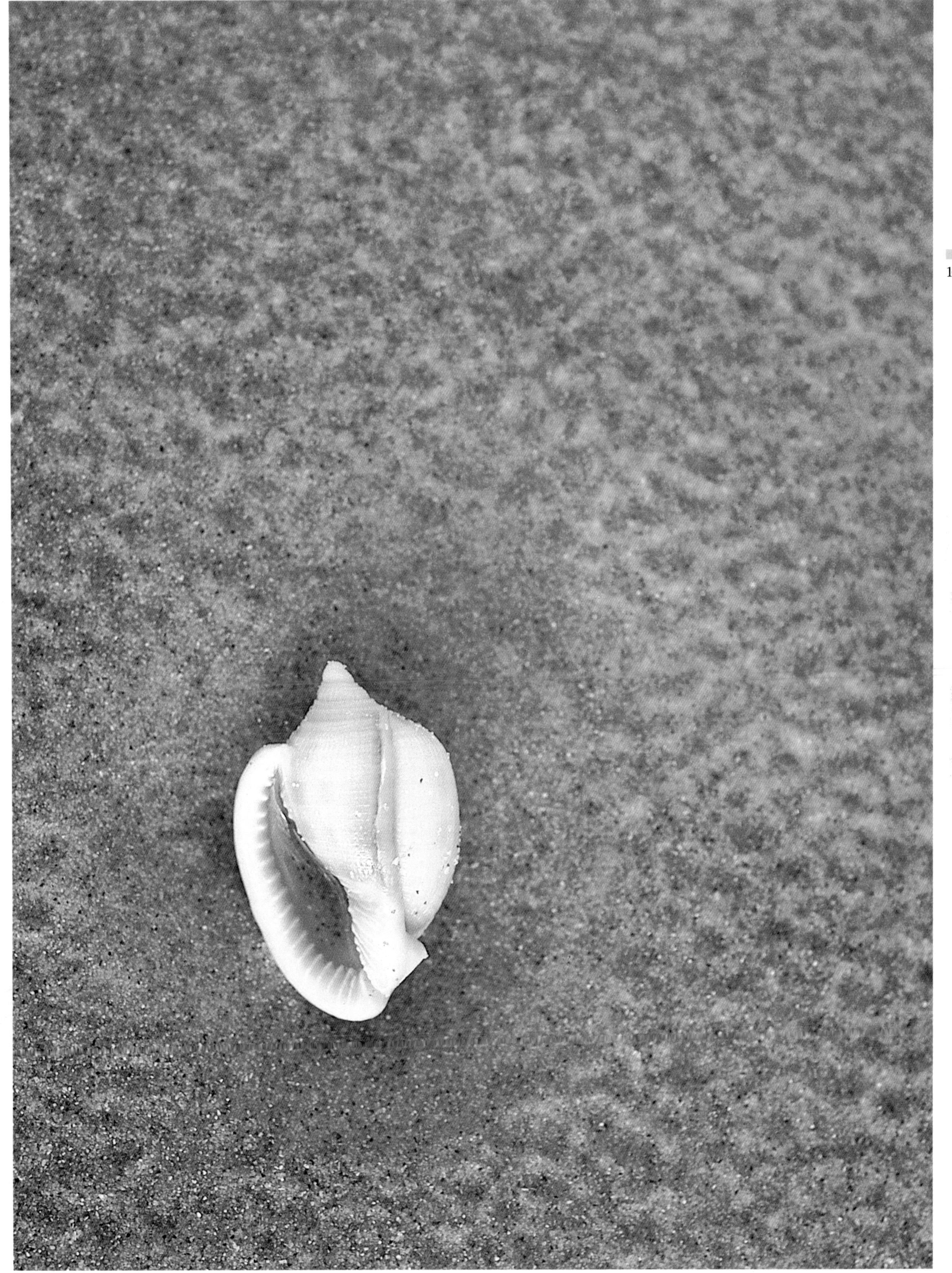

RAINDROPS BESIDE A SHELL, STRADBROKE ISLAND, QUEENSLAND.
125th sec., f8, 55mm micro, 64asa.

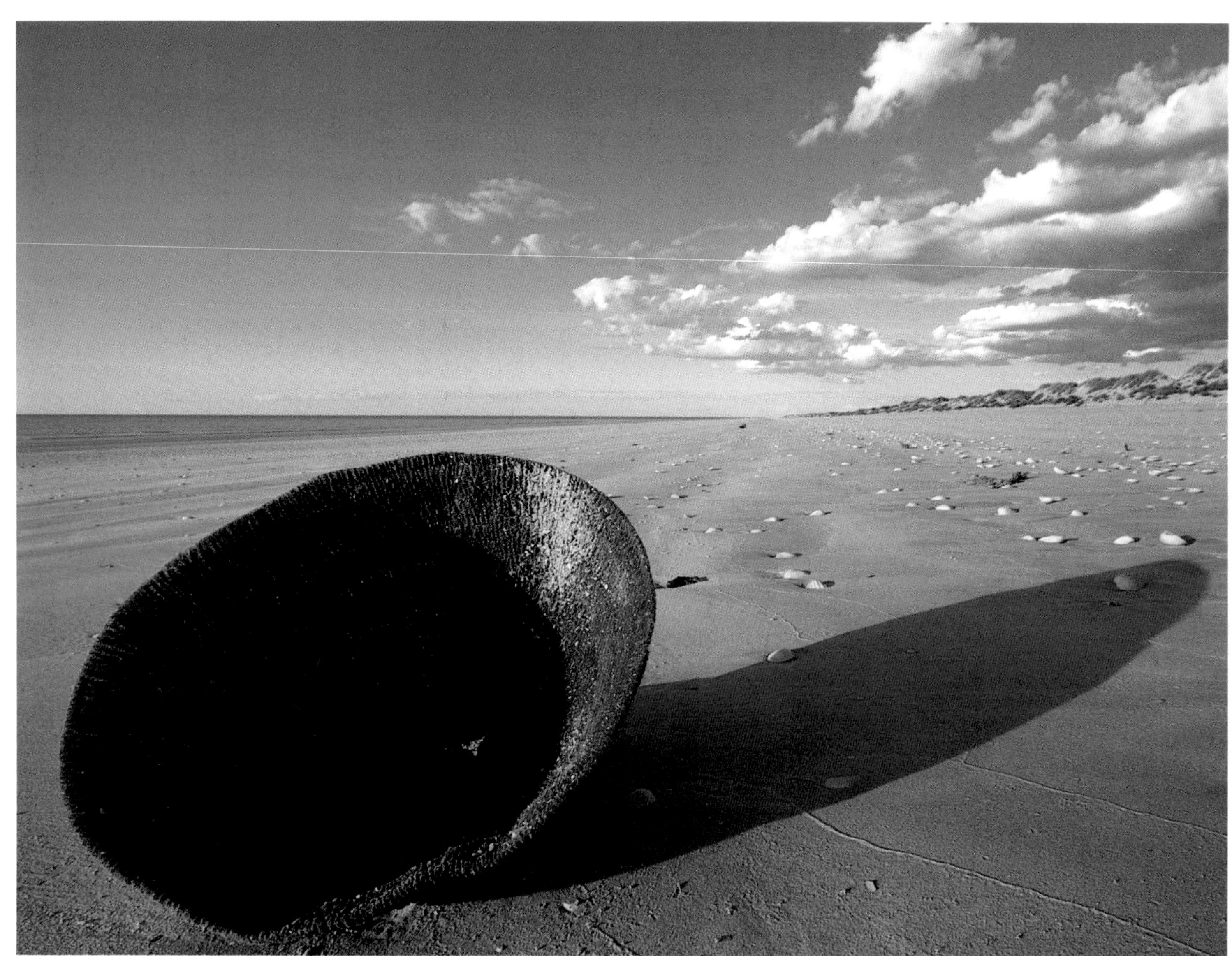

SPONGE, EIGHTY MILE BEACH, WESTERN AUSTRALIA.
125th sec., f8, 15mm, 64asa.

Although man likes to think that he is a power unto himself, he is, like all living things, under the control of nature's elements.

On my arrival in Broome, I was surprised to discover the colourful pearling industry in its death throes. Economic pressures, storms and disease had all but wiped out the industry.

Further south, cast ashore on Eighty Mile Beach, a sponge, lies lifeless, a silent testament to nature's control.

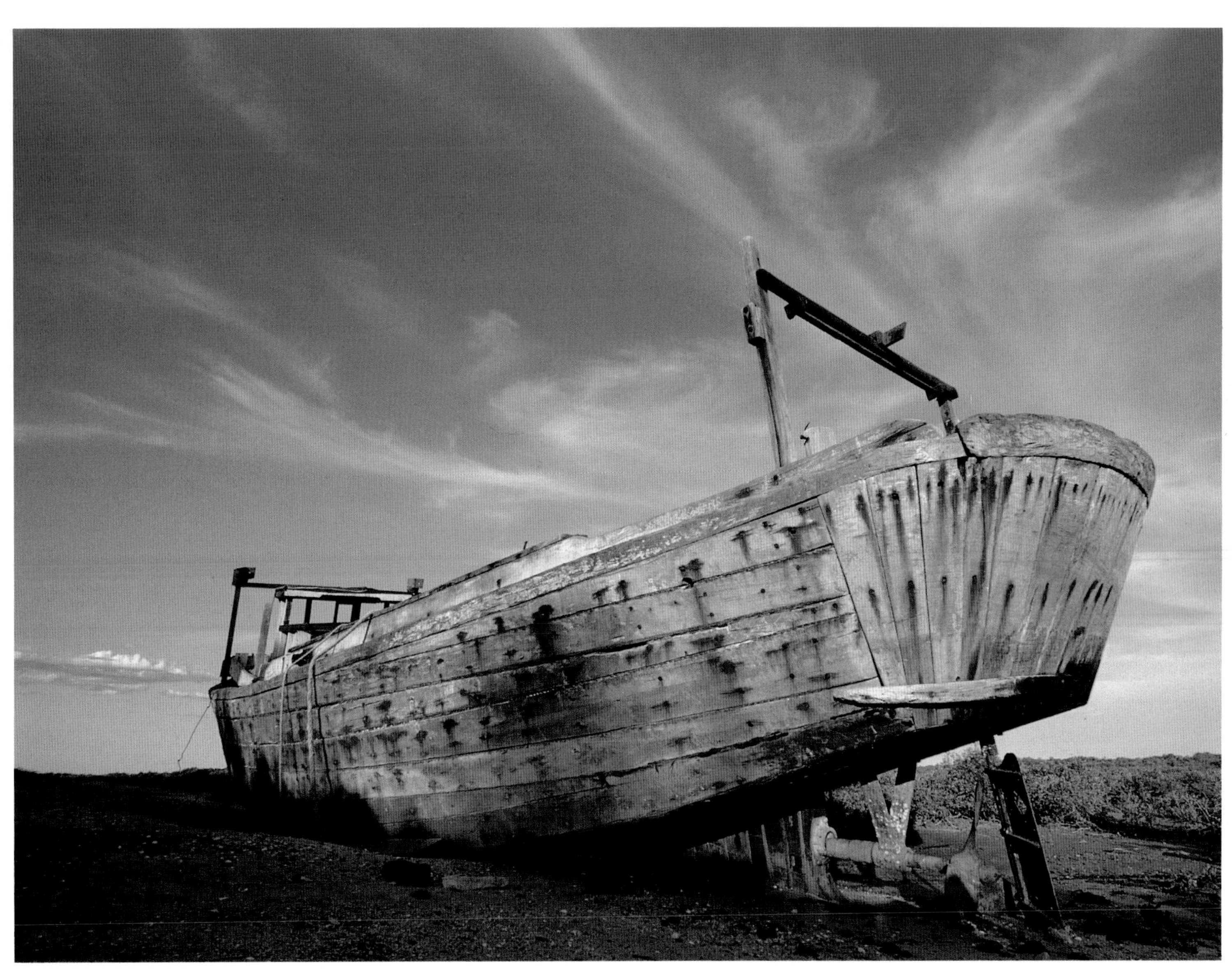

ABANDONED PEARLING LUGGER, BROOME, WESTERN AUSTRALIA.
125th sec., f8, 15mm, 64asa.

OYSTER CATCHER, CAPE ARID, WESTERN AUSTRALIA.
60th sec., f5.6, 600mm IFED, tripod, 64asa.

With a tripod, a 600mm lens and a long beach at dawn or sunset, I am as happy as I can be. I'll stroll along with the wind in my hair, the sand between my toes and the sea sounds all around. It is an experience available to anyone, just about anywhere. You do not need a 600mm lens, there are things to photograph every inch of the way with just about any combination of lenses.

Here, an Oyster Catcher works alone on an isolated wilderness beach in Western Australia. The solitude compelled a loose, free composition.

TERN SHAPES, CAPE ARID NATIONAL PARK, WESTERN AUSTRALIA.
250th sec., f5.6, 600mm IFED, tripod, 64asa.

These roosting terns presented an interesting interruption to the subtle wave patterns reflected in the tide-wet sand.

HINTING AT EARTH'S CREATION, TASMANIA.
15th sec., f11, 135mm, tripod, 64asa.

An hour earlier the landscape had so many colours, textures and patterns that my eye was confused. Under the twilight sky, I was deeply moved by the graphic simplicity of this scene.

COAST AT WILSON'S PROMONTORY, VICTORIA.
60th sec., f5.6, 600mm IFED, tripod, 64asa.

There were many kinds of birds in this area, but the one that really captured my imagination was the Banded Stilt. I soon discovered that every morning and afternoon, some 300 individuals would come together to form a raft. Then, roughly in a V-shape, they paddled back and forth feeding on microscopic life-forms on the water's surface.

I was so fascinated with their precision, and with their perfect co-operation, that I tried to capture the feeling by slowing down the shutter speed.

FITZGERALD RIVER NATIONAL PARK, WESTERN AUSTRALIA.
15th sec., f11, 600mm IFED, tripod, 64asa.

DINGO, CALOUNDRA, QUEENSLAND.
60th sec., f5.6, 600mm IFED, 64asa.

This Dingo became famous to the locals of Caloundra, a Sunshine Coast town north of Brisbane. Although wild, the dog regularly came to the edge of town to visit, and even to play with the local policeman's dog. It was a fine specimen, so armed with a 600mm lens, I paid this Dingo a visit.

Although fairly approachable, the animal played hard to get. What I was carrying must have looked like a gun. We played hide-and-seek in the heathlands for an hour before I made any shots at all. By this time the light was very low and the shutter reading was a 30th of a second. I was at the point of giving up when the Dingo walked out across a small peninsula in a watery depression, lowered his head and began to drink. As I raised the camera to focus, the sun broke out from behind a cloud. I had time to make just two exposures. The first one was out of focus, and the second gave me this image.

The Dingo has since been shot.

SEA EAGLE, BROOME, WESTERN AUSTRALIA.
125th sec., f5.6, 600mm IFED, tripod, 64asa.

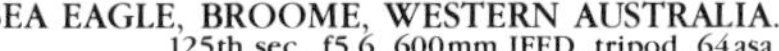

EGRET, CAIRNS, QUEENSLAND.
125th sec., f5.6, 600mm IFED, tripod, 64asa.

Mangroves grow virtually in the main street of Broome. This Sea Eagle was photographed at sunset 30 metres from the Roebuck Bay Hotel—one of the north-west's roughest pubs. On the other side of Australia, an Egret was photographed at sunrise on the mudflats along the Cairns shoreline.

I have made many wildlife pictures close to, and even in, towns and cities. If an animal is prepared to tolerate the noise and activity levels associated with human habitation, then it is probably going to offer a photographer the opportunity of working at close range, with time for deliberation over exposures and compositions.

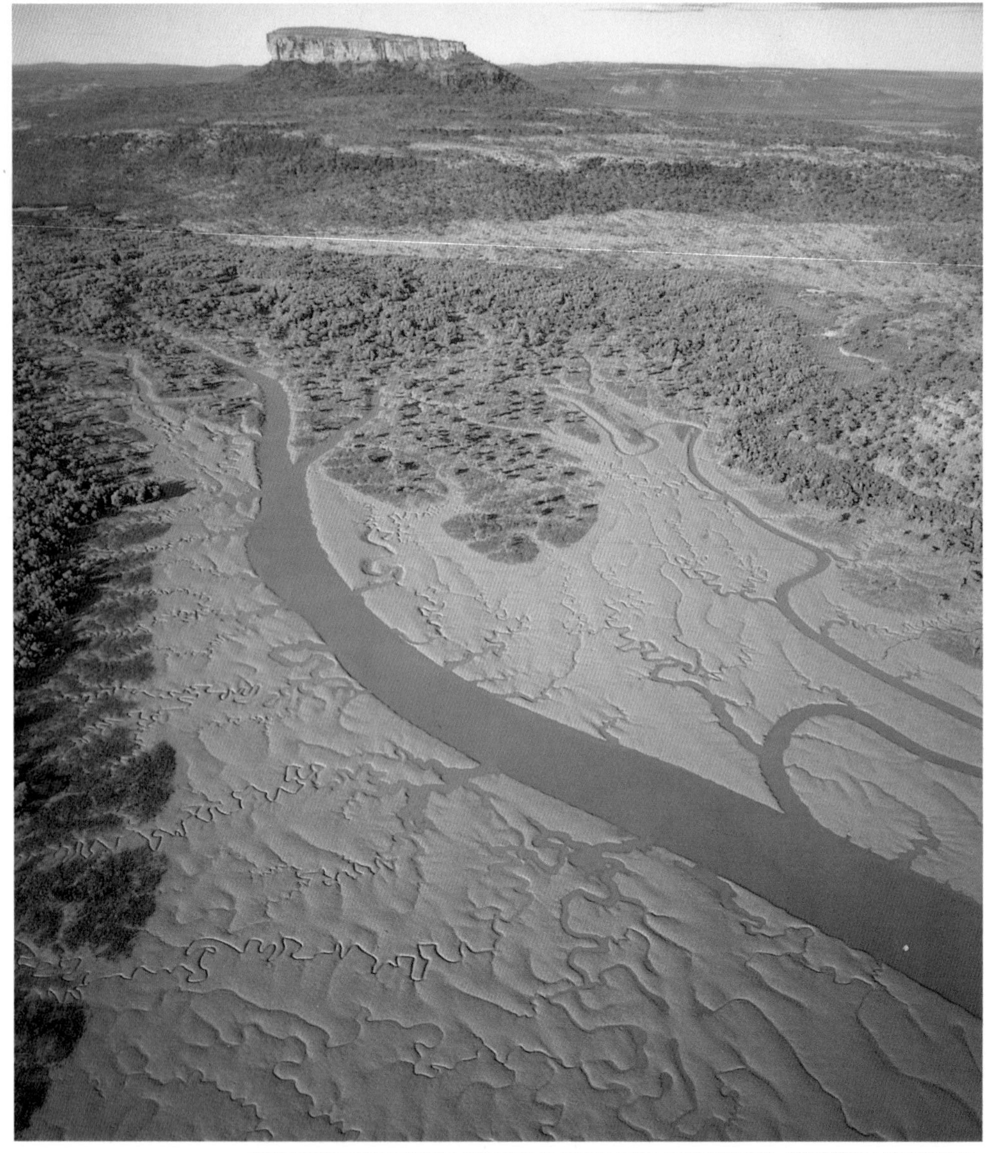

PRINCE REGENT RIVER NATIONAL PARK, THE KIMBERLEYS, WESTERN AUSTRALIA.
500th sec., f2.8, 24mm, air, 64asa.

While this is an image of one of Australia's most remote wilderness areas, there are many localities close to coastal urban centres that provide excellent venues for mud and mangrove photography. The only additional equipment necessary will be jungle boots and overalls, and probably some insect repellent.

Mangrove forests, usually adjacent to mudflats, are dependent on the high tide for life supporting nutrients. Generally the water is turbid, but off Stradbroke Island, near Brisbane, the combination of sand and mud flats provides low turbidity and so enables underwater photography. Here, a mangrove seedling surrounded by fish creates a rare picture.

MANGROVE SEEDLING, STRADBROKE ISLAND, QUEENSLAND.
60th sec., f5.6, 15mm, 64asa.

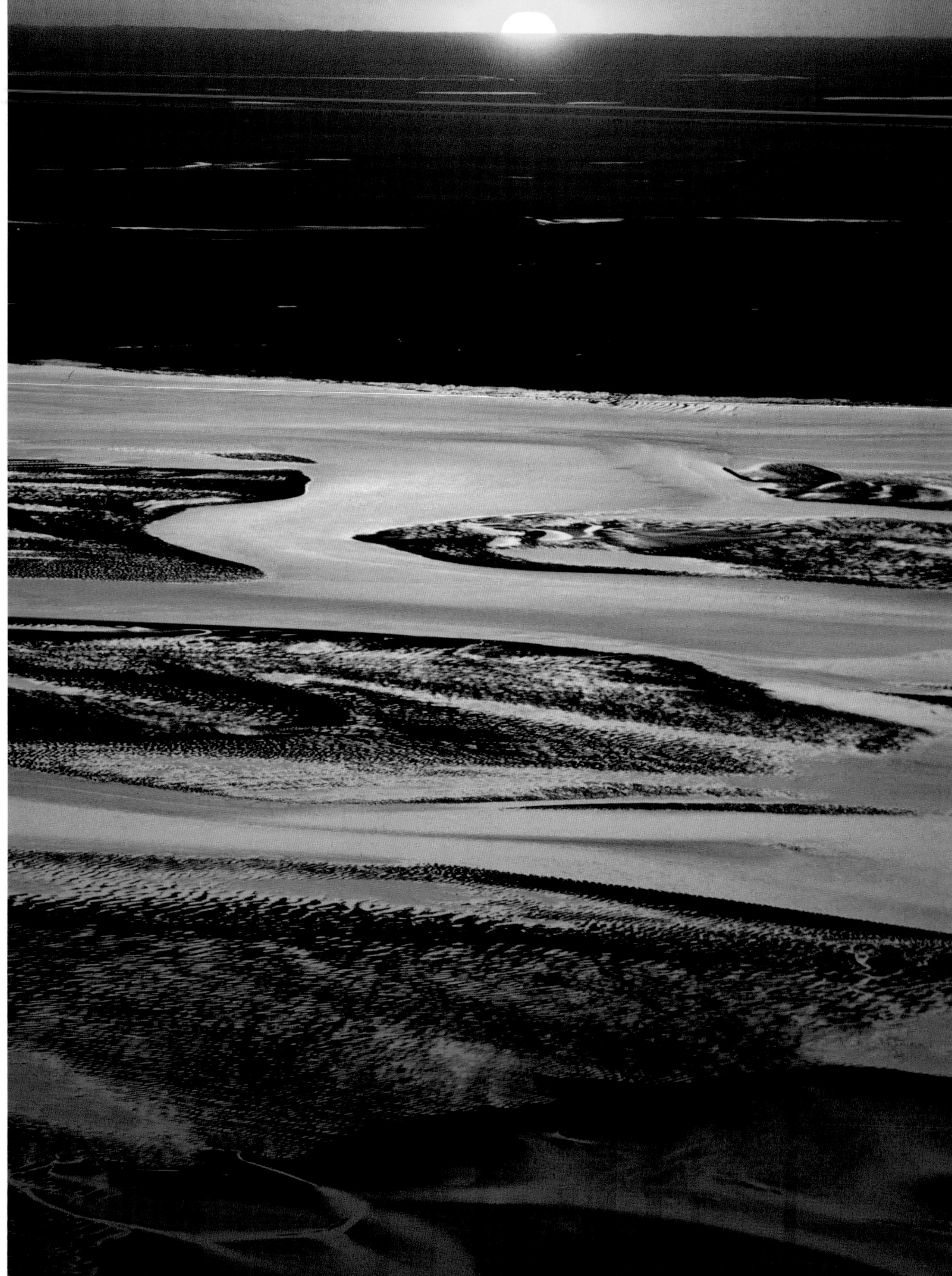

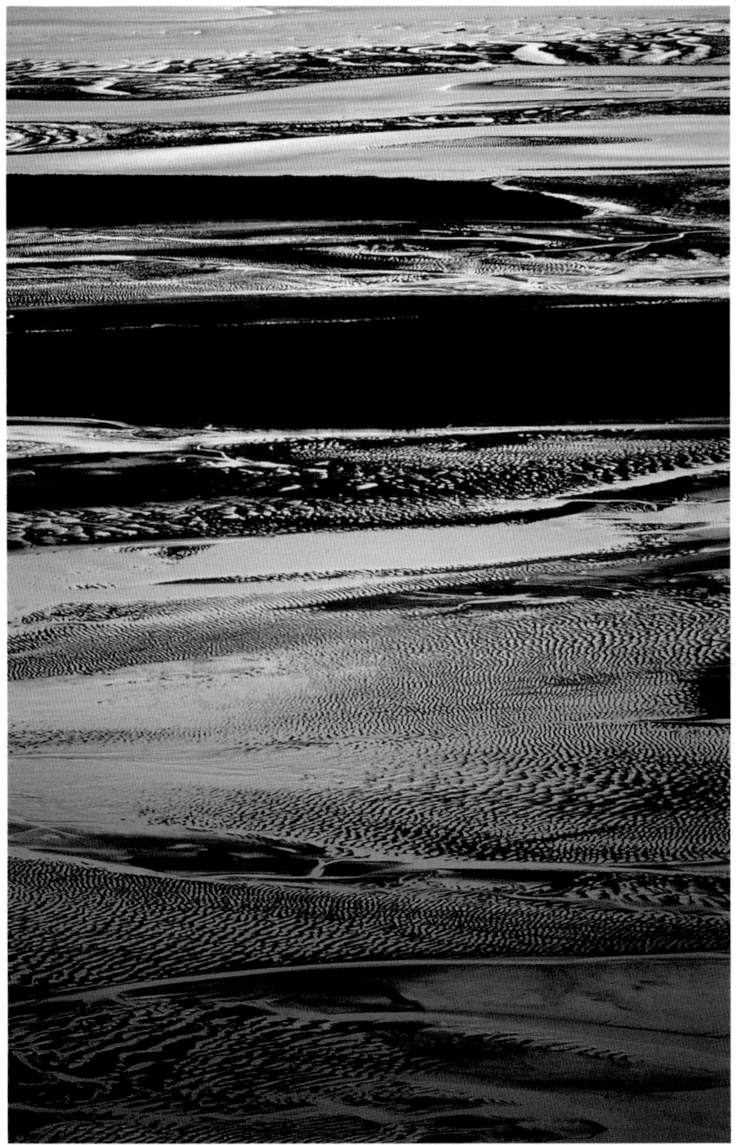

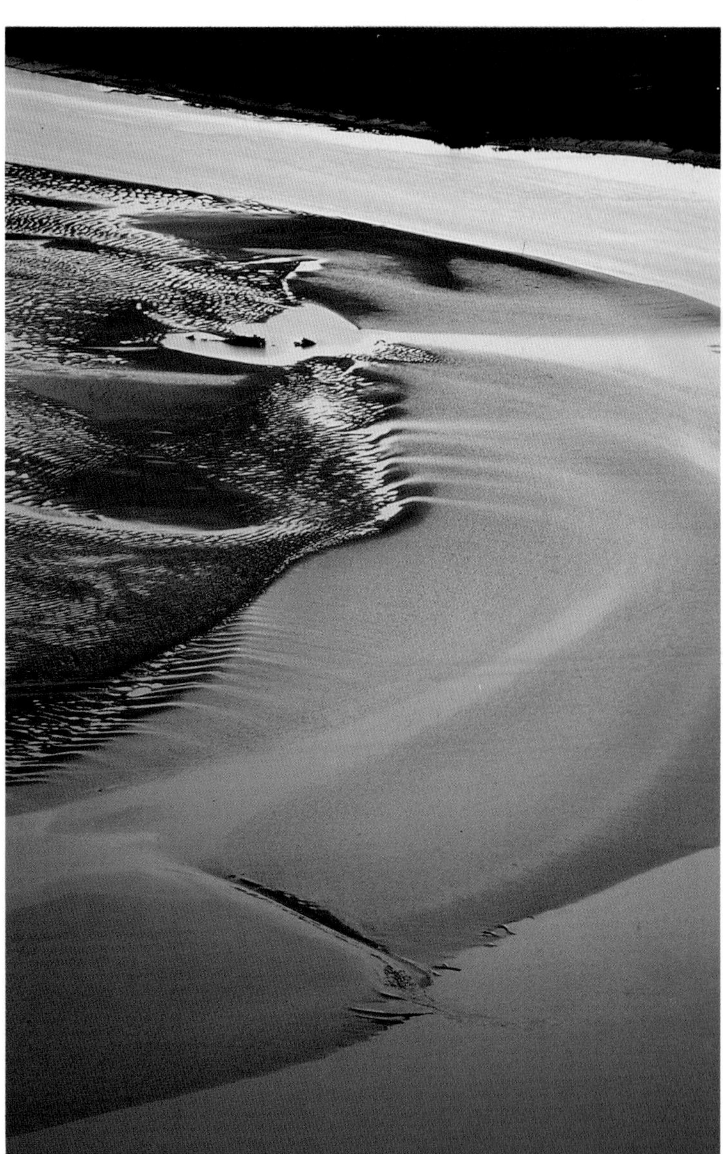

KING SOUND MUDFLATS, THE KIMBERLEYS, WESTERN AUSTRALIA.
250th sec., f2, 135mm, air, 64asa.

It was 4.30am when we took off from Broome on a four day aerial photo safari along the Kimberley coast. We had barely reached King Sound mudflats when, to my horror and dismay, the windscreen suddenly became obliterated with oil. Fortunately Derby airport was close by and the pilot, almost without vision, immediately began to make an emergency descent.

The three images here, made during that descent, are fine examples of how selective composition can change the feeling of a picture. It was one of those magic moments when light and landscape combine to create stunning imagery.

The scene before me was exhilarating, but I was terrified by our predicament. On landing, we discovered the oil cap had worked free and the engine was almost out of oil.

HEATH ON THE SLOPES OF THE STIRLING RANGES, SOUTH-WESTERN WESTERN AUSTRALIA.
125th sec., f5.6, 15mm, 64asa.

Heathlands are places which receive little attention. They are habitats which, like rainforests, are being destroyed at an alarming rate all over the continent.

The famed wildflower region of Western Australia's south west is rapidly disappearing as land is cleared for sheep grazing, and chemical enrichment programs improve the fertility of the soil.

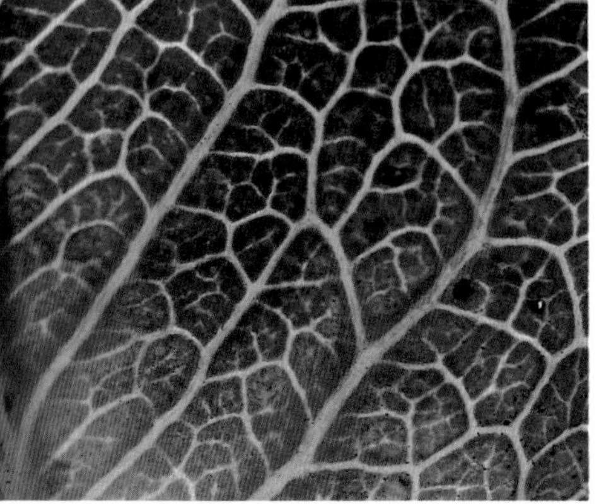

LEAF OF A ROYAL HAKEA,
FITZGERALD NATIONAL PARK, WESTERN AUSTRALIA.
125th sec., f8, 105mm micro, 64asa.

BANKSIA, WILSON'S PROMONTORY, VICTORIA.
125th sec., f8, 105mm micro, 64asa.

When I spotted this giant Praying Mantis perched on a large Banksia bloom beside the road, it was 4pm.

By the time I drove off it was 8pm. Heathlands have that sort of effect—once you start wandering among the bizarre plants, it is difficult to stop making pictures.

BANKSIA AND PRAYING MANTIS, RONSARD BAY, WESTERN AUSTRALIA.
60th sec., f11, 105mm micro, 64asa.

PANDANUS PALMS, HERON ISLAND, GREAT BARRIER REEF MARINE PARK, QUEENSLAND.
250th sec., f11. 15mm, 64asa.

ISLAND DELIGHT

THERE ARE FEW THINGS more exciting than arriving on an uninhabited island, particularly one that you have never been to before.

In 1976, I was fortunate to be part of a film crew which visited dozens of islands along the northern part of the Great Barrier Reef. The one thing that stands out most in my mind is just how vastly different such islands can be from each other; some have mangrove forests, others extensive mud flats, fringing reefs or tree coverage. Each different kind of habitat provides different kinds of animals which, in turn, provide a variety of experiences.

Everywhere you look there are images. In fact, it is sometimes difficult to concentrate on one thing in such a diverse environment.

ERSKINE ISLAND,
GREAT BARRIER REEF MARINE PARK, QUEENSLAND.
500th sec., f2.8, 35mm, polarizing filter, 64asa.

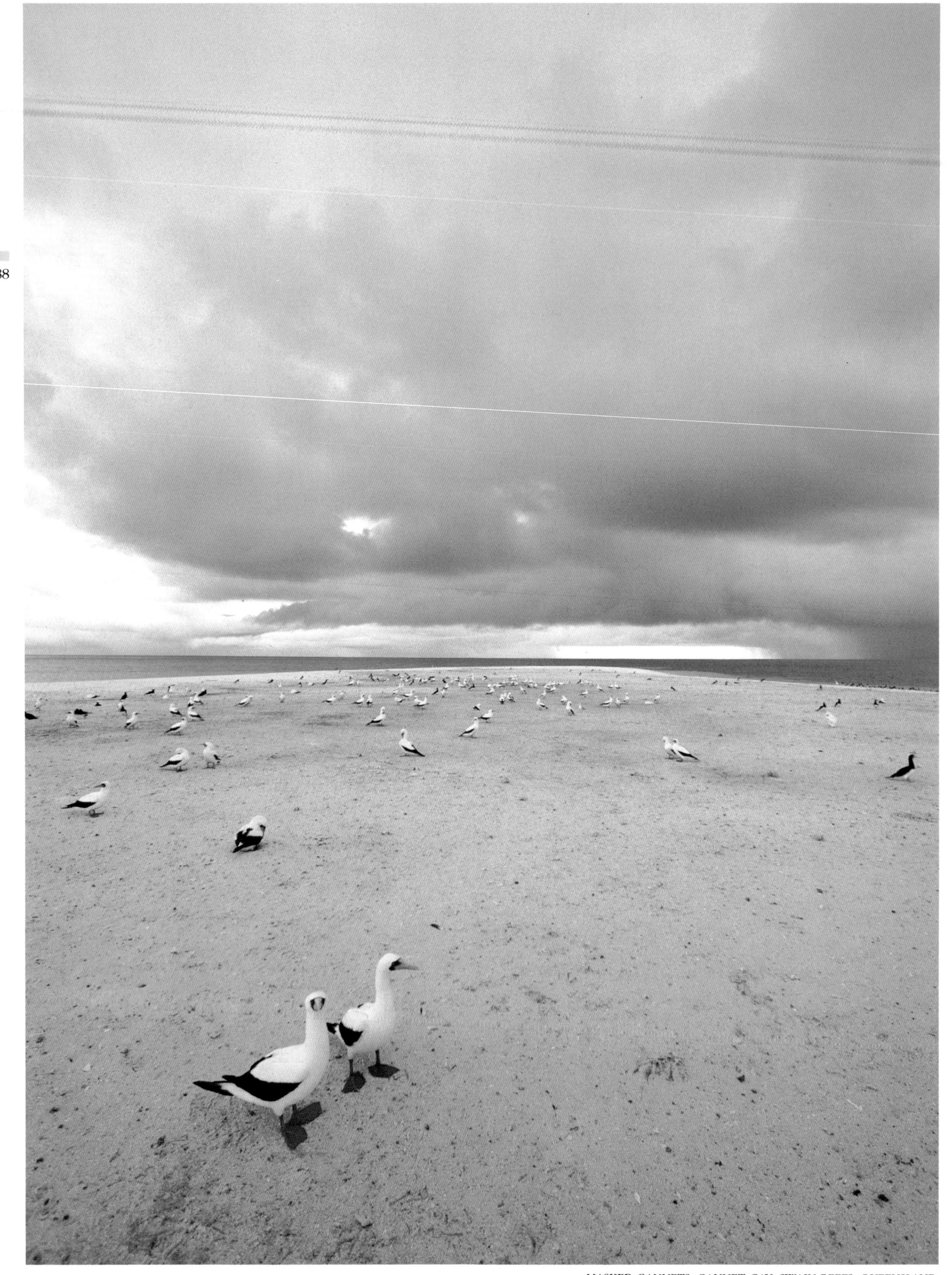

MASKED GANNETS, GANNET CAY, SWAIN REEFS, QUEENSLAND.
60th sec., f5.6, 15mm, 64asa.

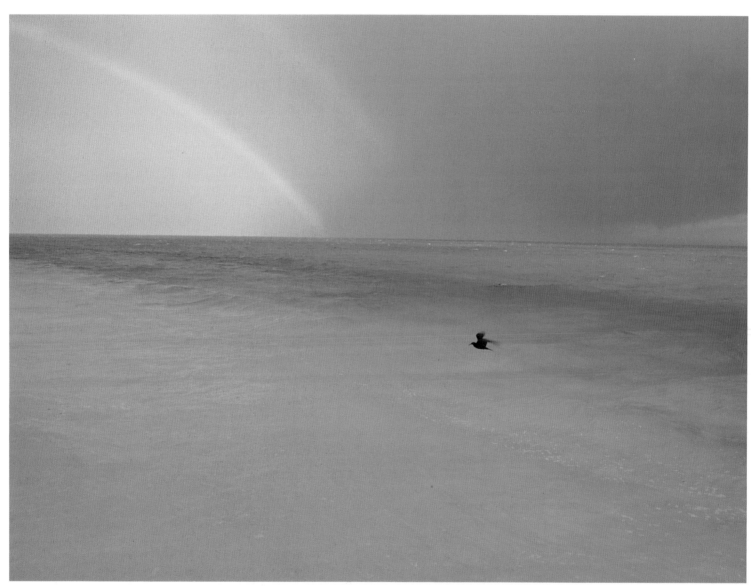

STORM, HERON ISLAND, QUEENSLAND.
125th sec., f5.6, 24mm, 64asa.

The Masked Gannets seemed to be aware of the approaching storm. Most had landed and there was an uncanny feeling of impending doom hanging over the tiny treeless cay.

I find grey skies, when the sun is still illuminating the foreground, almost irresistible.

This storm struck out of a clear blue sky. In fact it came so suddenly that I had to run to get a wide angle lens to make the picture. Seconds later it was pouring with rain, and within minutes, the sky was blue again.

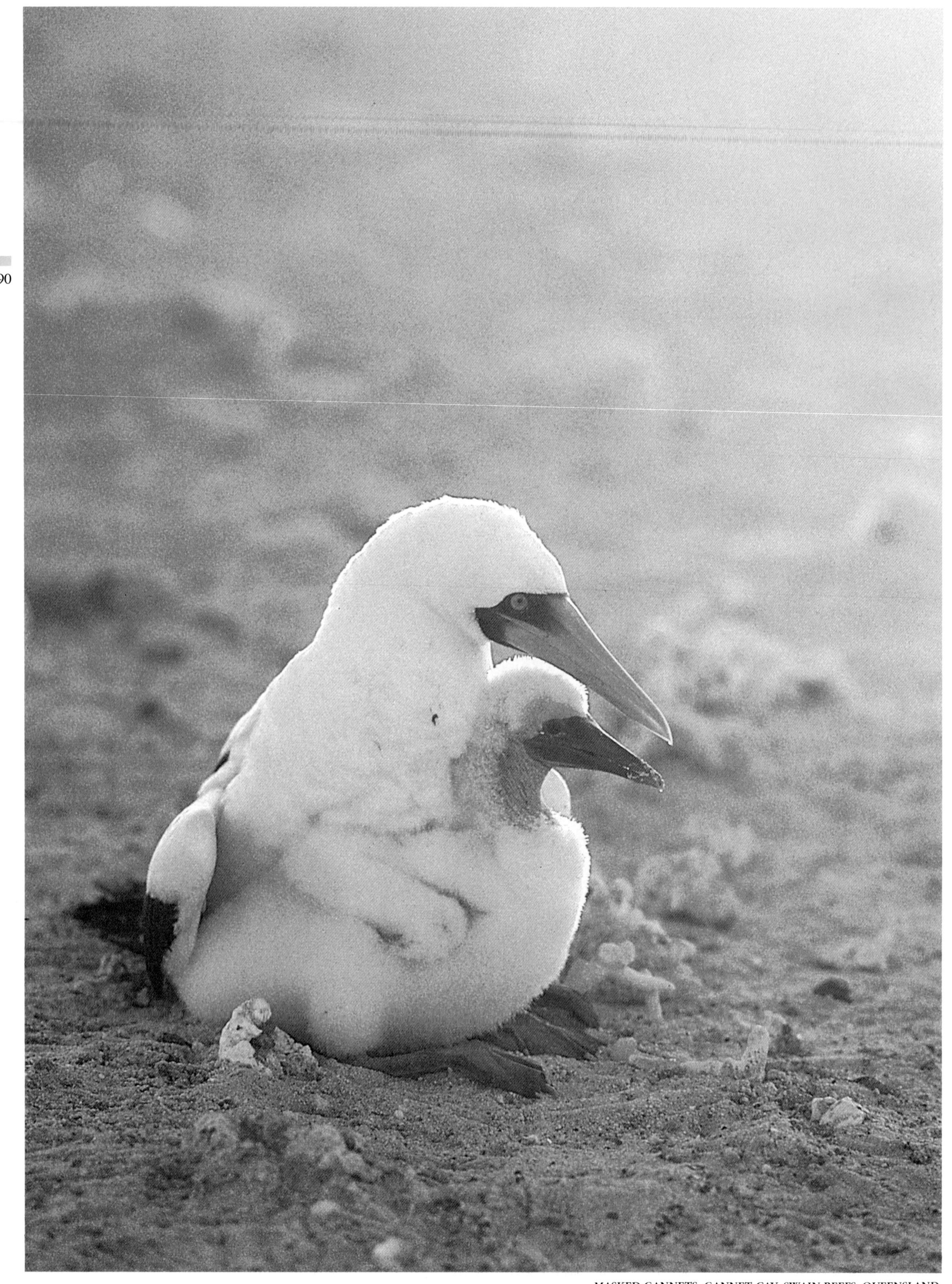

MASKED GANNETS, GANNET CAY, SWAIN REEFS, QUEENSLAND.
250th sec., f8, 135mm, 64asa.

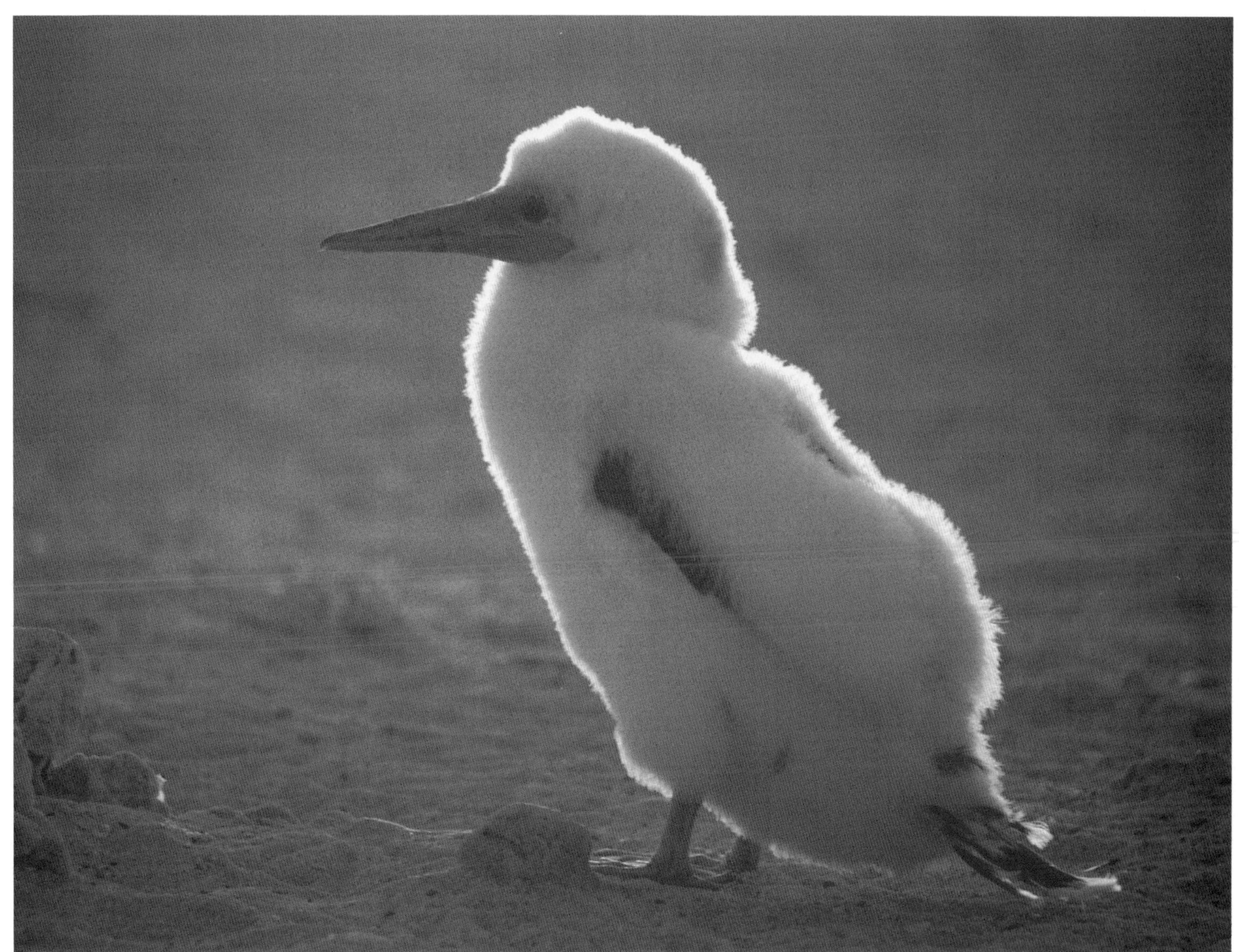

MASKED GANNET CHICK, GANNET CAY, SWAIN REEFS, QUEENSLAND.
250th sec., f8, 135mm, 64asa.

Shot towards the setting sun these back-lit birds seem to float in liquid orange. Shot from the opposite direction, away from the sunset, the pictures would not have the same feeling.

I always watch the sun and the way it casts light on things around me. Over the years I have learned how it will react with the particular film that I use. I have also learned to appreciate a different world, and to see things that others may not notice.

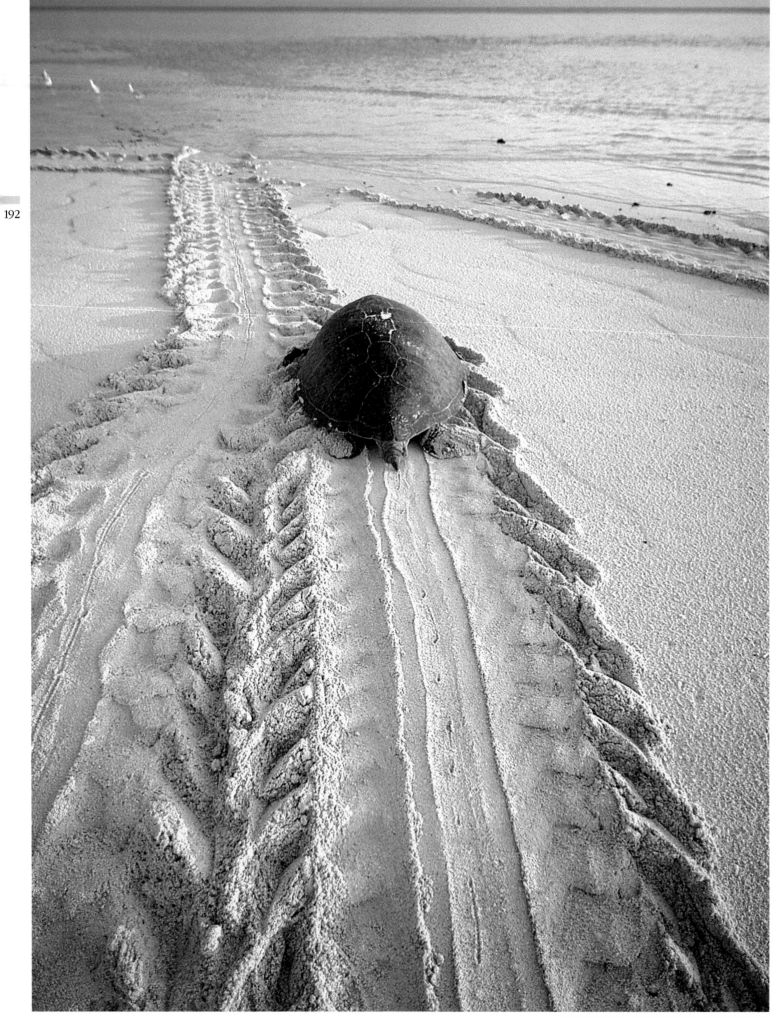

GREEN TURTLE, HERON ISLAND, QUEENSLAND.
125th sec., f5.6, 15mm, 64asa.

GREEN TURTLE, HERON ISLAND, QUEENSLAND.
250th sec., f8, 15mm, 64asa.

Photography is all about timing, not just in terms of shutter speeds and time of day, but also time of year.

On Heron Island, I was fortunate to arrive at the peak of one of the island's turtle nesting seasons. More than 140 turtles laid on the small island each night. While that was not a Great Barrier Reef record, it was a record for Heron Island.

The abundance of turtles coincided with extremely high tides at first light. So, by sheer coincidence, I was able to photograph a normally night-active animal, going through its entire egg laying ritual in wonderfully soft light.

After ninety minutes ashore, this Green Turtle followed its own tracks back to the sea. Then, lolling momentarily in shallow water to regain a little spent energy, the giant reptile headed seawards again.

DREAMS AND DISCOVERIES, QUEENSLAND.
30th sec., f11, 80 - 200mm zoom, 64asa.

It was 5am, first light on Heron Island. The tide was out, and the 30,000 resident Black Noddies were very active. Most were still on or around their nests, but some had already gone to sea, fishing.
There were small gatherings of birds on the beach, swallowing sand which aids their digestion.

Here on the beach, with an uncluttered background, I made many photographs as small gatherings came and went, poked and pried, fluttered and chattered.

BLACK NODDIES, HERON ISLAND, QUEENSLAND.
250th sec., f5.6, 600mm IFED, 64asa.

SHAPES FROM HERON ISLAND, QUEENSLAND.
125th sec., f5.6, 600mm IFED, tripod, 64asa.

The trees were literally filled with birds and I worked quickly—superimposing images, changing focus, camera angles, and exposures.

Although I could envisage the result each time I pulled the trigger, the actual image obtained did not really concern me. I was simply having some fun with a camera and a myriad delightful shapes and colours. These images represent an experience rather than a bird species.

BLACK NODDY COLONY, HERON ISLAND, QUEENSLAND.
125th sec., f5.6, 600mm IFED, tripod, 64asa.

The effects of ever-increasing human visitation to the Great Barrier Reef are of growing concern, particularly during the bird breeding season.

Many kinds of sea birds are easily disturbed and desert their eggs, leaving them to bake in the hot sun. Seagulls are predatory on deserted eggs, so if you are working with sea birds, try using a long telephoto lens. This will increase the camera-to-subject distance, and it will probably enable more relaxed, undisturbed studies.

BRIDLED TERN, MASTHEAD ISLAND, QUEENSLAND.
125th sec., f2, 135mm, 64asa.

The sun was fairly high when we arrived on Masthead Island. I had only a few hours to make pictures, and had to make do with light conditions which gave a great deal of contrast.

Here, to soften the Tern, I positioned myself so that the camera's view was interrupted by vegetation. Then, by using a short telephoto lens and a small aperture, I was able to photograph through the foliage as though it was not even there.

Sometimes it is possible to predict an action before it happens. When I saw one tern land, I expected others would soon join it. I was able to focus and compose the shot leaving the motor driven sequence to determine whether I had made an action image. The added involvement between the terns and a gull was a little extra bonus.

BLACK-NAPED TERNS AND SEAGULL, MASTHEAD ISLAND, QUEENSLAND.
500th sec., f5.6, 400mm IFED, 64asa.

While I usually prefer to make pictures early or late in the day, shooting fast action usually requires fast shutter speeds. For this, mid-morning or mid-afternoon is best. Using a hand-held 400mm lens, I was able to make a series of shots of Rosette Terns as they came in to land. This sort of photography, with tightly composed images and a small, fast moving subject, requires a lot of patience and a lot of film.

ROSETTE TERN, MASTHEAD ISLAND.
500th sec., f5.6, 400mm IFED, tripod, 64asa.

SEAGULL, MASTHEAD ISLAND, QUEENSLAND.
500th sec., f5.6, 600mm IFED, tripod, 64asa.

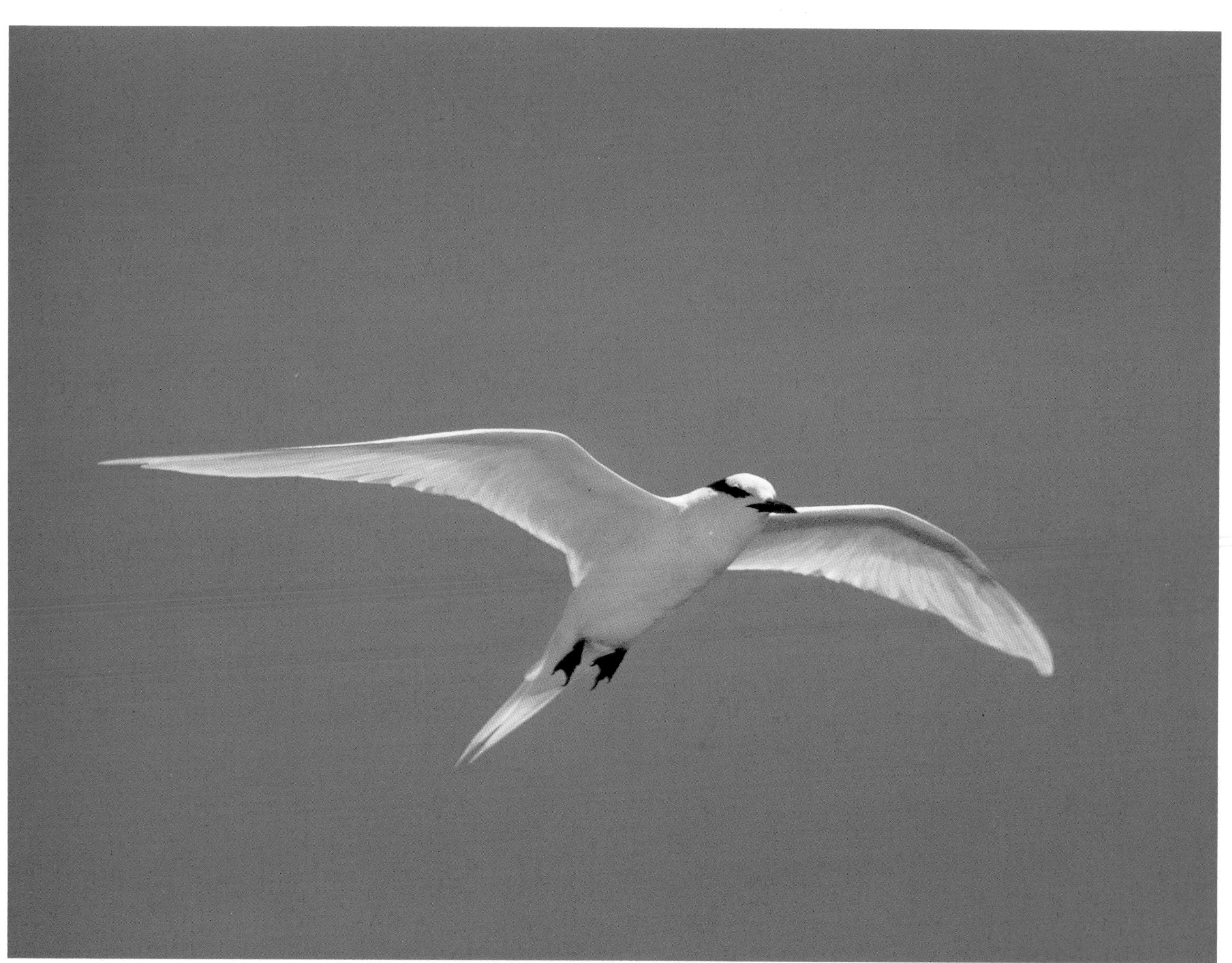

BLACK-NAPED TERN, MASTHEAD ISLAND, QUEENSLAND.
500th sec., f5.6, 600mm IFED, tripod, 64asa.

Here on the Great Barrier Reef, I noticed that every afternoon when a strong sea breeze sprang up, many birds would congregate on the island's windy side to 'hang glide'. Of course this made focusing a whole lot easier, even with a 600mm lens.

Under normal conditions pictures of birds in flight can be a matter of luck. I have made more exposures than I care to remember of birds without wings or heads, and many others hopelessly out of focus.

Like people, wild animals have aspects that lend themselves to powerful pictures. The Reef Heron has three main areas of activity: flight, roosting, and stalking prey. Here, I was after the latter.

I wanted to capture a Reef Heron at the peak of tension just prior to striking. I wanted the background clear, the image perfectly exposed and pin sharp.

There is a simple formula for making these sorts of pictures: you have to decide what you want; you have to be patient as you will have to watch your quarry for long periods; and you must have practice. Be prepared to accept failure without giving up, and use lots of film, because action shots pass so quickly that you can easily miss out.

REEF HERON, HERON ISLAND, QUEENSLAND.
125th sec., f5.6, 600mm IFED, tripod, 64asa.

CASUARINA AND TIDE-LINE, MASTHEAD ISLAND, QUEENSLAND.
125th sec., f8, 35mm, 64asa.

CORAL AND SKY, HERON ISLAND, QUEENSLAND.
125th sec., f11, 15mm, 64asa.

UNDERSEA FANTASY

I *FIND CONCEPTUALISING IMAGES,* before I make them, very stimulating. It is the sort of thing you can do on a train or bus going to work. You can do it in bed before you go to sleep. Making imaginary pictures helps exercise the brain and makes it more receptive to real pictures when they are encountered.

These images were conceived before I took them. They were made over two days, and the main factor I had to consider was the tide. The casuarina-tideline shadow and the underwater image required high tide, while the coral-sky picture required a tidal pool at low tide.

I wanted images with similar design elements that related life's essentials—sun, air, soil and water—to the Great Barrier Reef.

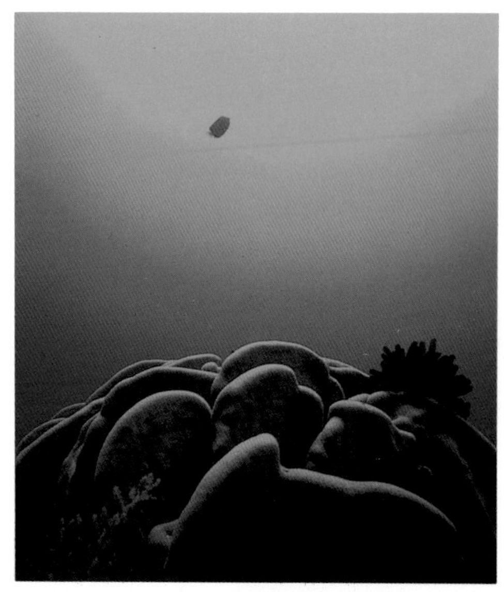

PORITIES CORAL AND FISH,
HERON ISLAND, QUEENSLAND.
60th sec., f5.6, 15mm, 64asa.

UNDERWATER FEELINGS, HERON ISLAND, QUEENSLAND.
60th sec., f5.6, 15mm, 64asa.

There are few artificially illuminated pictures in this book. My preference is for natural light because I find I can make images with more feeling.

Here, an artificial light source would have revealed a bright orange sponge; it would have turned the tiny fish silver; and it would have brought out a great many colours and textures in the foreground. That would would be fine if that was what I wanted to share; colour, form, texture and so on. But what I wanted to say here, and what I try to say through many of my pictures is simply, 'this is what it *feels* like.' Photography should communicate not just looking, but also hearing, touching and feeling.

Being underwater at sunset can feel like another time, another place, another galaxy.

Here, dinner-plate sized Batfish seem to be hanging like spacecraft, awaiting permission to land.

By over-exposing slightly, I was able heighten the surreal effect.

ANOTHER WORLD, HERON ISLAND, QUEENSLAND.
125th sec., f5.6, 15mm, 64asa.

SUN, SEA-SURFACE AND SEA-LIFE, FEELINGS FROM A METRE DOWN, SWAIN REEFS, QUEENSLAND.
125th sec., f5.6, 15mm, 64asa.

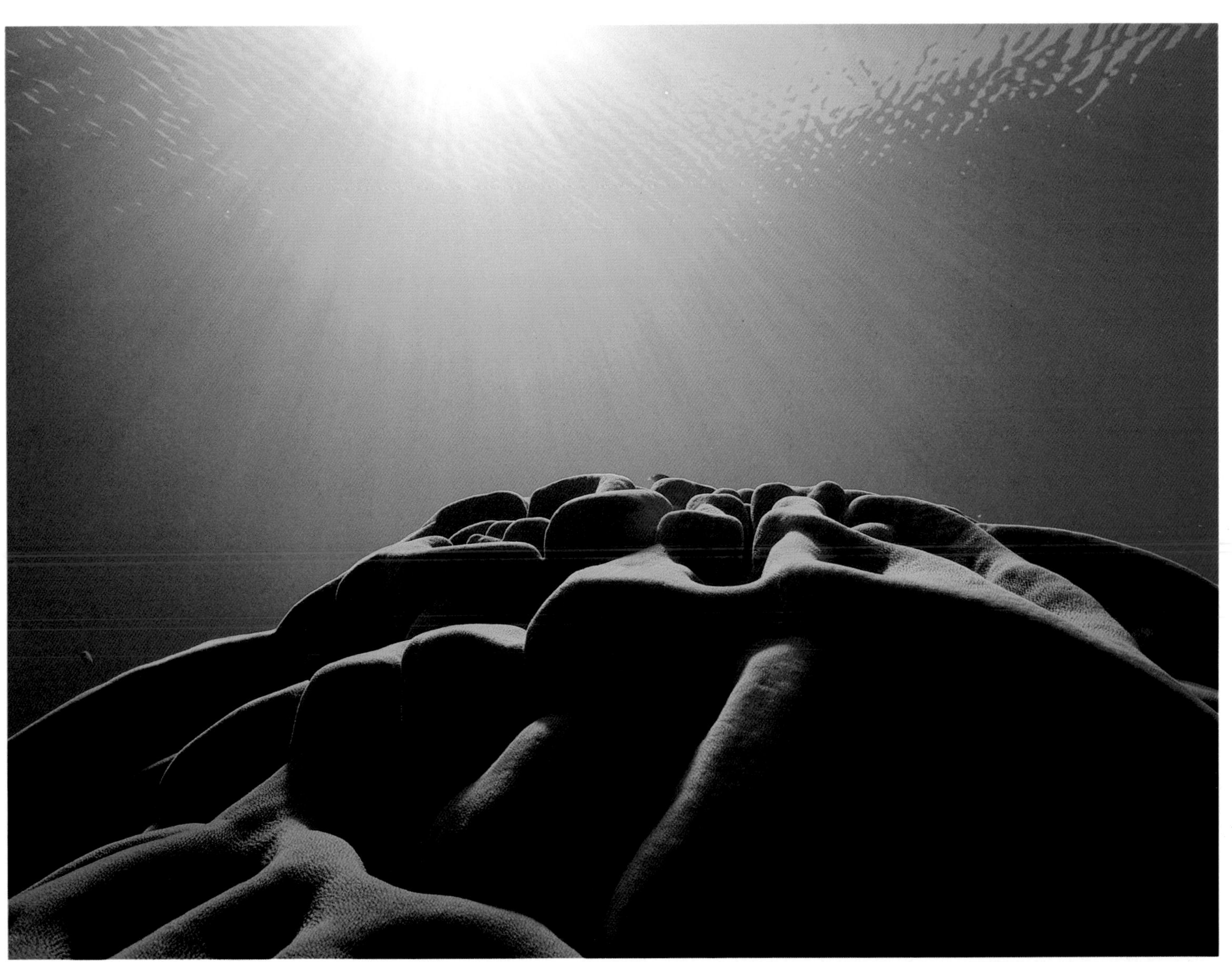

SUN, SEA-SURFACE AND CORAL, FEELINGS FROM THREE METRES DOWN, SWAIN REEFS, QUEENSLAND.
125th sec., f5.6, 15mm, 64asa.

YOUNG SEA LION, BARRENJOEY ISLAND, BASS STRAIT, TASMANIA.
125th sec., f2.8, 15mm, 64asa.

One of the most memorable and exciting encounters I have ever had with wild animals was with Sea Lions.

I had contracted 'flu while on a lecture tour in Tasmania, and the local divers thought that the best way to rid me of my affliction would be to drown it.

As we arrived at Barrenjoey Island, a hundred young Sea Lions leapt off the rocks and swam towards our boat. It was my first encounter with the animals, so it was with some apprehension that I fell backwards into the icy ocean.

Within seconds my 'flu had vanished. Several hours, two tanks of air, and many rolls of film later, we left the water. The Sea Lions had grown quite bored with nipping hands, pulling off swim fins, peering into face masks, and blowing bubbles in our faces!

GOING TROPICAL

D*AWN HAD SCARCELY* cast its first feeble rays across the landscape as I waded ankle deep in the warm water of the paperbark swamps that fringe the main billabong.

As though stepping back through aeons of time, I broke through the thick vegetation at the edge of the billabong. There before me was every size and shape of bird imaginable; a bird fanatic's dream come true. There was hardly a log or patch of bank vacant. The activity was intense with birds stalking, preening, feeding, stretching, drying their wings, diving for food, squabbling and even sleeping!

The visual delights soon found competition with the sounds. As though pumped through a giant quadraphonic sound system, the clappings and chirpings, whoopings and whirrings, and guttural cluckings and clickings filled the air. Above the canopy of trees the air hummed with constant winging.

I froze, not wanting to disturb a thing, and the hair on the back of my neck bristled with excitement as I became totally enveloped.

From my diary, October 21st 1978, the first time I 'went tropical.'

ROYAL SPOONBILLS, THE KIMBERLEYS, WESTERN AUSTRALIA.
125th sec., f5.6, 600mm IFED, 64asa.

DUCKS, YELLOW WATERS LAGOON, KAKADU NATIONAL PARK, NORTHERN TERRITORY.
30th sec., f5.6, 600mm IFED, tripod, 64asa.

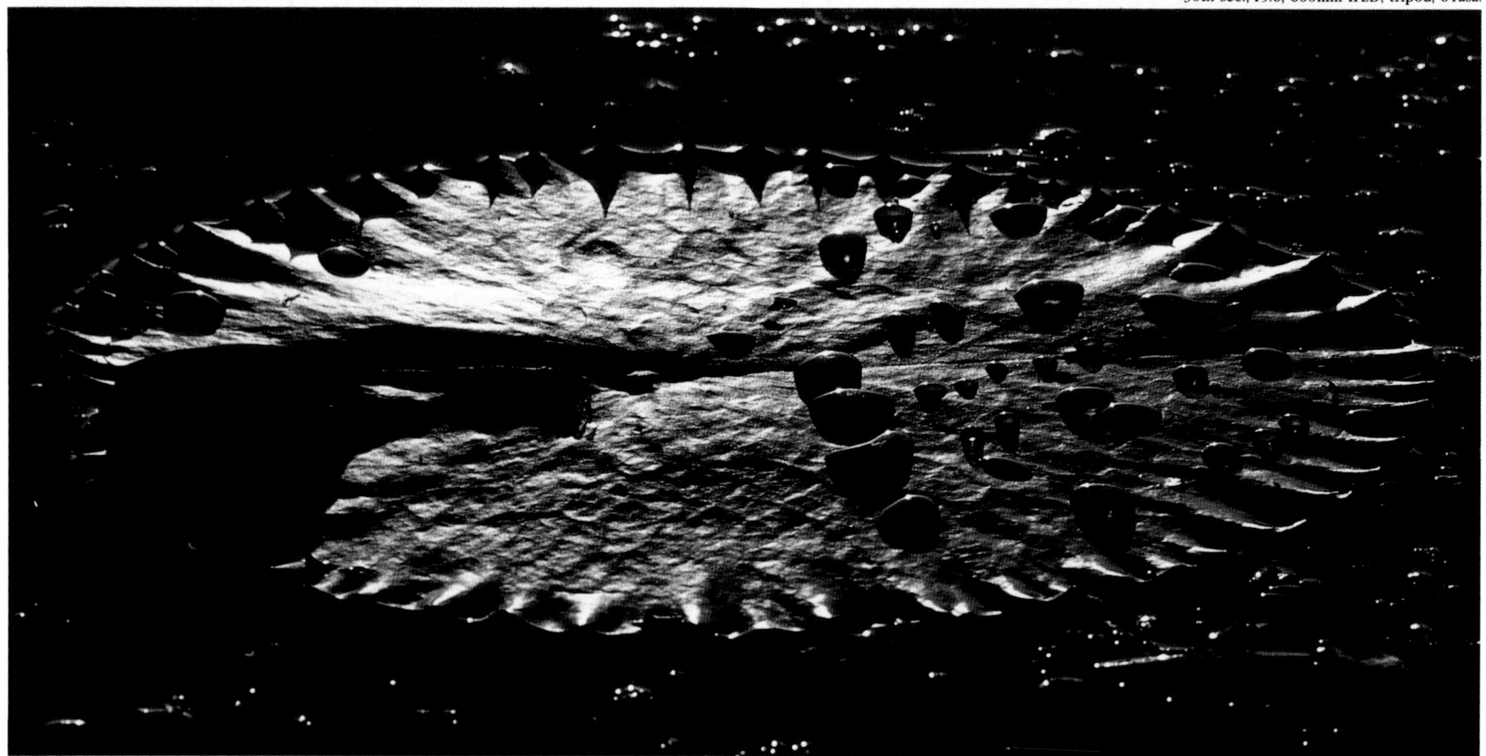

RAINDROPS ON A LILY PAD, KAKADU NATIONAL PARK, NORTHERN TERRITORY.
125th sec., f5.6, 135mm, 64asa.

Sunset and sunrise colour the watery world of billabongs and floodplains reflective pinks, reds and oranges.

While you may have seen images like these a thousand times, it is almost impossible not be be moved when surrounded by them.

FLOODPLAIN, KAKADU NATIONAL PARK, NORTHERN TERRITORY.
125th sec., f5.6, 600mm IFED, tripod, 64asa.

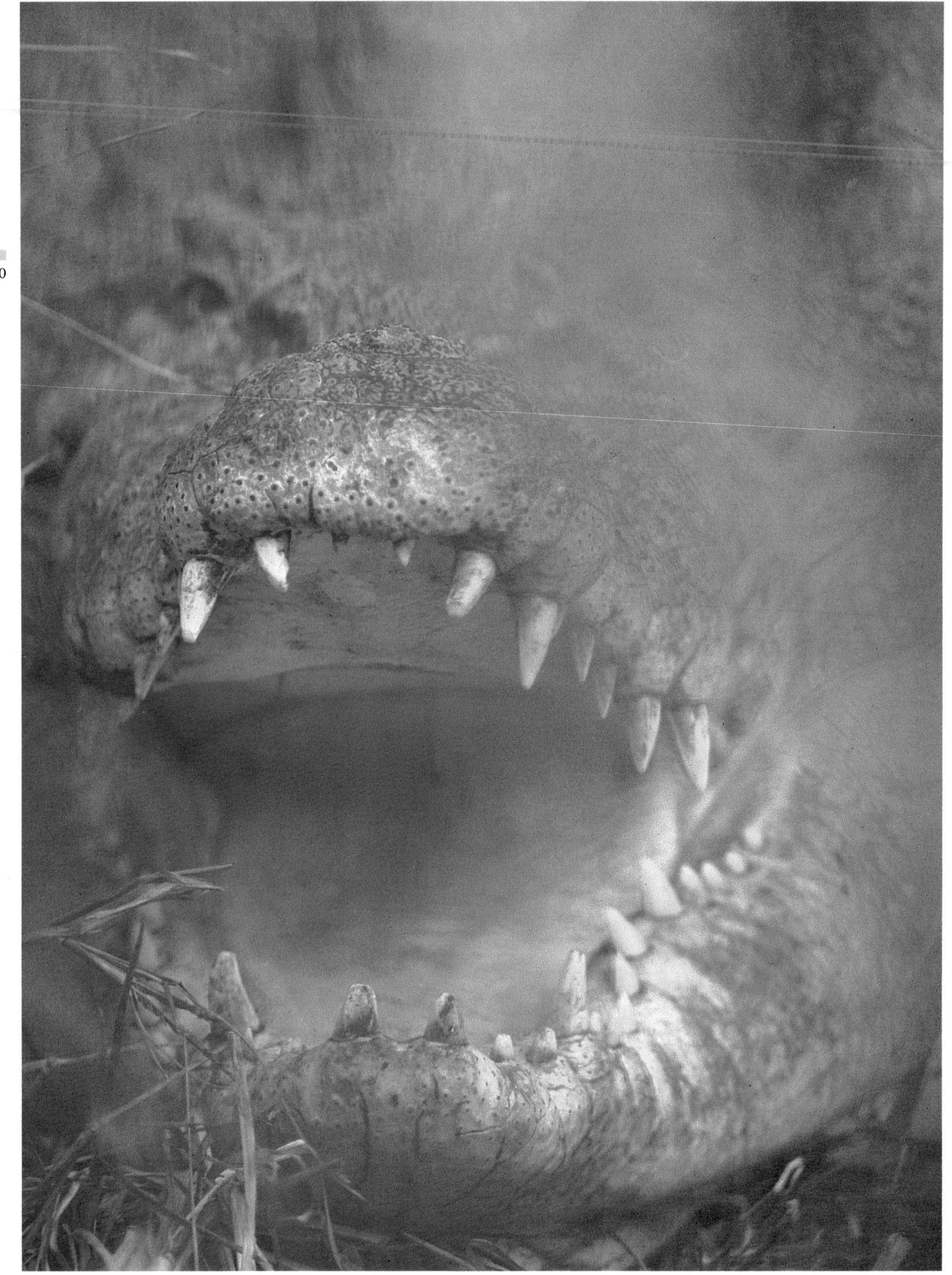

SALT WATER CROCODILE, CAPE YORK, QUEENSLAND.
60th sec., f5.6, 600mm IFED, tripod, 64asa.

PAPERBARK SWAMP AND MAGPIE GEESE, KAKADU NATIONAL PARK, NORTHERN TERRITORY.
125th sec., f5.6, 600mm IFED, tripod, 64asa.

Few habitats in Australia compare with wetlands for sheer diversity of both plant and animal species.
I find the Paperbark by far the most striking plant, and the Crocodile would have to win the high impact award for animals.

Crocodiles as large as 5 metres have been recorded. I estimated this individual to be 3 metres, and I almost tripped over it on a river bank on Cape York Peninsula.

I chose this picture in preference to a sharp, side-on shot because it portrays something of the elusiveness of the animal. Crocs are common, but to all but skilled observers, they are not commonly seen in the wild.

WATER LILIES UNDERWATER, KAKADU NATIONAL PARK, NORTHERN TERRITORY.
125th sec., f8, 15mm, 64asa.

Most billabongs and floodplains in the tropical north are rimmed with a delightful array of water lilies.

Like chocolates in a candy store, I find these sorts of habitats irresistible, and have spent many hours wading in them with a micro lens.

My first choice of lens is a 105mm micro lens. Being a short telephoto, the 105mm enables me to photograph frogs, beetles, bugs and dragonflies from a moderate distance. Shorter lenses, like the 55mm micro, are good, but the necessity to work closer can disturb the subject. Frogs do have a habit of hopping just at the moment you are about to press the shutter release!

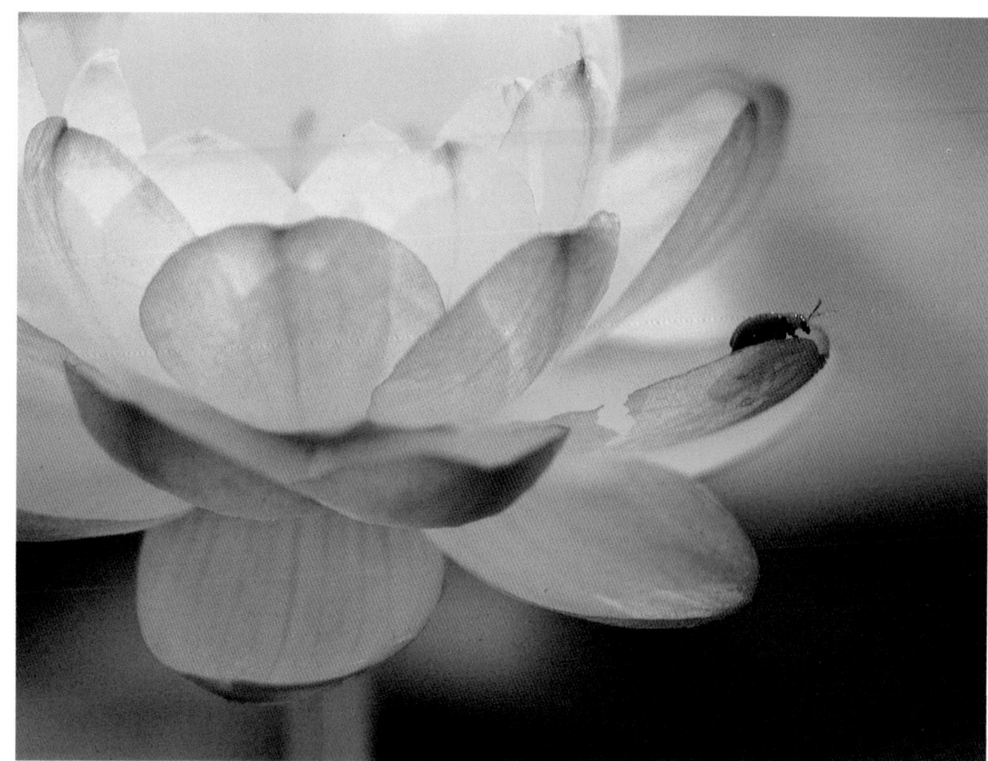

BUG ON A WATER LILY, KAKADU NATIONAL PARK, NORTHERN TERRITORY.
125th sec., f8, 105mm micro, 64asa.

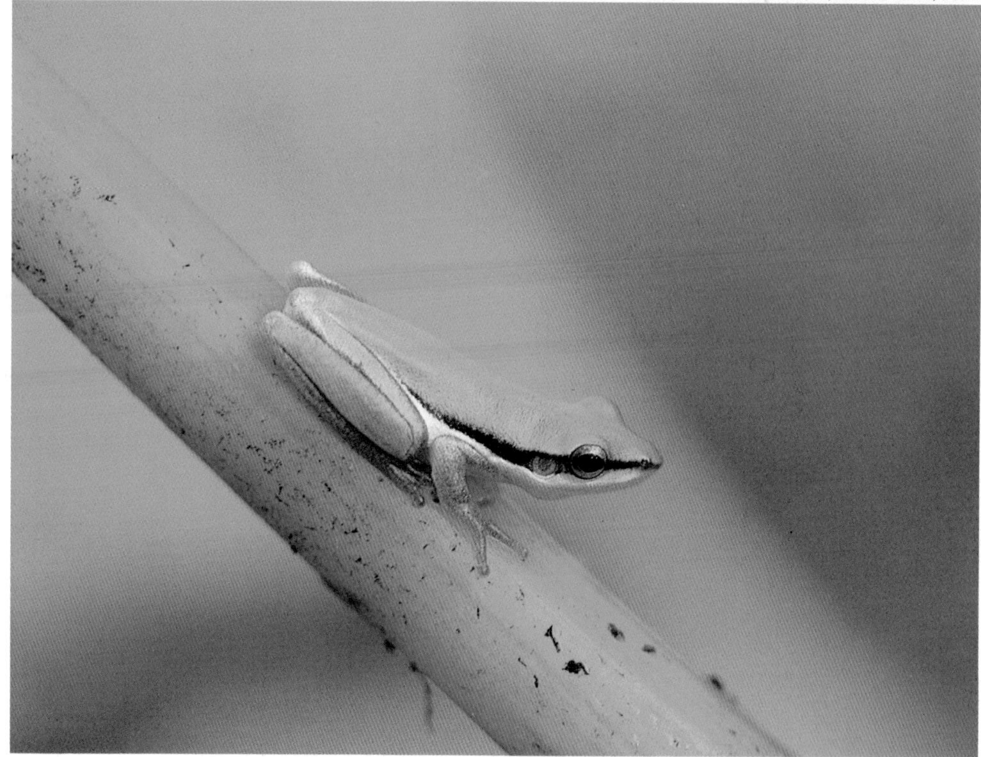

FROG ON A WATER LILY STEM, KAKADU NATIONAL PARK, NORTHERN TERRITORY.
125th sec., f8, 105mm micro, 64asa.

LILY AND SEDGES, KAKADU NATIONAL PARK, NORTHERN TERRITORY.
125th sec., f5.6, 600mm IFED, tripod, 64asa.

While all these pictures are of the same kind of subject in the same habitat, each conveys a quite different feeling. This is due primarily to the choice of lens, although lighting and colour also play a part.

My preferences in lenses are 400mm to 600mm telephoto, 55mm or 105mm micro for close up work, and 15mm or 24mm wide angle.

The soft, ethereal feeling above has been achieved with a 600mm lens positioned so that its view is interrupted with sedges. Then, by using a short depth of field and selective focus, the green wash effect is achieved.

The pink Lotus Lily has been portrayed close up with a 55mm micro lens. The crisp detail and bright colours add to the impact of this striking image.

The lily landscape was created with a 15mm ultra wide angle lens.

LOTUS LILY, LAKEFIELD NATIONAL PARK, CAPE YORK, QUEENSLAND.
125th sec., f8, 55mm micro, 64asa.

LAKE NUGA NUGA, QUEENSLAND.
125th sec., f8, 15mm, 64asa.

LEMON-BREASTED FLYCATCHER, NOURLANGIE BILLABONG, KAKADU NATIONAL PARK, NORTHERN TERRITORY.
125th sec., f5.6, 600mm IFED, tripod, 64asa.

Both of these birds are classic examples of 'now-you-see-me, now-you-don't'. They are fast moving, elusive little birds, but they both have the habit of remaining perfectly motionless while you set up your tripod. They may even wait while you focus and compose the picture. Then just before you pull the trigger they vanish, leaving you with an empty frame.

The best way to outwit these small creatures is to compose the picture on a vacant perching branch. If you watch closely, you will often notice that the birds prefer certain branches around their feeding site. Then, with the image carefully composed on such a perch, you can settle down to wait. That is how both of these images were obtained.

AZURE KINGFISHER, NOURLANGIE BILLABONG, KAKADU NATIONAL PARK, NORTHERN TERRITORY.
125th sec., f5.6, 600mm IFED, tripod, 64asa.

Of all Australian birds, I find the Sea Eagle the most dramatic to be with. Here, I have attempted to capture something of the drama of the bird in flight by slowing down the shutter speed. The stately silhouette then provides a marked contrast..

SEA EAGLE, LAKEFIELD NATIONAL PARK, QUEENSLAND.
60th sec., f5.6, 400mm IFED, 64asa.

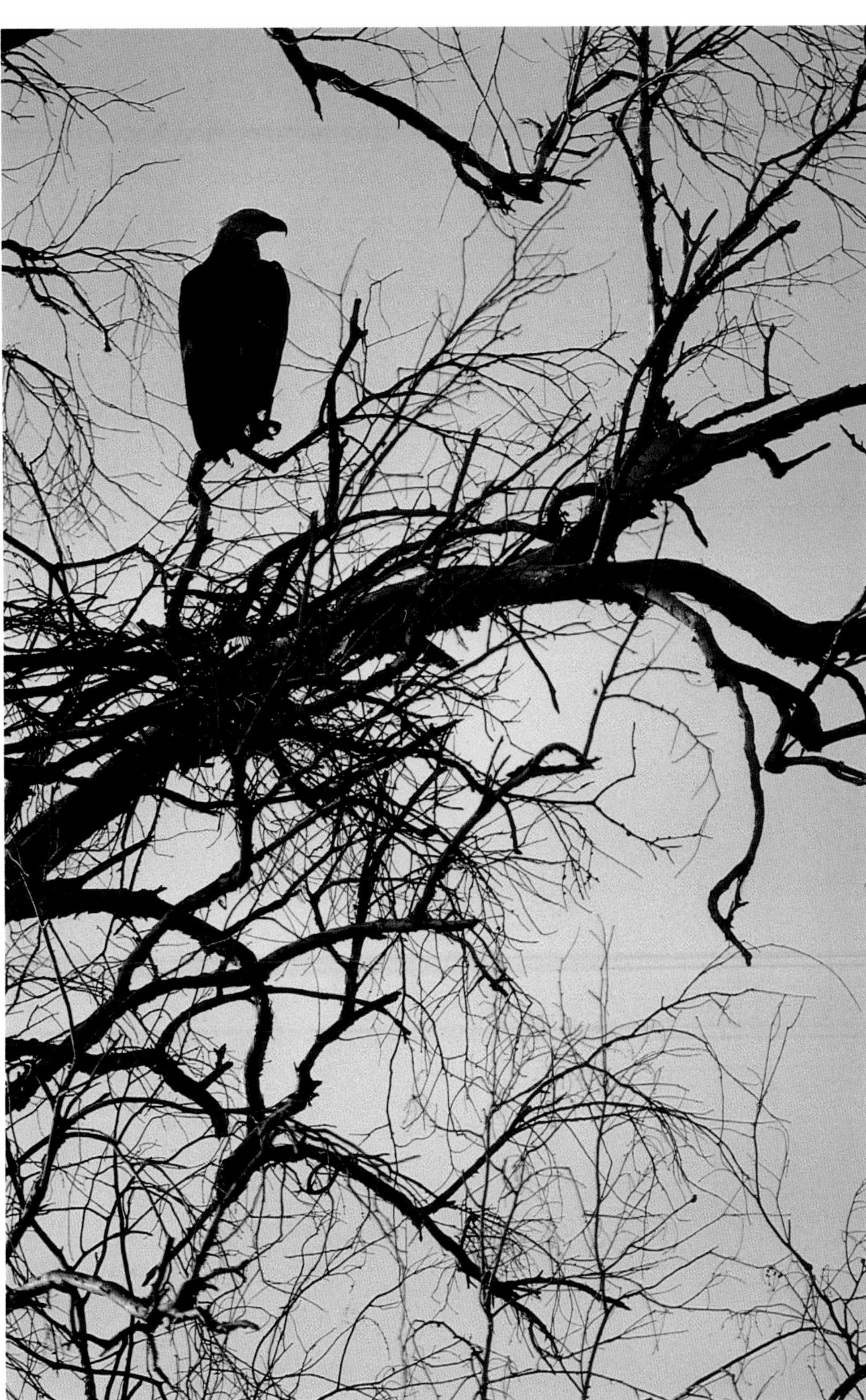

SEA EAGLE, KAKADU NATIONAL PARK, NORTHERN TERRITORY.
125th sec., f5.6, 600mm IFED, tripod, 64asa.

JABIRU, KAKADU NATIONAL PARK, NORTHERN TERRITORY.
250th sec., f5.6, 600mm IFED, 64asa.

JABIRU, NOURLANGIE BILLABONG, KAKADU NATIONAL PARK, NORTHERN TERRITORY.
15th sec., f5.6, 600mm IFED, tripod, 64asa.

Tropical billabongs ooze with life. Here an Egret lands behind a Jabiru. The blur is accomplished by using a slow shutter speed. I did this in an attempt to capture the dreamtime qualities of the scene and to add a little mystery.

JABIRU, EGRET AND PIED HERON, NEAR DARWIN, NORTHERN TERRITORY.
125th sec., f5.6, 600mm IFED, tripod, 64asa.

This photo was taken near a homestead billabong on a cattle station. I have found that cattle stations can provide excellent sites for wildlife photography.

On one particular station in the Kimberleys, where shooting had been banned for more than fifty years, the reactions of the birds were almost unbelievable.

For the first time I was able to approach quite close to huge flocks of Whistling Ducks. These are normally very shy birds.

It is always advisable to approach station owners prior to setting up camp.

FLOODPLAIN FROG, KAKADU NATIONAL PARK, NORTHERN TERRITORY.
125th sec., f5.6, 600mm IFED, 64asa.

AUSTRALIAN PRATINCOLE, LAKEFIELD NATIONAL PARK, QUEENSLAND.
125th sec., f5.6, 600mm IFED, 64asa.

When I made this picture of a floodplain frog I was particularly impressed with the relationship of size between the tiny animal and its habitat. Unlike many of its kind, this species is active during the day, and I was amused to watch hundreds of tiny heads duck underwater each time the threatening shadow of an Egret passed over.

Few areas of Australia present such vast seasonal variations in their landscapes as do the tropics.

Floodplains, particularly in the shallow back waters, are fine examples of this. During the dry, frogs, reptiles, and fish hibernate deep in the wet mud of river floodplains. When the wet season comes, they emerge to feed.

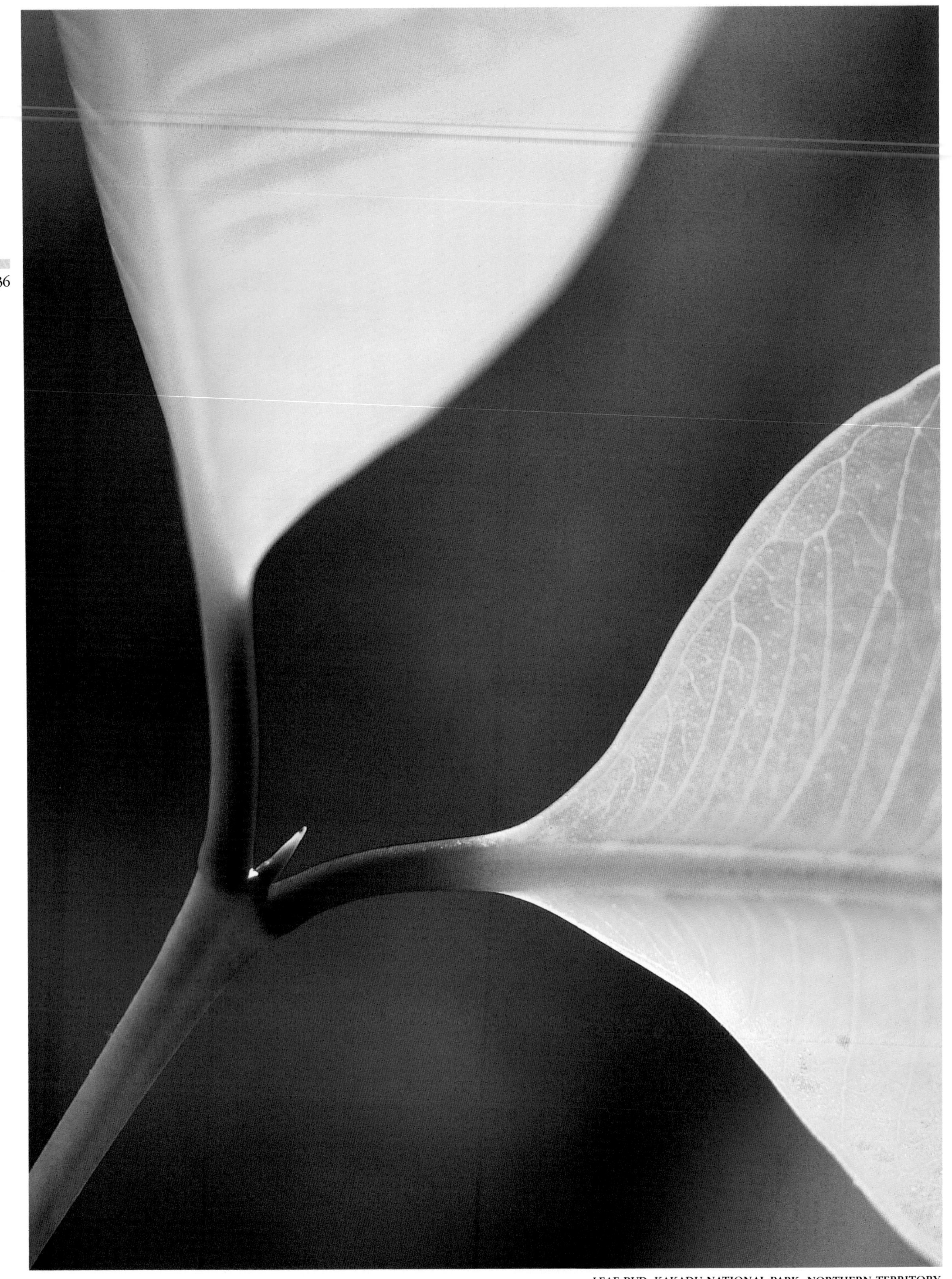

LEAF BUD, KAKADU NATIONAL PARK, NORTHERN TERRITORY.
125th sec., f8, 105mm micro, 64asa.

TROPICAL WOODLANDS

T*HE TROPICAL WOODLANDS* that stretch right across the top of this country are sparsely covered with low vegetation, unlike the tall timber woodlands in the temperate south of Australia. In fact, while they are both loosely referred to as 'the bush,' these two habitats are quite different kinds of places.

A friend of mine trains young aborigines as rangers in the Northern Territory, and as part of his program he takes his students south to see the rest of the country. On one such trip he took his group for an outing into the giant timber woodlands of eastern New South Wales. He tells of their incredulous reactions. Never before had they seen such a place, and never in their wildest dreams did they imagine that gum trees grew so big! The trainees' behaviour, which was usually free and easy in the bush, became very subdued, and the group stuck closely together. They were obviously feeling closed in.

For that reason alone I find tropical woodlands a much better place to work with a camera. Light penetrates more freely and, during the dry season when the tall grasses have browned off and died back, there is room to move and to make thousands of discoveries.

MAYFLY ON PADANUS PALM,
KAKADU NATIONAL PARK, NORTHERN TERRITORY.
125th sec., f5.6, 600mm IFED, tripod, 64asa.

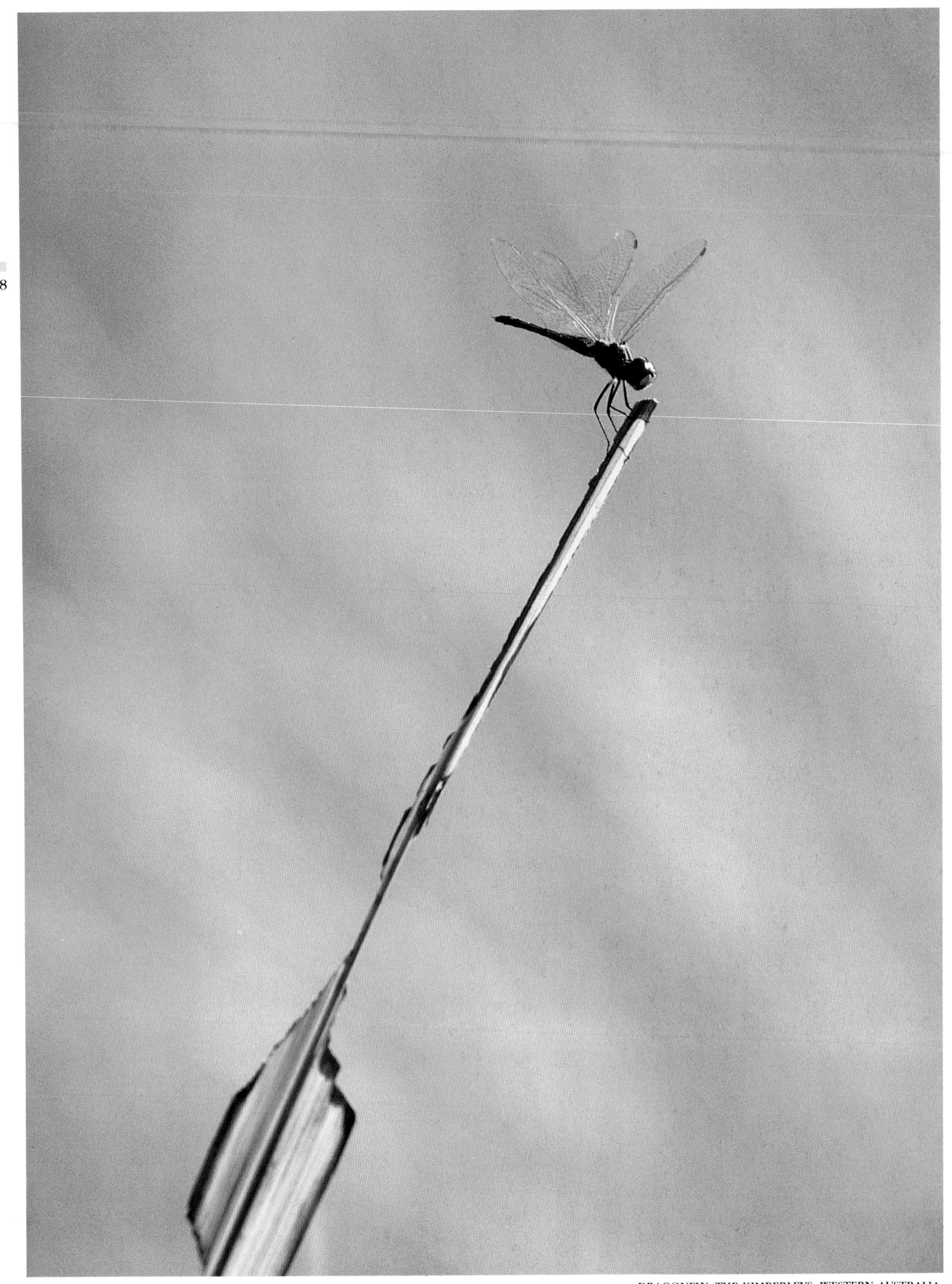

DRAGONFLY, THE KIMBERLEYS, WESTERN AUSTRALIA.
125th sec., f5.6, 600mm IFED, tripod, 64asa.

PRAYING MANTIS, CAPE YORK PENINSULA, QUEENSLAND.
125th sec., f5.6, 105mm micro, 64asa.

I made this image of the Dragonfly with a 600mm telephoto lens. The lens has provided two distinct advantages. Firstly, the short depth of field has washed the background, adding emphasis to the animal and its perch. Secondly, it has enabled me to work from some distance away because Dragonflies have a nasty habit of 'buzzing off' just as you are about to pull the trigger.

The Praying Mantis on the other hand is very easy to approach. Here, with a 105mm micro lens, I positioned my camera between the animal and the sun to heighten the drama of the mantid's striking shape.

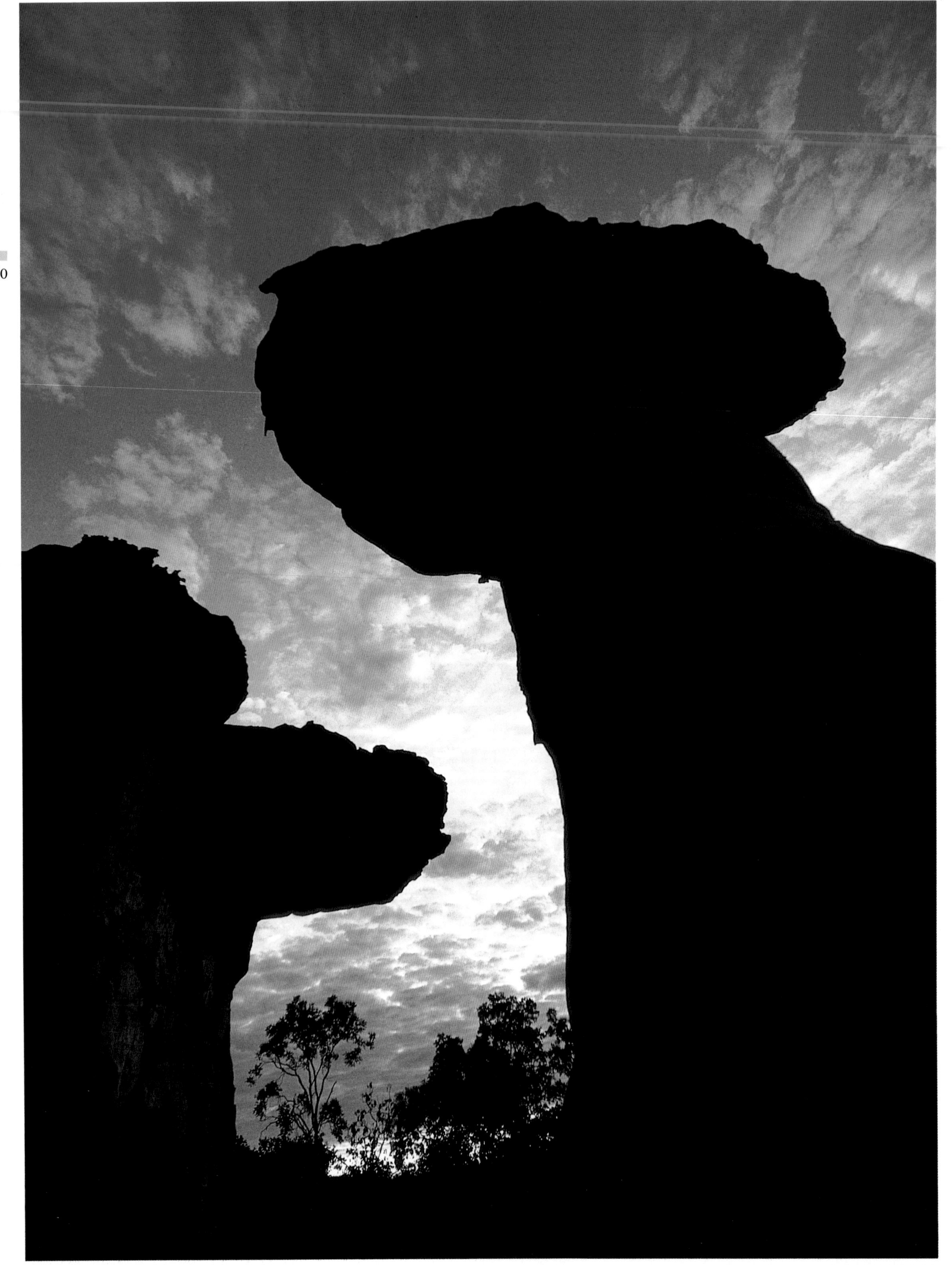

ROCK FORMATIONS FROM UBIRR, KAKADU NATIONAL PARK, NORTHERN TERRITORY.
60th sec., f5.6, 15mm, 64asa.

STONE COUNTRY

THROUGHOUT THE TROPICAL AREAS of Australia there are thousands of places that bear spiritual significance for Aboriginal people. Such a site may be a dynamic formation, a cave, a waterhole, or simply a group of pandanus palms on a floodplain.

In some areas travellers will notice *'Sacred Site. No Entry'* signs posted. Unfortunately signs like this can act more as a magnet than a repellent. I have always taken the attitude that, unless invited by the local people, I do not intrude. There are hundreds of other places for me to go and make pictures without causing a disturbance.

SHAPES FROM THE STONE COUNTRY,
KAKADU NATIONAL PARK, NORTHERN TERRITORY.
125th sec., f5.6, 600mm IFED, tripod, 64asa.

BIG BILL NEIDJIE, KAKADU NATIONAL PARK, NORTHERN TERRITORY.
125th sec., f2.8, 50mm, 64asa.

Big Bill Neidjie is one of the three remaining elders of the Bunitj clan Gagadju language group. He was born in the 1920's in an area known today as Kakadu National Park, the word Kakadu having been derived from Gagadju.

I first met Big Bill in 1980, and consider myself fortunate to have had the opportunity to sit with him among his stone galleries listening to his stories. The stories that had the greatest impact were those which related to the landscape. Bill expressed great concern for its future.

As I roamed his country, watching the brolgas and geese flocking over floodplains, stalking silent rock wallabies, poking and prying among the sedges and water lilies, I always felt that I was documenting history; a history that goes back thousands of years.

At the end of one visit in 1981, Big Bill came to me just as I was about to leave. He put his big flat foot on mine and, standing inches from my face, with a sombre expression, he said, "Steve, you put 'em ina book. Put 'em ina book soon. Next time you come back, my land be high rise looking way over there."

Today, within the Kakadu National Park region, there is a uranium mine, a support town of 1,200, 180km of bitumen roads, and an annual visitation of 100,000 people. There are plans for further tourist development.

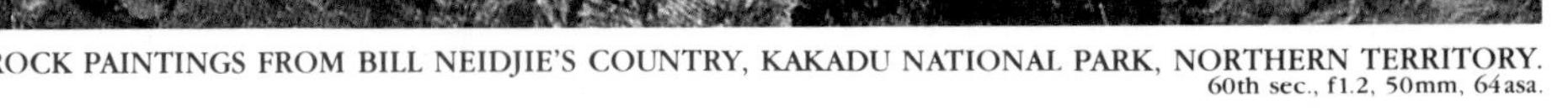

ROCK PAINTINGS FROM BILL NEIDJIE'S COUNTRY, KAKADU NATIONAL PARK, NORTHERN TERRITORY.
60th sec., f1.2, 50mm, 64asa.

"Our story is in the land . . .
it is written in those sacred places.
My children will look after
those places, that's the law.
Dreaming place . . .
you can't change it, no matter who
you are. No matter you rich man,
no matter you King.
You can't change it."

Big Bill Neidjie. 1983

UBIRR, STONE COUNTRY AND FLOODPLAIN, KAKADU NATIONAL PARK, NORTHERN TERRITORY.
125th sec., f8, 15mm, 64asa.

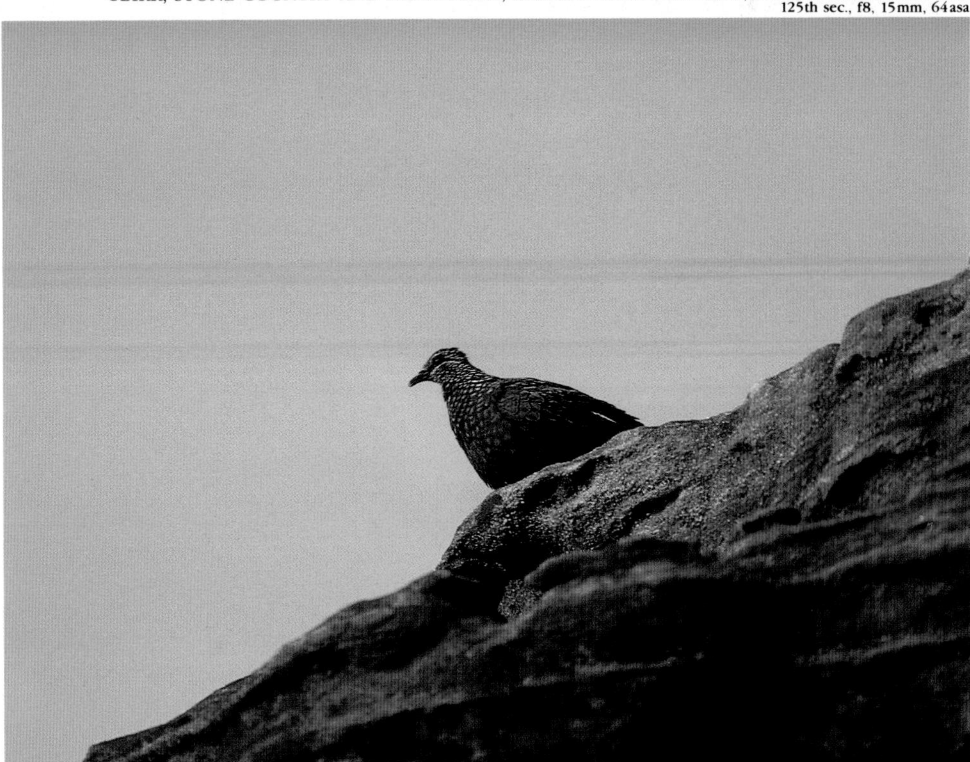

CHESTNUT QUILLED ROCK PIGEON, FOUND ONLY IN THE STONE COUNTRY, WESTERN ARNHEM LAND, NORTHERN TERRITORY.
125th sec., f5.6, 600mm IFED, tripod, 64asa.

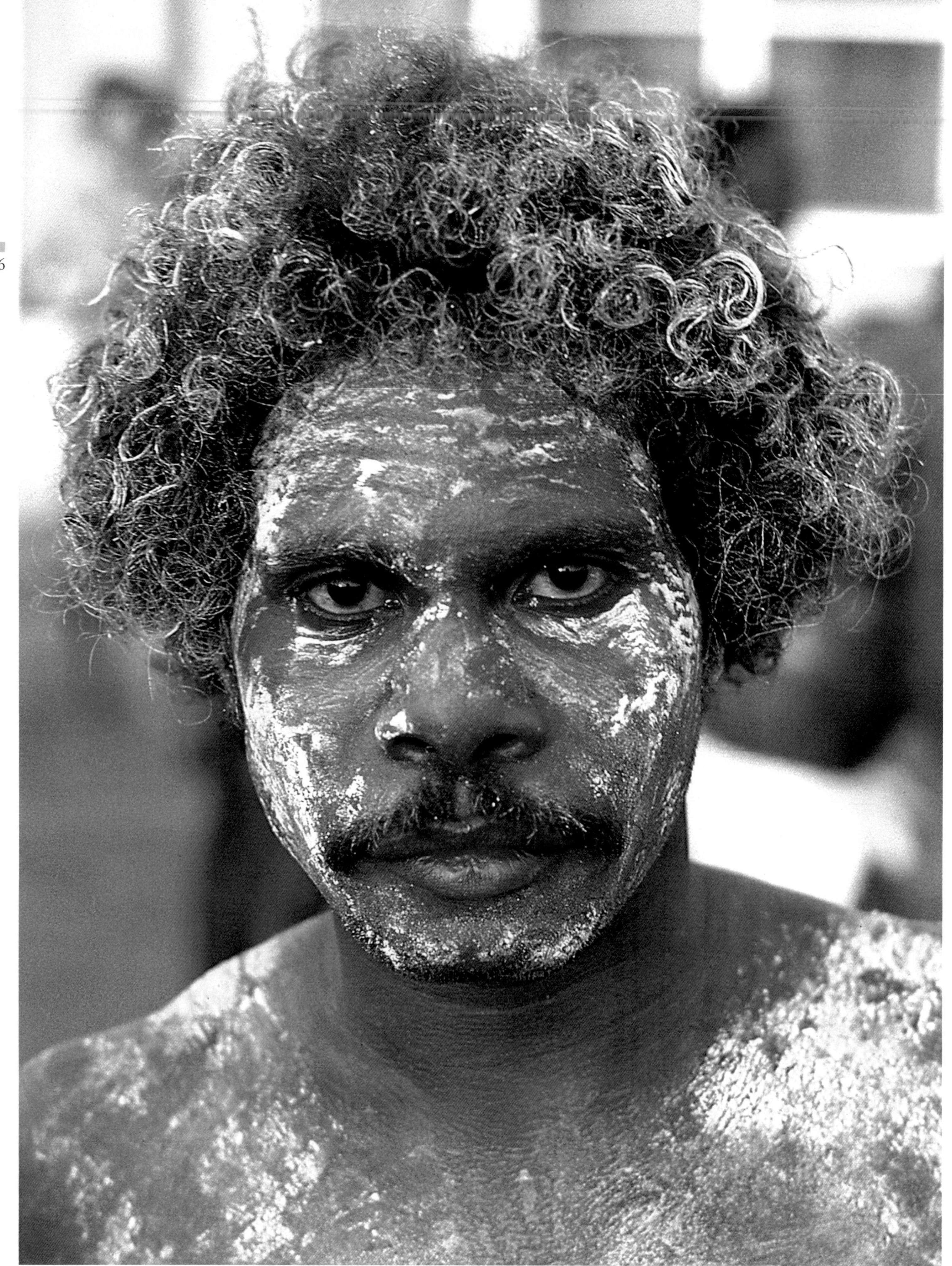

AT BIG BILL NEIDJIE'S CORROBOREE, KAKADU NATIONAL PARK, NORTHERN TERRITORY.
125th sec., f5.6, 135mm, 64asa.

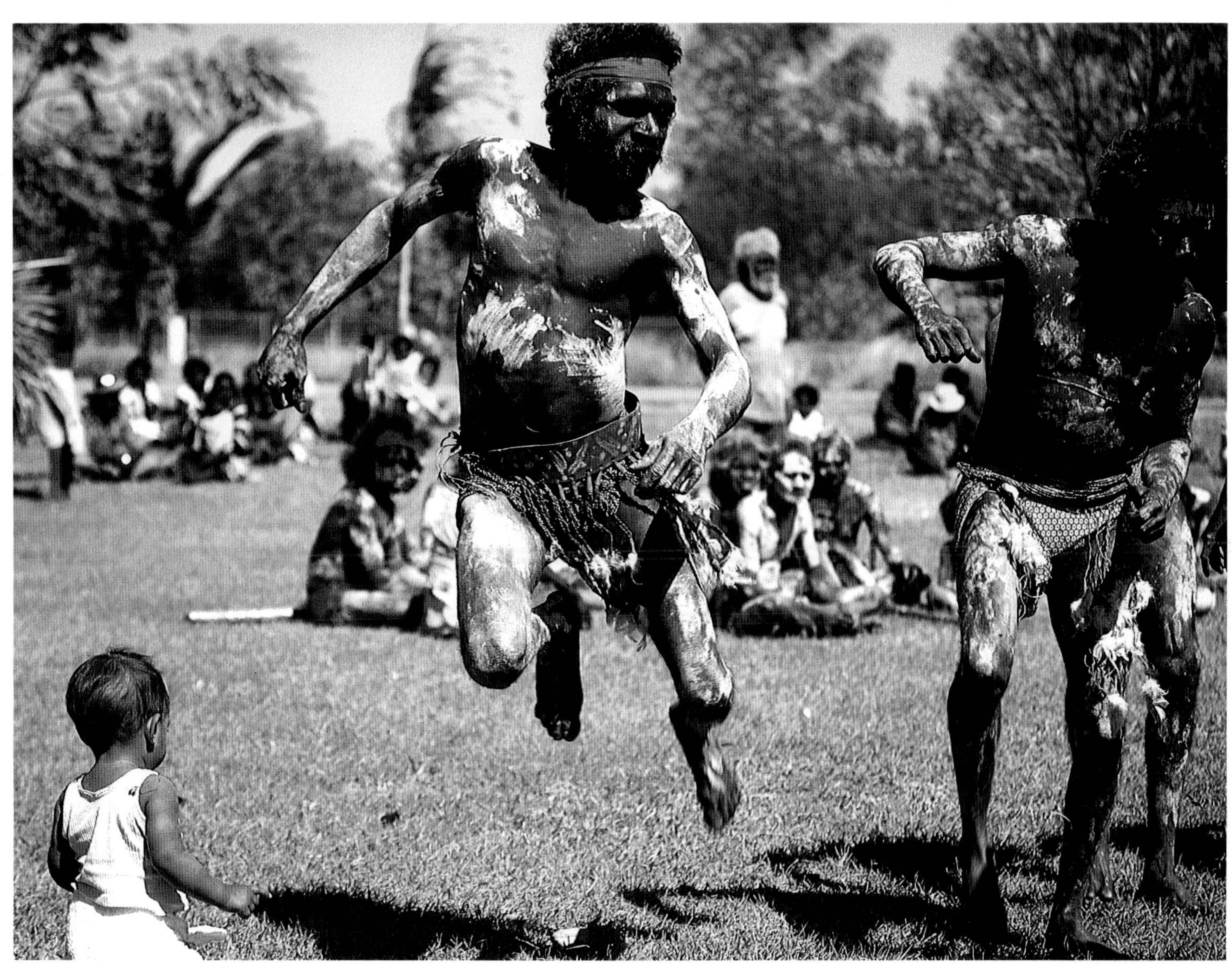

KALANDO FESTIVAL, KATHERINE, NORTHERN TERRITORY.
125th sec., f5.6, 15mm, 64asa.

"*We have to keep pressure on*
young people to learn.
They must learn these things.
I have to stay on to teach
my children. But, young people
spread out [go elsewhere to towns].
It like that everytime we have
meetings for business [ceremonies].
We make arrangement . . .
you know . . . appointment,
about business, secret.
Young people all in town."

Big Bill Neidjie. 1983

Big Bill's concern is shared in many aboriginal communities. At Katherine, the Kalando Community hosts a 'top end' festival every year. Their objectives are twofold. They want to show Europeans that their culture is not dead, and they want to bring young people together to teach them about the old traditional ways.

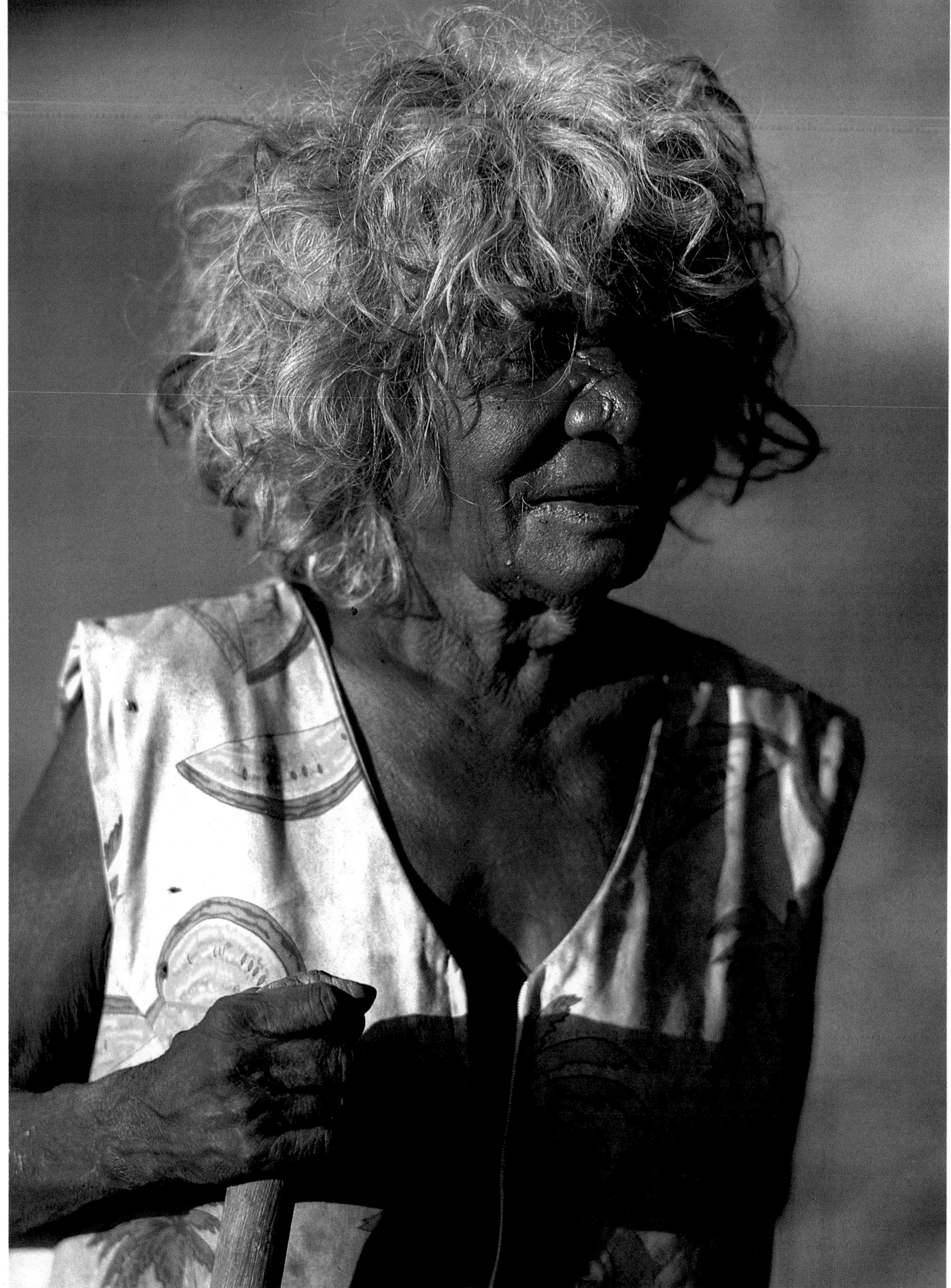

BLIND WOMAN, WESTERN AUSTRALIA.
125th sec., f5.6, 135mm, 64asa.

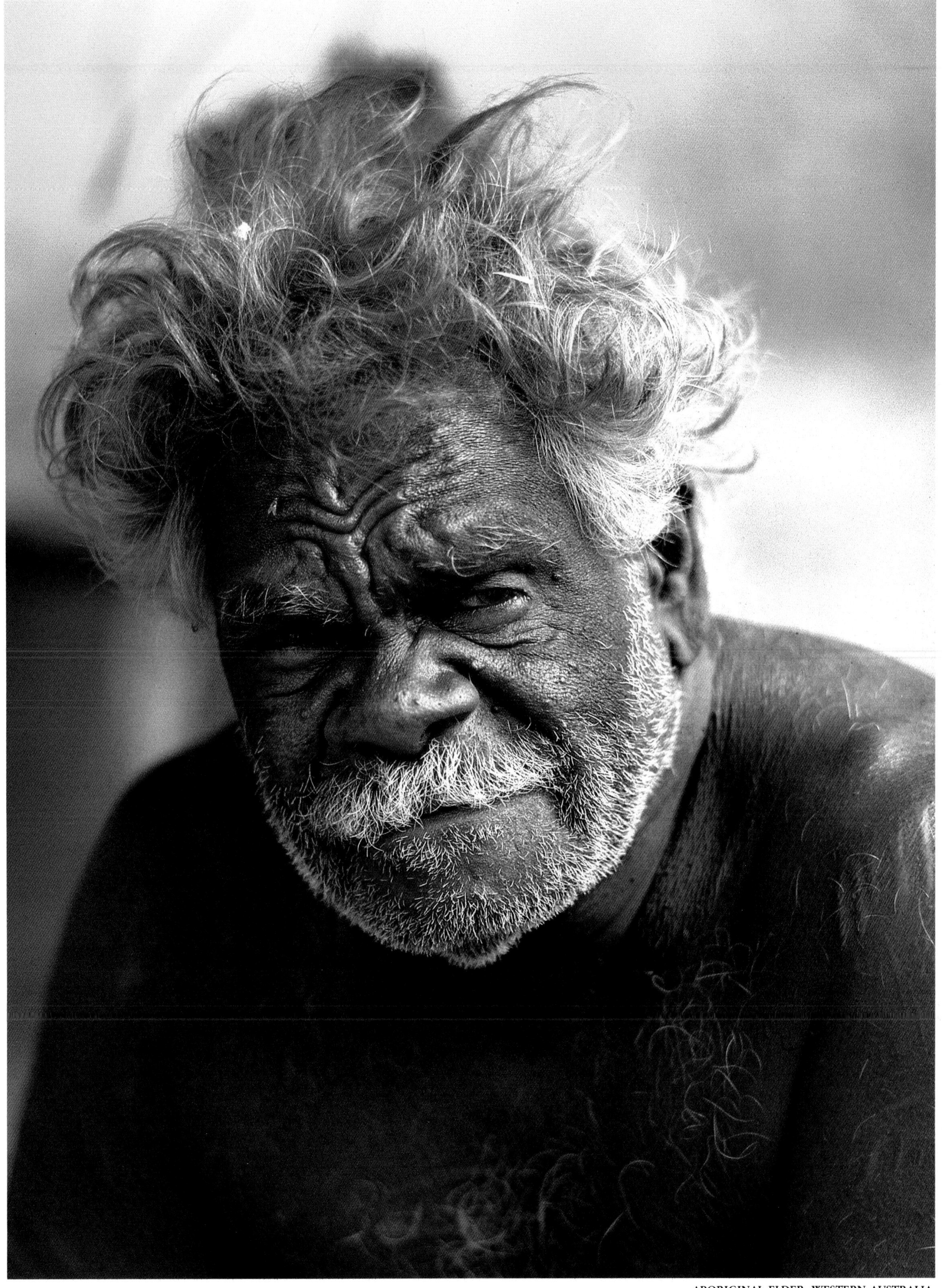

ABORIGINAL ELDER, WESTERN AUSTRALIA.
125th sec., f5.6, 135mm, 64asa.

FRINGE DWELLERS, THE KIMBERLEYS, WESTERN AUSTRALIA.
125th sec., f5.6, 135mm, 64asa.

"First people come to us,
then they started to run our life . . .
quick. They bring drink.
First they should ask about fish,
cave, dreaming, but . . . they rush in.
They make school . . . teach.
Now Aborigine losing it,
losing everything.
Nearly all dead my people,
my old people gone."

Big Bill Neidjie. 1983

When Big Bill spoke of his dying culture it had tremendous impact. It made me realise that, as a photographer, I have a responsibility. Even when I took Bill's picture, I was photographing a history that goes back 50,000 years!

Now, as I wander Australia with my camera, I feel that I am more aware of the great change that is occurring in this country. It is affecting not just the Aboriginal people, but the very basis of their culture . . . and the land itself.

SYMBOLS OF THE 'NEW' CULTURE.
125th sec., f8, 80 - 200mm zoom, 64asa.

"I feel it with my body,
with my blood.
Feeling all these trees,
all this country.
When this wind blow,
you can feel it.
Same for country . . .
You feel it.
You can look,
but feeling . . .
that make you."

Big Bill Neidjie
on the subject of feeling . . .

IMMERSED IN WILDERNESS, LAKE NUGA NUGA, QUEENSLAND.

BEHIND THE PHOTOGRAPHS

A*LL OF THE PHOTOGRAPHS* in this book were taken with Nikon 35mm cameras. The range of bodies included Nikkormat, Nikon F2, Nikon ELW, Nikon FE, and Nikon FA. The variety was due to upgrading as new models became available. A Nikonos III with a 15mm corrected lens was used for all underwater pictures.

I use motor drives for several reasons. Firstly they are faster to work with. Secondly, motor drives frequently enable me to capture action that would otherwise be missed. And finally, motor drives enable me to work with one hand—the other hand is often clinging for dear life to some kind of support.

The lenses most frequently used to illustrate this book were 15mm, 135mm and 600mm. My favourite method of working, particularly for wildlife, is with a 600mm IFED f5.6 lens in association with a motor drive, cable release and tripod. Other frequently used lenses are 24mm, 35mm, 50mm, 55mm micro, 105mm micro, 24mm to 85mm zoom, 80 to 200mm zoom, and 400mm.

Film stock used to illustrate this book was entirely Kodachrome 64 A.S.A. 36 exposure film, processed in the normal way through Kodak's service in Melbourne. I choose to use this film because of its resistance to heat and scratching. It is by far the most economical in terms of cost, and when you use it like I do, that does matter.

It will probably be evident that I prefer not to use artificial light. Because I prefer natural light, I use tripods extensively. I find that in low light the use of a tripod and cable release produces sharp pictures even when shutter speeds are very slow.

My only other accessories are gadget bags and items of personal clothing. I occasionally use polarizing filters, and each lens is fitted with a UV filter for protection.

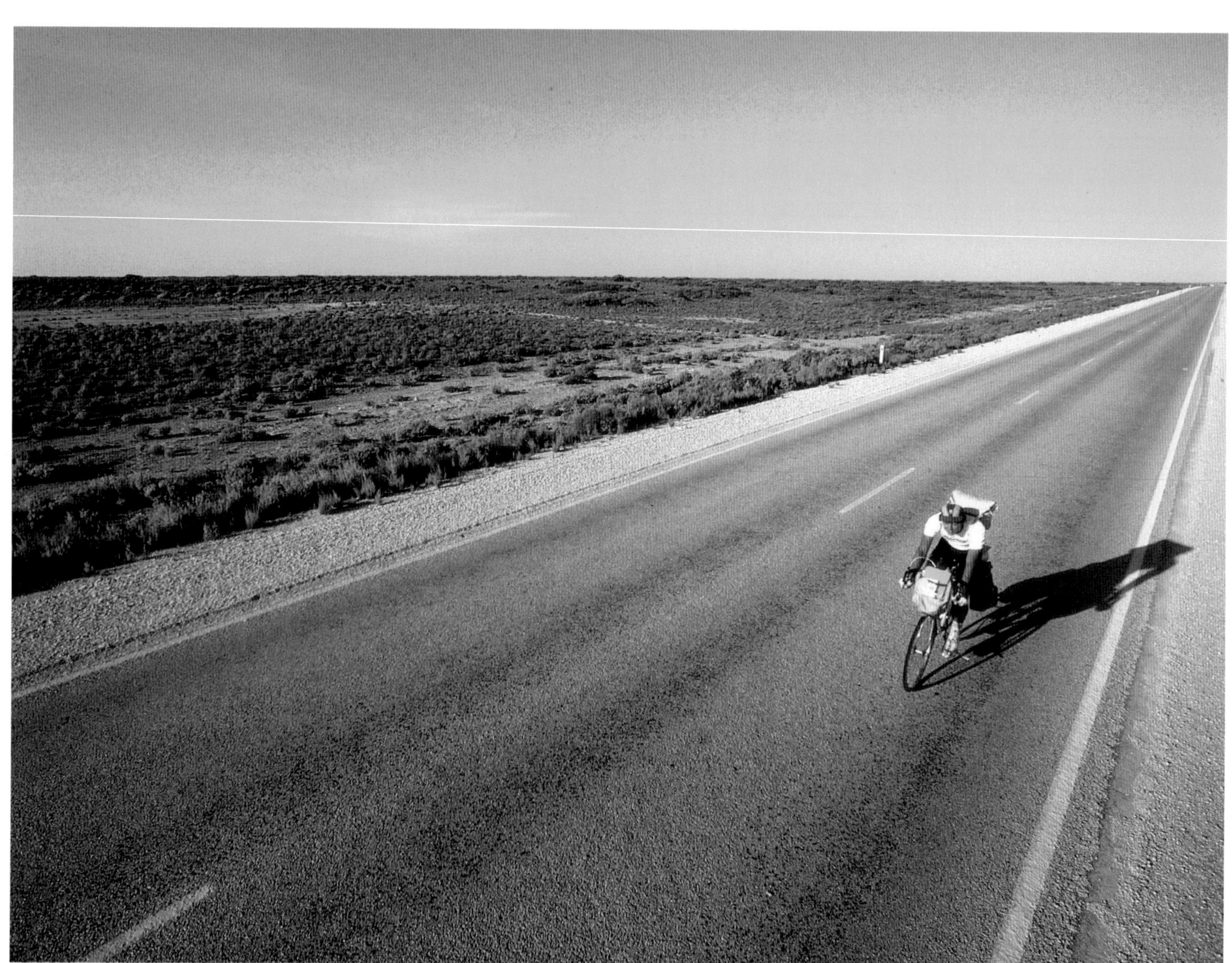

MAKING TRACKS, NULLARBOR PLAINS, WESTERN AUSTRALIA.

MAKING TRACKS

I *HAVE DIVIDED* this book into four main sections based on two criteria. Firstly, I wanted to broadly group the kinds of experiences that specific areas offer. For example the space and aridity of the outback as compared with the dripping green, secret feelings that mountains can provide. Secondly, I felt that by grouping the images into specific areas, I may well motivate interest more directly in particular habitats.

We have all gone through the decision-making process when we know we want to go somewhere. Just where to go is often the problem. Space does not enable me to fully discuss the times of year, modes of transport or even to give a detailed description of all of the venues. So, to assist you in making your own plans, I have provided the names and addresses of organisations in each state that can provide you with details regarding travel, accommodation and possible destinations. I have also provided an anecdotal map which shows most of the areas that I have specifically dealt with. Studying this map will provide you with some idea of the destinations that I have preferred.

A.C.T. GOVERNMENT TOURIST BUREAU
P.O. BOX 744
CANBERRA CITY 2601

N.S.W. DEPARTMENT OF
LEISURE, SPORT AND TOURISM
G.P.O. BOX 7050
SYDNEY 2001

NORTHERN TERRITORY
TOURIST COMMISSION
P.O. BOX 2532
ALICE SPRINGS 5750

QUEENSLAND TOURIST AND
TRAVEL CORPORATION
G.P.O. BOX 328
BRISBANE 4001

SOUTH AUSTRALIAN
DEPARTMENT OF TOURISM
G.P.O. BOX 1972
ADELAIDE 5001

TASMANIAN DEPARTMENT OF TOURISM
G.P.O. BOX 3990
HOBART 7001

VICTORIAN TOURIST COMMISSION
G.P.O. BOX 1328L
MELBOURNE 3001

WESTERN AUSTRALIAN
TOURISM COMMISSION
G.P.O. BOX X2261
PERTH 6001

1. Cape York
2. Coen
3. Voilet Vale Station
4. Lakefield National Park
5. Atherton Tableland
6. Cairns
7. Swain Reefs
8. Heron Island
9. Stradbroke Island
10. Brisbane
11. Lamington National Park
12. Girraween National Park
13. Bunya Mountains
14. Carnarvon Gorge
15. Jericho
16. Longreach
17. Winton
18. Stonehenge
19. Welford Downs
20. Birdsville
21. Sturt's Stony Desert
22. Bulloo Downs
23. Lightning Ridge
24. White Cliffs
25. Mootwingee National Park
26. Broken Hill
27. Darling River
28. Sydney
29. Canberra A.C.T.
30. New South Wales Alps
31. Murray River
32. Wentworth
33. The Grampians
34. Daylesford
35. Melbourne
36. Tasmanian Wilderness
37. Hobart
38. Morgan
39. Adelaide
40. Flinders Ranges
41. Lyndhurst
42. Marree
43. William Creek
44. Oodnadatta
45. Coober Pedy
46. Cook
47. Simpson Desert
48. Uluru National Park
49. Finke Gorge
50. Alice Springs
51. Tennant Creek
52. Barkly Tableland
53. Daly Waters
54. Katherine
55. Victoria River District
56. Darwin
57. Kakadu National Park
58. Kulumburu Mission
59. The Kimberleys
60. Derby
61. Broome
62. Eighty Mile Beach
63. The Pilbara
64. Nambung National Park
65. Perth
66. Fitzgerald River National Park
67. Stirling Ranges National Park
68. Kalgoorlie
69. Norseman
70. Cape Arid National Park
71. Eucla

0 100 200 300 km

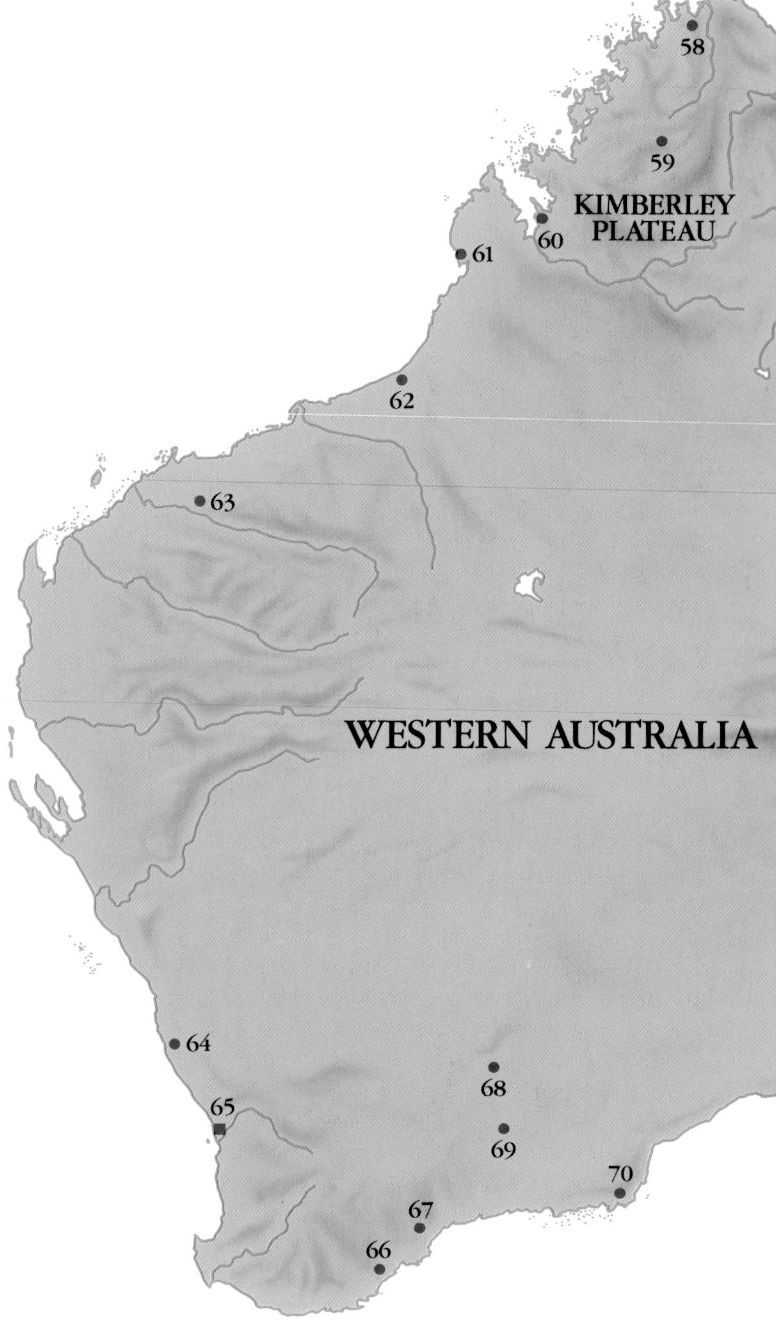

NORTHERN TERRITORY
QUEENSLAND
SOUTH AUSTRALIA
NEW SOUTH WALES
VICTORIA
TASMANIA
CAPE YORK PENINSULA
MACDONNELL RANGES
GREAT DIVIDING RANGE
CHANNEL COUNTRY
1
2
3
4
5
6
7
8
9
10
11
12
13
14
15
16
17
18
19
20
21
22
23
24
25
26
27
28
29
30
31
32
33
34
35
36
37
38
39
40
41
42
43
44
45
46
47
48
49
50
51
52
53
54
55
56
57

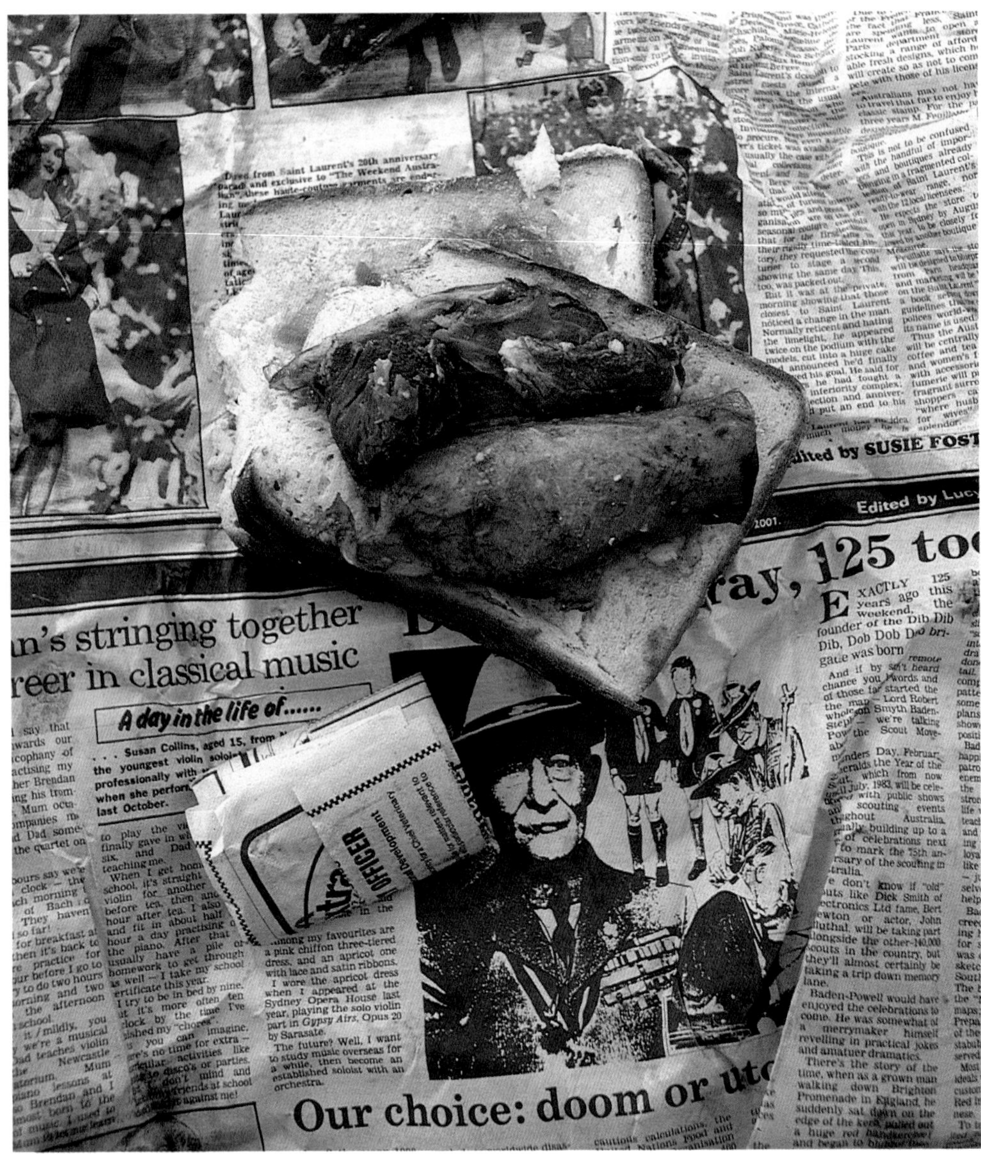

The fact that I could not face this steak sandwich prepared by a bunch of outback ringers resulted in a great deal of ribbing. I promised the boys that one day I would share their lunch with the world.

Thanks to all the ringers who helped me find my way around some pretty rough country.

THANKS FOR HELPING

MAKING PICTURES is impossible without the support and enthusiasm of a great many people and, as the images in this book span half a decade, there have been literally hundreds who have helped. I have been given accommodation, directions, meals, scientific advice and lots of encouragement along the way. I could not possibly thank everybody here, but there have been several people who have been largely responsible for making this book happen.

Foremost I thank Robert Tolmie, Managing Director of National Photographic Marketing. As publisher of the book, Robert has always shown undying enthusiasm, even when I drove him potty with incessant telephone calls.

Connie, my wife and partner in work and play, gave her usual undying support. She was with me when many of the images in this book were made.

Katrina Hergstrom edited my scribbles with amazing results and her partner, Dennis Veal, has taken my images and designed a superb book.

Irene Amos helped me to discover the 'thin line' between what was, and what was not a photographic image, although I take full responsibility for all images selected and presented here. Allan Fox and Steven Davis gave permission to quote from their unique book, *Kakadu Man Bill Neidjie.* Thanks also to 'Big Bill' for opening my eyes to what being aboriginal in the 80's really means.

I thank Ian Morris and Damien McGreevy for helping me to adjust my thinking to terrestrial ecosystems after fifteen years spent underwater. Peter Slater and Jon Marr made comments which gave direction to the text during its early days. Joan Sorrensen and Les Parish provided considerable support in running my business while my head was totally absent.

Students on workshops also played a major role in the development of this book. I trialled many of my thoughts on them before committing them to paper.

Communication . . .

. . . and friendship.

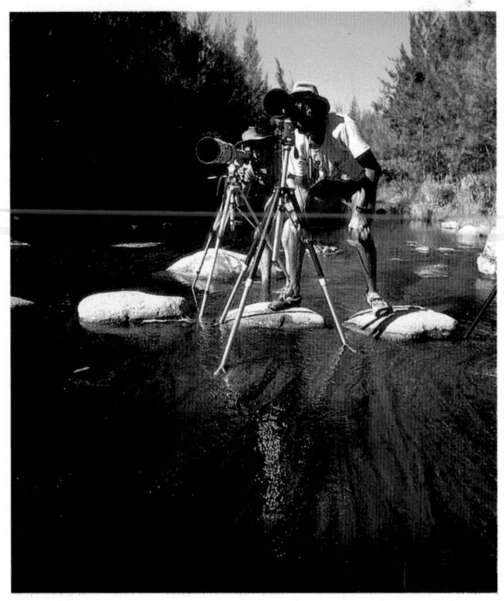

First published in Australia in 1986 by
National Photographic Marketing Pty. Ltd.
30 Hinde Street, Southport, The Gold Coast, Queensland 4215.

National Library of Australia Cataloguing in Publication data.

Parish, Steve **Photographing Australia**
ISBN 0 9588217 0 4
1. Photography — Australia
I. Title

Produced by Steve Parish & Associates Pty. Ltd., Brisbane, Australia.
Compiled by Prime Design, Brisbane, Australia.
Typeset in Garamond ITC by Prime Type, Brisbane, Australia.
Printed by Dai Nippon Printing Company, Japan.

Photography: **Steve Parish**
Text: **Steve Parish**
Editing: **Katrina Hergstrom**
Design: **Dennis Veal**
Artwork: **Cherie Kaouklis**
Typography: **Phil Taylor**

Front Cover
AYERS ROCK, ULURU NATIONAL PARK, NORTHERN TERRITORY
125th sec., f2.8, 35mm, 64asa.

Back Cover
FRILL-NECKED LIZARD, KAKADU NATIONAL PARK, NORTHERN TERRITORY
125th sec., f11, 105mm micro, 64asa.

Page 1
SHELL ON SAND, WILSONS PROMONTORY NATIONAL PARK, VICTORIA.
60th sec., f11, 15mm, 64asa.

Pages 2 & 3
AYERS ROCK, ULURU NATIONAL PARK, NORTHERN TERRITORY.
125th sec., f5.6, 15mm, 64asa.

Pages 4 & 5
EMU, SOUTH AUSTRALIA.
125th sec., f5.6, 15mm, 64asa.

Pages 6 & 7
NOEL AND ANNE PERRIER, SILVERTON, NEW SOUTH WALES.
125th sec., f11, 24mm, 64asa.

Pages 8 & 9
REEF HERON, HERON ISLAND NATIONAL PARK, QUEENSLAND.
500th sec., f11, 600mm IFED, 64asa.

Page 10
GUM TREE BARK IN TWILIGHT, KATHERINE GORGE NATIONAL PARK, NORTHERN TERRITORY.
30th sec., f11, 105mm micro, tripod, 64asa.

Pages 12 & 13
"KEGO," WILLIAM CREEK, SOUTH AUSTRALIA.
250th sec., f5.6, 135mm, 64asa.

Page 14
MAKING TRACKS, STRADBROKE ISLAND, QUEENSLAND.
125th sec., f8, 135mm, 64asa.